SPECIAL CRIMES

Kenny Rodgers

Special Crimes Press

Words of praise for *Special Crimes*

"In *Memoirs of a DA Investigator,* Kenny Rodgers, former Investigator in the Office of the District Attorney of Harris County, Texas lays out the varied, and frequently unusual and dangerous, duties of this very specialized breed of peace officer. These experienced men and women are relied upon by prosecutors in major cities to help them prepare for trial and, in the organization in which Rodgers worked, actually performed initial investigations. The Special Crimes unit put together a varied array of prosecutions including an organized crime murder of a witness in a federal fraud case in Arkansas, the bribery of a district judge in Houston, safe housing for an essential witness during the trial of a contract killer. It was in these and other similar cases that Kenny gained the experience and knowledge required to accurately relate the hard work, patience, fortitude, and perseverance required to do the DA Investigator job. Every reader will find this book to be a learning experience about the criminal justice system."

— **Robert "Bob" Bennett**
former Harris County Assistant District Attorney
and Chief of the Special Crimes Bureau

"A very entertaining and insightful read. Kenny Rodger's book is reminiscent of stories from Joseph Wambaugh, gritty, often humorous, and brutally honest. The book details the unfortunate and sometimes deadly results for the victims of 'special' criminals."

— **Jim McLain**
Retired Louisiana Probation and Parole Agent

"This book is a must-read for anyone interested in the true crime stories of Harris County, Texas. Sometimes gritty and salty, this book offers firsthand details and the backstories of some of the most interesting and infamous crimes and criminals in Harris County history. Former Chief DA Investigator Kenny Rodgers hasn't lost his "old school" touch. An entertaining read for sure."

— **Mark W. Stephens**
Retired Houston Police Investigator

"WOW, what insightful stories of true crimes! Awesome! Magnificent! Well written, great reading, a police-police officers' story. I thoroughly enjoyed reading each story."

— **Linda Bell-Robinson, Ed.D.**
Former Houston Area Police Officer

"In Houston, Texas, the 1970s and 1980s was a time of flamboyant criminality and flamboyant criminals. Kenny Rodgers was on the front lines of the prosecution of many of these characters. His memoir of those efforts is engrossing reading."

— John Boone
Retired Harris County Assistant District Attorney

"When it comes to well-known police procedural fiction writers and protagonists, Michael Connelly gave us Los Angeles' Detective Harry Bosch; John Sandford gave us Minneapolis' Lieutenant Lucas Davenport; and James Patterson gave us New York City's Detective Michael Bennett. Now comes Houston, Texas' Harris County District Attorney's Office Investigator Kenny Rodgers, albeit, in the divergent genre of non-fiction. His book, *Special Crimes,* is an addictive and prodigious real-life police procedural response to Lord Byron's 'truth is stranger than fiction' axiom. Kenny Rodgers' copiously written chapter-by-chapter investigative exploits are from an era long gone – not always politically correct in context by today's standards – but nevertheless he remained dedicated to his sworn duty with exemplary fortitude. Crime fiction authors like Connelly, Sandford, and Patterson often leave the reader anxiously waiting for the next book – I look forward to reading Kenny Rodgers' next book. It would be a crime if he did not write another book."

— Mike Grabowski
Retired Criminal Justice Professor
and Former Houston Area Police Officer

"This book brings back the glory days of the Harris County District Attorney's Office when the only thing that mattered was getting justice for victims and holding offenders accountable. This book reads like a best selling fiction novel but it's all true stories of the dedicated professionals who tried to keep Harris County safe without the benefit of today's modern technology."

— Amy Smith
Former Director of the Victim Witness Division
at the Harris County District Attorney's Office

"I have always loved listening to Kenny's stories and I found reading these chapters so captivating that I couldn't put it down! They are in true 'Kenny fashion' complete with all the laughs! I have always admired his dedication to law enforcement and so pleased that Kenny has chosen to commit to history these stories for all to read."

— Lynn Robideau
Retired Police Sergeant, Houston Police Department

"I love this book! The cases delve into some of the masterminds of criminal behavior. Fortunately, their lives of crime were brought to an end by Kenny and some of the other awesome investigators in the DA's Office."

— Debbie Mills
Retired Dispatcher Harris County District Attorney's Office

"A bird's eye view of a major jurisdiction's prosecutor office written by a bird that was a part of the flock. Accurate, entertaining, and a good read."

— John B. Holmes, Jr.
Former Harris County District Attorney, Houston, Texas

"Kenny Rodgers, in his book, *Special Crimes - Memoirs of a DA Investigator*, gives the reader a behind-the-scenes look at a criminal justice system that doesn't always work perfectly. The experiences he shares range from the bizarre to the downright funny. He has an amazing ability to make the reader feel that he is an actual part of the investigation. This is one of those 'hard to put down' books and is a thoroughly enjoyable and insightful read."

— Eddie Macaluso
Major Detective Bureau Retired

"A compilation of more interesting than fiction events in the career lifetime of one of the most colorful and competent characters to ever work at the Harris County District Attorney's Office. Kenny records the history of some of the more exciting cases and situations that puts you behind the scenes of crime solving and prosecution in the third largest jurisdiction in the United States. He takes you along for the ride as his career began as a rookie police investigator and culminated with his ascension to the vaunted position of Chief Investigator supervising over 100 senior peace officer investigators."

— Bert Graham,
**Former Harris County First Assistant District Attorney
and Chief of the Trial Bureau and Chief of the Special Crimes Bureau**

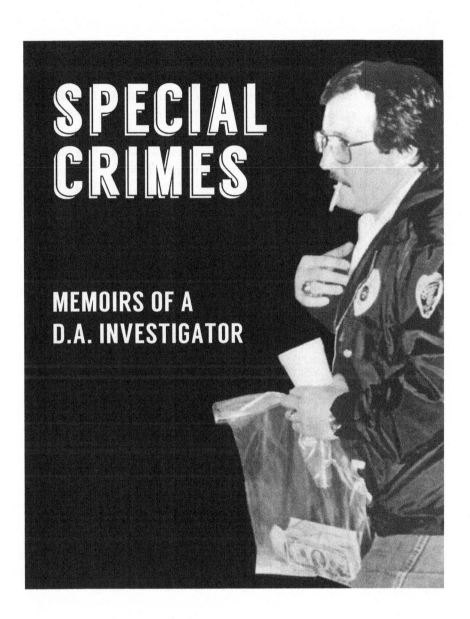

SPECIAL CRIMES

MEMOIRS OF A D.A. INVESTIGATOR

Kenny Rodgers

with Tom Kennedy

Special Crimes Press

Special Crimes Press
www.specialcrimesbook.com
information@specialcrimesbook.com

ISBN 978-0-578-70304-6

Some of the explicit language and culture depicted within the criminal justice environment may be offensive to some.

Please consider the context of the time, place, and events described respectively of the individuals and organizations as means of maintaining the authenticity and impact of the non-fiction genre.

Dedication

To my family and friends

Especially to my family, who put up with my late nights,
long hours, and being away from home.

A special thanks to my parents –
Burford and Jean Rodgers Haymon and step-father Jim Haymon –
and my children Kyle, Kristin, and Keith Rodgers.

This book was written for my six grandchildren –
Carson, Jackson, Hunter, and Garrett Rodgers,
and Coy and Bali Smith – so they can know
what their Pawpaw did as a young man.

Special thanks to my editor and good friend, Tom Kennedy,
a former *Houston Post* crime reporter and columnist.
He wrote many of these stories in the newspaper.

CONTENTS

ACKNOWLEDGMENTS

This book is dedicated to the men and women who serve and served as Investigators for the District Attorneys and state prosecutors across the United States.

They are the people behind the scenes who make things happen with their hard work and dedication — which are rarely acknowledged. You rarely hear about their feats and accomplishments.

Most people don't realize that criminal cases could not be prosecuted or tried without the defendants and witnesses. These investigators have spent many an hour searching for witnesses and defendants in order to ensure that justice be done. They have sacrificed time with their friends and families. They spend countless hours and late nights in places where no one would want to be and are usually by themselves.

They also investigate specialized and complicated cases that most police agencies do not have the time or manpower to investigate.

I was honored to work with these fine investigators and attorneys. I was involved because it was my job to dislike crooks and get them off the streets, especially those who sneak around in darkness harassing innocent victims.

I hope my book will inform those who have no knowledge or information on the inside workings of a prosecutor's office.

■ ■ ■

I would like to thank former Harris County Assistant District Attorney Rowland Elder for hiring me on September 11, 1972.

I also would like to thank former District Attorneys Carol Vance and John B. Holmes, Jr.

Texas and Caroline was the location of my office in the Special Crimes Bureau, where most of the "high profile" cases were investigated and prosecuted during the 1970s and 1980s. I began working in that division in 1976, when I was only twenty-five years old and spent nearly twenty years assigned there during my thirty-three year career.

I would like to also thank then Bureau Chief, Assistant DA Robert "Bob" Bennett, for allowing and trusting me to work there.

I would also like to express my appreciation to all the Assistant District Attorneys who I had the pleasure to work with. Most worked long and hard hours for little pay compared to attorneys who didn't and don't work for the government.

I owe Austin fiction author, George Wier, a debt of gratitude for the final copy-editing and formatting of both the ebook and trade paperback versions of this book.

SPECIAL EFFECTS

The Harris County District Attorney created the Special Crimes Bureau in 1972 through the use of a federal-funded grant that enabled local prosecuting agencies to combat organized crime. Our cause was to investigate and prosecute members of groups involved in narcotics, pornography, gambling and other "organized" criminal activities.

My story begins in Special Crimes. I can't tell it without introducing the unforgettable cast of law enforcement characters who were dedicated to the hard work of tracking down the bad guys and putting them away.

Special Crimes took all walk-ins and phone calls regarding complicated cases that local police agencies couldn't or wouldn't handle. We also worked closely with the Intelligence, Vice, Narcotics, and Homicide divisions of the Houston Police Department and the Harris County Organized Crime Unit, which included multiple police agencies.

Our office was in a grey gothic-looking building located on the corner of Texas Avenue and Caroline Street in the northeast corner of downtown Houston. It was two blocks away from the Criminal Courts Building. This quasi-remote corner building was occupied on the lower two floors by the Crispin Company, an import/export operation. The structure was the one-time home of the U. S. Federal Reserve. It had large pillars and the words *U. S. Federal Reserve* engraved across the façade.

Special Crimes was located on the third floor, which a person could access through an unmarked glass side door on Caroline. On many occasions some of our "shifty" characters and informants would enter through Crispin's entrance on Texas Avenue, no doubt causing Crispin employees to wonder what in the hell was going on upstairs. Another investigator and I shared a large corner office with several large windows that overlooked the streets below. The downside of our locale was that investigators and the assistant district attorneys – the ADAs – would have to walk two blocks in the infamous Houston humidity to get to a courtroom.

The upside of our tucked-away lair was that it was virtually free of the always high human traffic of the criminal courts. This made some of our criminal-element friends feel far more comfortable in spilling the beans on a partner in crime. Many times, we'd have a bank president sitting by a former hitman, pimp, or embezzler in our waiting room.

Our file cabinets were locked every night with a coded padlock and steel bars that extended through the handles. The code was the last four digits of our county phone number. Don't tell anybody but my family and I still use the code in many of our passwords and combination locks.

We had buzzers, locks, and alarms on all the doors and windows. I thought I was working for the CIA. We probably had as many intelligence files as the Houston Police Department and the FBI put together. But nobody ever counted.

We kept files on suspected Mafia members, hitmen, major drug dealers, gamblers, book makers, organized crime figures, crooked cops, pornography dealers, and pimps. We had a special phone line that was used for undercover operations. If we got a call on that line, we had a standard answer: "Austin Street and Bridge Company. May I help you?"

One weekend, ADA Chuck Cottingham, our major fraud prosecutor and an expert in financial crimes, answered the phone with "District Attorney's Office, Cottingham." Chuck's absent-mindedness inadvertently ended our long-running undercover operation.

It never failed that we always had some big case or newsworthy investigation that began or ended on a Friday. Most of the cases I detail here happened on a Friday. There was either an arrest made or a nighttime shootout right as we were looking forward to a weekend. Quite simply, it was the most "high pressure" job I ever had. The people in Special Crimes knew that if you didn't produce or get your assignment completed and locked in the file drawers, you were gone. I loved it! So did the others on the third floor.

What I'm saying here is that Special Crimes investigations usually screwed up our weekends. I used to ask my partner, Bobby Blaylock, every Friday morning, "I wonder what's going to happen today." We always knew *something big* was going to unfold. Most of us worked sixty to eighty hours a week. We didn't keep time sheets or comp time or overtime records. It was a calling, really.

At 9 a.m. sharp every Friday, Special Crimes had its weekly staff meeting. We would sit around a table in our conference room. The large varnished table probably cost more than the county car I was driving. Each of us took turns naming our investigative targets and, in general, our accomplishments of the week. If our target was a government official or a high-profile character, what was said in the room stayed there. You were not to even share it with others in the DA's office. If you did, you'd be transferred out.

■ ■ ■

Sam Robertson was the first Chief of the Bureau. Sam later became District Attorney Carol Vance's first assistant before being named a state district judge. When Sam got his promotion to first assistant, his successor was Bob Bennett, a tough veteran prosecutor who had the reputation for not tolerating bullshit. Or – put in newspaper terms – Bennett effected a no-nonsense air.

I'm introducing some of the characters in this memoir and the story of Bob Bennett is a good beginning. Bennett was born in Corpus Christi and drifted around the oil patch with his family as a child. He graduated from De Quincy High School in Louisiana and became a Texas Aggie when Aggieland was all-male. This made him a member of the Corps of Cadets, as the school required. Even though this cadet was only five-foot-six and weighed a mere 145 pounds, he went out for the vaunted Aggie football team. He suffered a concussion on the first day of fall training. Undaunted, he joined the school's rodeo team, riding bulls and broncos. A slender man with sunken cheeks and a square jaw, Bennett could pass for the little David pitted against the gigantic Goliath. He also had David's determination to beat the odds through hard work and grit. During the summers as a teenager he worked in the oil fields. After A&M he worked hard and graduated from George Washington University Law School in 1965. After he joined the Harris County DA's office, his colleagues soon began calling him "Little Napoleon" behind his back because of his stern and serious ways. He wore this determination on his face and in his step.

Shortly after I was assigned to Special Crimes, I checked out on the two-way police radio for lunch at my grandparents' house, located east of downtown – in the 5800 block of Rusk. I had nothing to hide and radioed the precise address. When I returned to work, Bennett called me into his office and asked me why I checked out at that location. I told him that my grandparents lived there and he got a funny look in his face. He said, "Oh my God, C.C. Rodgers is your grandfather?"

My memoir won't be complete until I tell you about my family. When I began my career in the DA's office, my grandfather, Clarence Carter Rodgers, was serving ten years' probation for felony bookmaking. He'd been sentenced by Judge Miron Love, who had the reputation for handing out lighter sentences than most of the other criminal district judges in Harris County. During my junior year at Sam Houston State University, where I majored in Criminal Justice, my grandfather was arrested and charged for selling "football cards" used in his bookmaking operation. Bennett had written the search warrant for my grandparents' house and HPD vice officers Joe Singleton executed it along with Bo Norris. Both of these lawmen later became my close friends.

I will be telling you about many infamous Harris County criminals on these pages. It looks like the first one will be the story of my grandfather. I remember sitting on my couch in my apartment in Huntsville when a TV newsflash alerted viewers to the "Major bookmaker arrested by HPD vice officers." There he was on the screen – my grandfather!

And here I was with Bob Bennett in an assignment that quite likely would result in investigations of people in the very same business.

I have to continue my flashback. In my childhood I remember while we were on vacation in Colorado and being pulled over by the Colorado State Police. They had an all-points bulletin on our car because my grandfather had been arrested for bookmaking and needed my dad, Burford Rodgers, to call home. Dad was a Houston city official for Mayor Louie Welch and carried a city-issued badge. We had to return home and cut our vacation short to help my grandfather. My dad was a complete opposite of my grandfather. He was an honest and very good person, and my grandfather was a criminal.

You can pick your nose, but not your family. My dad lied about his age in order to enlist in the U. S. Marine Corps to get away from his dad. They later found out and gave him an honorable discharge, so when he became of age, he enlisted in the U. S. Air Force, where he played on their baseball team. Prior to that he was signed by the New York Yankees in 1947 and was assigned to play for the Longview Texans in the Texas League. He was released in 1949, when he "threw out his arm." Doctors discovered that my dad had lymphoma cancer. He died three months later on my seventeenth birthday in 1967.

I remember the smell of stale cigar smoke when I was seven years old and made the rounds with my grandfather. I sat in the front seat and between us was an old cigar box that contained several rubber-banded rolls of large bills. Those "football cards" were in the glove box. He was always puffing on a cigar. I never complained because he'd always slip me a $5 or $10 bill not to tell Granny Rodgers about smoking. She probably knew because he always smelled like a stinking old cigar.

He was only five-foot-five but wasn't too fat. His face was always a flush red under curly slicked-down red hair parted right down the middle. He never spoke softly, a trait that every member of the Rodgers family has. His "HPD rap sheet," which was several pages long, said that his alias name was Sea Sick probably because his initials were C.C.

I had an explanation to Bennett for my sign-out to the Rusk address. I told him that I was only eating lunch there with my grandmother. My "football cards" came with bubble gum. I also told him that I didn't gamble and that my grandpa died in February 1975.

■ ■ ■

Bob Bennett was not the only extraordinary prosecutor in Special Crimes. Johnny Holmes was head of the Organized Crime Division of "the Bureau." Holmes was as feared by the other staff members as much as Bennett was. In their day both were two of the smartest ADAs and crimefighters that I ever knew. I wasn't the only one who felt that way, either.

Because Special Crimes had the best quality investigators, prosecutors, and equipment, most of the other employees in the DA's office called us the "Special Effects Bureau." They disliked us because they thought we got special treatment. You know what? We did!

To be selected as an assistant DA or investigator in Special Crimes was an honor. So the resulting jealousy in the other sections of the DA's office was to be expected. As I have said, it also was the most tireless, stressful job inside the courthouse complex. Your performance had to be excellent or you were relieved of duty. Practically all the other DA's employees figured that we thought we were better than everyone else. You can bet that no employee ever used the term "special effects bureau" to Bennett or Holmes. No. They would have been too scared.

Carol Vance, the elected district attorney, described Holmes as a guy who *calls it like it lies, intelligent, decisive, a man who can get the job done.* Vance also liked using the moniker "Bad John."

Holmes was born in Houston, graduated from Lamar High School in the fashionable River Oaks, a varsity letterman who was chosen an all-city guard, earning a football scholarship to the University of Texas. He was a starting guard as a freshman but was injured in practice before his first year on the varsity. The injury was serious enough to end his college career.

Johnny's dad, John Sr., was a wildcatter oilman who hit it big and had more money than God. Johnny grew up in River Oaks and was a neighbor to Bud Adams, an oilman in his own right and also owner of the Houston Oilers, which later became the Tennessee Titans when he moved them out of Houston.

Johnny began flying airplanes when he was fourteen and soon became known as "Sky King" in honor of the hero of the 1950s Saturday afternoon television series. After graduation from UT he worked as a full-time pilot who flew groups on fishing trips to Canada. He also piloted the plane that carried the Houston Apollos professional hockey team and the UT basketball, track, and baseball teams. He proved to be as reliable as the DC-3 that he flew.

While in law school Holmes worked as a reserve deputy sheriff for Harris County, he performed traffic control duties for paving contractors, and worked as a bank guard. Through this connection he became very interested in law enforcement. After passing the bar in 1969, he wanted to become an assistant DA but was given the run around. He applied time and time again but on each occasion was told, "We'll let you know." Finally, on the Friday night of September 12, 1969, Johnny got the call from First Assistant DA Neil McKay, who asked him to be in the office at 8 a.m. the following Monday.

Johnny's trademark became his well-groomed bushy handlebar mustache. Big John had a tell-it-like-it-is attitude. He never minced words and you always knew where you stood with him. He later became one of my closest and most trusted friends. I ended up becoming his chief investigator while he was the Harris County District Attorney in the 1990s. The only time I ever saw him without his mustache was when he had to shave it when it caught fire while he was working on his Jeep's engine. One of Johnny's favorite quotes from the 1937 radio show was, "Who knows what evil lurks in the hearts of men? The Shadow knows!" I used to also hear him say, "I hate crooks a lot."

Another standout in the bureau was Mike Hinton, aka "Machine Gun Mike." He got his nickname because of his consistently hyperactive, rapid-fire ways.

Vance described Mike as *volatile, sensitive, intelligent, hard-working, the life of the office.* Hinton was born in Kansas City, Missouri, but grew up in Liberal, Kansas, at one time serving as the mascot of the Volunteer Fire Department there. He spent most of his childhood in Liberal and later Amarillo in the Texas Panhandle. Mike's dad was an oil consultant and played the drums, inspiring Mike to also start out with the sticks at age eleven. He became a professional and used his earnings to pay his way through college.

Shortly after earning his law license, he became the City Attorney in Amarillo. He then served as assistant DA for Potter County. Hinton heard Vance speak at several seminars at the Texas District and County Attorney's Association meetings and applied for a Harris County ADA job. Vance hired him and he began work on September 8, 1972.

Mike was also a high school graduate of New Mexico Military Institute, where I graduated from junior college. He played the drums for the marching band and was known as a damn good drummer.

Police loved Mike because of his eagerness to get involved early in investigations. In other words: *shoot first and ask questions later.* His two big cases were Vernon McManus and the "Candy Man," Ronald Clark O'Bryan. McManus killed his wife's parents in order to collect insurance money. O'Bryan laced his son's Halloween candy with cyanide in order to collect his insurance money after the ten-year-old boy died.

Mike was a well-dressed, short, stocky fellow who never sat still. I remember that soon after we got new two-way radios, which included a phone "patch," I'd hear Mike on the radio calling his wife at the time, Dixie, and saying, "Dixie, it's Mike, do you need anything from the store?" He did that every single day.

■ ■ ■

The other investigators assigned to the bureau were Bill Hubbell and Don Baker. Hubbell was a retired Navy man, who later went to work as a deputy in the warrant division of the Harris County Sheriff's Office. He was a crusty old fart in his late fifties whom I highly respected. He stood about five-foot-eight and looked great for his age. Hubbell was hardcore and tough as nails. He was as no-nonsense as the rest of the bureau staff. He had the energy of a twenty-year-old.

For some reason unknown to me, I followed him as his replacement any time he transferred. Initially in Special Crimes, I worked alongside him. One of the best complimentary memos placed in my personnel file was from ADA Stu Stewart when he called me a "little Bill Hubbell." Hubbell nicknamed me "The Kid." I'd always hear him tell Bennett or Holmes, "I'll send 'The Kid' out there."

Baker was a retired detective from the Houston Police Department. He was a hard worker but seemed to complain about everything. The bureau had sent Baker to electronics school so he could "wire" our informants and witnesses with a transmitter to enable us to monitor and tape record the conversations of the "bad guys." Some years later, this became my responsibility for about twelve years.

One of the reasons I was selected as an investigator was because of my talent for finding people who had disappeared from the crime scene radar. My first DA assignment was in the Welfare Fraud Division. The problem there was that we had no defendants to prosecute because none of the arrest warrants had ever been executed.

I sent out more than two hundred letters to these people advising that they needed to come to our office to discuss a pending criminal investigation. Within two or three weeks I'd arrested more than ninety percent of the wanted defendants. I spent a lot of time walking these people to the county jail that month.

The most memorable arrest that week was when I told the Borden milk delivery man that he was under arrest while in the waiting room of our office, which then was located on the fifth floor of the old Citizen's Bank building at Preston and Main streets. He fainted, prompting me to immediately call the Houston Fire Department paramedics to get him revived.

I also was responsible for serving civil citations to people behind or simply not paying their child support. In general, the complaining party resided in another jurisdiction. I called most of these folks "diaper dodgers" or "bad daddies," among other nicknames.

Back in those days there were no computer databases or the Internet where you could go to find these people. Your best "high-tech" tool was a telephone book. There were other sources: Cole's Criss Cross directory, the Houston City Directory, and utility records.

It took a lot of gumshoe work in those days. There were no cell phones then, but almost everyone had a land line, so the security guys at the phone company were always a big help. I also had a great "source" at the light company, as well. Without them, you'd be lost. I got these resources when I began looking for defendants in welfare fraud cases and "bad daddies" and/or "baby dodgers" in non-support cases.

I learned most of these investigative methods from my first partner, Frank K. Wilson, who was a former bus driver for the only bus company in Houston and later became its investigator. He later became a deputy for the Harris County Sheriff's Office and was assigned as the court bailiff and process server in the court of Judge Miron Love, where my grandfather was sentenced. He did such a good job of locating and serving subpoenas that he was later hired by the DA's office.

In 1978 we learned that we were getting a new investigator in the bureau. Usually you were transferred in from another division because you had to "prove yourself" as an investigator before coming to our group.

DA Carol Vance called Holmes and said, "You're getting a new investigator, Bobby Blaylock, and if you don't like it, it's just too bad." That didn't sit well with Holmes as well as the other staff members – not only the bureau, but the entire investigative staff of the DA's office.

Shortly after hiring me, the office started hiring younger investigators instead of older retired police officers as so often had been the case. So, there were quite a few of these young guys who would "die" just to work in the bureau.

I remember Blaylock's first day like it was yesterday. This big tall Herman Munster lookalike came into my office and introduced himself. I took an immediate liking to him but no one else in the office would even speak to him because he came straight to Special Crimes without "working his way up the ladder."

Since he was an electronics expert, he was probably going to replace Baker as the electronics or "wire" guy, which pissed off a lot of people, especially Baker. I kind of understood his feelings in the matter, but there was no one better than Blaylock when it came at wiring someone or picking a lock.

Bobby stood well over six-foot-four and had a thin build. He wore a mustache with his lips turning down on the edges. He had an unforgettable laugh that I'll always remember because it made me laugh. Blaylock, a twenty-year veteran of the Houston Police Department, had spent most of his years assigned to the Intelligence Division and, years earlier, had been found not guilty of wiretapping in a federal charge along with eight other HPD officers. Testimony was very damaging for the officers, but the jury heard that several lives were probably saved because they prevented armed robberies and murders.

Blaylock was also involved in the Texas Southern University and Black Panther riots during the late 1960s and early 1970s. He still had a bullet in his butt from the TSU event. I used to tease him and would sometimes call him "lead ass." He also killed Carl Hampton, the lead rioter and Black Panther leader who was firing on the officers, in the police effort to quell the riot. Blaylock's policing peers held him in high respect throughout his career in HPD and the DA's office.

The bureau hired Blaylock on a federal grant but forgot to ask for monies to provide him a vehicle, police radio, and office space. I volunteered to share my office and phone with him. I called Chief Investigator Johnny Fox and asked him about getting Bobby his DA investigator identification card and was told that Vance's administrative chief, Lloyd Frazier, a former chief deputy for Harris County Sheriff Buster Kern, made them and he was on vacation. So, Blaylock would have to wait.

I got off the phone and told Blaylock, "You've got to be shittin' me." He had to use his retired HPD ID for almost a month. I just couldn't believe it.

Fox hated Special Crimes because he'd never been asked for his advice or expertise when the bureau was formed. Johnny Fox was another "tough old bird." He wasn't that tall and had a large belly. He always wore suspenders and kept his Colt .45 ACP tucked in his waistband on his left side. He probably hadn't seen the head of his pecker for years without looking in the mirror.

I'd hear him talking about the lawyers as "those fucking cocksuckers" while shaking his index finger. Every time he'd say that, I'd think, "Who the hell do you think we work for?"

Fox was reared between Waco and Marlin in Central Texas. He left home when he was sixteen and made his way by horseback and freight trains through Texas, New Mexico, Arizona, Utah, and Nevada for the next two years. While traveling, Fox worked for a group of guys who had a wild horse camp. He spent most of his time making a lot of money branding wild horses. When he was nineteen, he came back to Texas and went to work in the Brazos River bottom raising cattle and livestock. The owner of the livestock was the sheriff and got John interested in law enforcement because of cattle rustling. This sheriff was appointed a Deputy U. S. Marshal in 1933 and Fox worked for him as a field deputy until 1941. A year later, Fox volunteered for the U. S. Army after the bombing of Pearl Harbor.

While in the Army, a colonel who also was from Marlin recognized Fox and had him assigned as a military policeman in Camp Wallace, outside Galveston. After the war, John went to work for the Galveston Police Department and attained the rank of Chief of Detectives. He later resigned to join Sheriff Buster Kern in Harris County and later worked for the Harris County DA.

I really liked and respected Fox. In 1975 I spent three months working for Alcohol Tobacco and Firearms in Washington, D.C. and upon my return was assigned to Fox as his assistant. I took a lot of shit from the other guys, but they knew it really wasn't my choice.

One day while assigned to Fox, I noticed that he wasn't sitting down all day, so I asked him what was up with that. He admitted to me that the day before while getting into his county car, he reached into the back seat to hang up his coat. Something caused his Colt .45 ACP to discharge and blow a hole clean through his buttocks. Apparently, the safety on his pistol had worn down and caused the gun to discharge when the door hit him on his hip.

Fox hated Special Crimes so much that he took my police-equipped 1974 blue Plymouth Fury when I transferred there and assigned me a 1968 metallic green Ford Fairlane station wagon that was used to transport mental patients on a weekly basis to Austin. The damn thing was still equipped with the caged screen across the back seat that would keep the passengers from choking the ever-living shit out of the driver. This piece-of-shit vehicle still had the Texas Exempt license plates displayed on it and had been driven over 220,000 miles.

I took the car to Holmes' residence, located in Briargrove, an upper middle-class neighborhood on the west side, and he helped me remove the cage and plates. Holmes, a gadget freak like me, helped install a police radio in the vehicle. I got a Florida license plate from the Harris County tax assessor/collector, who regularly got out-of-state plates from new Texas residents.

In those days you'd drive a clunker like this everywhere as if it were your own car. I was totally embarrassed to be seen in it. I even had to drive Adrienne, my wife at the time, to the Methodist Hospital while she was in labor with our daughter Kristin. I'm surprised that she didn't give birth on the way because the car would start shaking once it reached about forty-five miles per hour. That's probably why Kristin used to rock herself when she was young because she was rocking and rolling on the way to the hospital.

Thank God that I got another vehicle after it broke down for the last time. I don't even think Harris County found it fit enough to auction off. The "new" car that I got wasn't much better. It was a 1973 Army green Plymouth Fury with well over 100,000 miles on it. It had been driven by investigator Charlie Isbell, a very large man whose size had crushed the springs toward the floorboard. I looked like a midget in it and had to put a large phonebook on the seat so I could see over the dash. Charlie was later shot and killed by his wife, Emily, who worked for the county as an elevator operator.

The car had been wrecked and couldn't be properly aligned after it was repaired, so when driving down the North Freeway it appeared as if I were going sideways. I knew that when Blaylock started in our unit that he'd get the same treatment as I did, so I was excited to see what kind of shit car he'd be assigned. It turned out that I was right! He got a 1970 grey AMC Condor that would barely go fifty-five miles an hour. At least he didn't need a phone book.

Blaylock and I became very good friends and shared office space for several years even though we could've had separate offices. He kept the rifle he used in the Hampton shooting under his desk in case he ever needed it. His laugh made me laugh and vice versa. We spent a lot of time laughing.

I taught him about being a DA investigator and he taught me all about electronics and picking locks. He taught me so much about electronics that when I attended a CIA electronics school in 1978, I passed the final exam on the first day of class. The next day they offered me a job. I can't tell you how many file cabinets or desks that I unlocked in my career because of a lost key.

Bobby never drove anywhere slowly. Any time I wanted to scare anyone, I'd make them ride in the front seat. Funny thing is that Bobby would pull over people who'd pass him on the freeway and give them a tongue lashing for speeding and threaten to get on the police radio and call for a "marked unit" to write them a ticket.

I'd tell him, "Hell, Bobby, you're speeding, too." He'd say, "Yeah, but he's going faster and that pisses me off."

On one occasion when driving to Hempstead to check for hidden electronic devices – also known as "bugs" – in a paranoid witness' home, I told Bobby that he'd better slow down because there was a chicken-shit state trooper who patrolled Highway 290. I told him that this trooper would write his own mother a ticket for going one mile an hour over the speed limit and that he'd written citations to HPD officers and Harris County deputies as well.

"Fuck him," Bobby retorted, while going about ninety-five MPH.

I don't know how he got that Concord to travel that fast, but about the time he said that, I saw the trooper parked along the highway. Bobby just pulled over and let the trooper catch up to us on the side of the road.

Bobby got out of the car with his Colt .45 ACP tucked in his waistband as the trooper, ticket book in hand, was approaching the car. He towered over this individual, pulled out his badge and said, "We're on the job." Before the officer could say anything, Bobby got back in the car and sped off, throwing loose gravel in his tracks. I know that some of the gravel hit the ticket-happy state highway patrolman.

As I turned in my seat to see what the trooper was doing, I said, "Shit, Bobby, we're going to jail." The trooper just stood there with a funny look of disbelief on his face. He must've stood there for several minutes before I lost sight of him. Then I turned to Bobby and said, "You know the son of a bitch is going to be waiting for us when we're heading back to Houston." Bobby got that big Herman Munster smile and hesitated a second, then said, "Fuck that son of a bitch."

Sure enough, about forty-five minutes later, on our way back to the office, there he was parked on the shoulder of the highway while we were doing a hundred. I don't know what scared me more, the trooper taking us to jail or going that fast in a car that shitty.

As we flew past him, I waited for the trooper to turn on his red lights and give chase. But he never moved.

Bobby and I were inseparable and worked on tons of cases together. We spent more of our off time together as well. He was a truly great friend and human being, as I detailed in my eulogy at his funeral in 2008.

Bobby and these other characters were just a few of the main ones in my story as a district attorney investigator. We missed some of our "targets" but I have to say we hit the bull's eye on most of them. I hope the stories I'm telling you here will prove this point.

Carol Vance

Bob Bennett

John B. Holmes, Jr.

"Machine Gun"
Mike Hinton

Burford Rodgers

Former Chief Investigators, left to right: Kenny Rodgers, Bill Hubbell, Bobby Blaylock, along with ADA Henry Oncken and DA Johnny Holmes

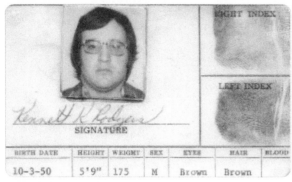

Kenny Rodgers, Investigator ID
September 1972

Kenny Rodgers, Investigator Special Crimes ID
March 1978

CHAPTER 1

THE BLACK WIDOW

Catherine Mehaffey had a bad temper. If you doubt my veracity, let me supply plenty of evidence. When I first got to know about her, she was an intern in the DA's office assigned to the Grand Jury Division. The word was that she apparently had gotten into a fight with her live-in boyfriend, Ferris Bond, who was a law student like she was, he at South Texas School of Law in downtown Houston and she at the University of Houston on the near eastside.

At the height of her anger Mehaffey went to their garage apartment while Bond was gone, put all of his law books and class notes in a garbage can, and set them on fire. The flames also caused extensive smoke damage to the apartment unit. Mehaffey stole Bond's car as she left the scene, only to be later arrested. However, the now former live-in refused to file charges. Even so, the DA fired the volatile intern.

Few people knew at the time but would later learn that what happened to Bond was part of a pattern in Mehaffey's young adult life. She married a Navy lieutenant, Matt Quinlan, in 1969. In a court proceeding just more than ten years later, Mehaffey admitted that once during the marriage she was holding her husband's handgun in their home when it discharged. A Quinlan relative later told authorities the future ex-wife was aiming the gun at her husband.

The pattern developed early and stayed the same: Mehaffey would be infatuated with a lover, assess the benefits he could bring to her life, display a fiery attitude that grew to be violent, and end with a violent act that included gunfire or arson.

Sometime after her dramatic bout with Bond, she began dating Dr. George Tedesco, an Argentinean anesthesiologist about her same age. An off-and-on relationship in the late 1970s with Mehaffey sometimes spending the night at the doctor's townhouse unfurled until Tedesco decided he'd had enough. He instructed her to get her things and remove herself from his premises. Then came a master gambit in the Mehaffey scheme of operations. She used her growing legal acumen to forthrightly allege that the two had a "common law marriage." In order to be done with her, Dr. Tedesco would have to go through a divorce, complete with the division of community property. It proved to be the Argentine-born anesthesiologist's initiation into the American legal system.

The Tedesco case went down as the first fatal example of the Black Widow's methodology and, especially, her seemingly endless survival streak. On the date that Tedesco and Mehaffey – who tried unsuccessfully at calling herself "Mrs. Tedesco" – were set to appear in court, the doctor failed to show up. Dr. Tedesco's family called police and asked them to check on his welfare. Officers found him bludgeoned to death in his garage. One in-depth report of the case said, "A metal pipe with a rag wrapped around one end was found beside the body; whoever had wielded the pipe had done so in a frenzy. Repeated blows to the doctor's head had splintered his skull," the autopsy showed. His right eye had been crushed, his nose fractured, and several of his teeth knocked out." The medical examiner ruled the death a homicide due to "blunt force trauma to head."

The five-foot-six wisp of a man apparently was taken by surprise and never had a chance.

Later, Houston police detectives met with Special Crimes to discuss the murder case. The assistant DAs told us that there just wasn't enough evidence to charge Mehaffey, even though she was the only suspect. One of the detectives told me Mehaffey had a violent past, saying that her first husband, Lt. Quinlan, re-enlisted in order not to come home to her. *I was thinking that was probably a good idea.*

Mehaffey got a license to practice law in 1977 and, like hundreds of her contemporaries, set up shop in the hallways and courtrooms of the Harris County Criminal Courts Building. Those who grew to know her almost to a person believed she was an expert lawyer but seldom used her talents for the good of her clients. Plenty of evidence and back hall talk has clearly shown that Catherine Mehaffey began to use her sexual prowess to help earn her living in the courts.

To put it quite simply, she would do anything to get a court appointment to represent an indigent defendant. You can use any euphemism you like; she used her skirt, flirted with court coordinators or judges, or made it known she was available to satisfy any manly needs to influential court personnel.

Traditionally, in Harris County and any other large county with innumerable criminal cases, there was an increasing demand for court-appointed attorneys.

The judges involved had their own ways of performing this task. In at least one felony court, the court coordinator was in charge of "shuffling the cards." When appointment opportunities arose, he would shuffle the business cards of attorneys anxiously awaiting their next paycheck. The attorney with the first card drawn got the next court appointment.

Mehaffey caught the coordinator in mid-shuffle one day and pleaded for her card to be the first drawn from the top of the deck. The coordinator protested, citing his own fairness doctrine. Undaunted, lawyer Mehaffey said, "Would this help?" She proceeded to hike her loosely-fitting skirt up to her chest and showed the coordinator that she wore no panties.

Purely coincidental, of course, Mehaffey started getting appointments in this court, and others as well.

Mehaffey continued using this feminine astuteness at every turn and, one might say, on every floor where there was even a misdemeanor court.

Sometime after the Tedesco case rested in the laps of frustrated Houston homicide detectives, I received a phone call from a Harris County deputy sheriff, Steve Melinder, who was working as the bailiff and process server for one of the county's misdemeanor courts, located a floor below our office. The bailiff told me that he had slept with Mehaffey – *surprise, surprise!* – on a few occasions. At one point she told him she was pregnant with his baby and demanded money for her medical expenses. She also threatened to call his wife if he didn't pay, which she ended up doing anyway despite his $300 monthly payments to her.

In our meeting Melinder said he understood that I was the "electronics guy" in Special Crimes and wanted someone with my expertise to "wire me up" in order to catch her lies on tape. The next morning, I put the wires in place as I had on numerous occasions by this time in my career in Special Crimes. Melinder was ready for the task.

Several hours later he returned with a recording. He did a great job. We had some evidence! You must understand that when many folks around the courthouse, particularly those of us with badges, know the Catherine Mehaffeys of the world, they (we) know it's just a matter of time before the protective shroud is lifted or the house of cards caves in. I told him that I would get with one of the ADAs and let him know what we could do. About an hour later, he called me and said he didn't want us to pursue any charges.

What?

Lordy, I hate to tell you in this early chapter, but this became a pattern in the Mehaffey saga, which is now in its forty-third year! A growing number of honest-to-goodness victims have come to believe they will die at her hand or that of a henchman if they provide enough evidence for, say, felony charges.

As I write this, I can firmly state that the number grows almost by the day or week. Most of them are so scared of Mehaffey that they want their identities erased from her memory bank.

This whole pregnancy situation continued to get more complex. An assistant district attorney, James "Slug" Lombardino, was a very good friend of Mehaffey, close enough to funnel cases to her when defendants came to court without an attorney. He got his nickname because he looked like a sloth. Lombardino's two-year tenure in the DA's office raised the eyes of many of his fellow ADAs, DA investigators like me, and, more significantly, the bosses that looked into his modus operandi.

The last thing any decent prosecutor, investigator, or secretary, for that matter, wanted to do was attract the attention of the boss, in this case, Harris County District Attorney Carol Vance. Carol ordered an investigation of Lombardino, whom I still more often refer to as "Slug." Slug had joined the DA's office in 1977 but, lo and behold, he was listed as an attorney in private practice in the Houston White Pages in 1978 and 1979. You can't do that. If you were caught at this particular "double duty," you were subject to being fired. You just can't serve two masters in our publicly-funded office.

Even more significant was the learned fact that Slug had a working relationship with Catherine Mehaffey. High-ranking ADAs could verify the habits of this dynamic duo. I know what you're thinking and I have to say at this point of the story that there was no evidence, or even "talk" that the relationship was sexual in nature. Although Slug was assigned to a county court at law, so called misdemeanor "no-attorney defendants" always needed representation. Well, Mehaffey got five in short order in Slug's court, raising the suspicions of the presiding judge therein.

As an investigator I can recite for you one of the oldest investigative adages in the book: One thing leads to another. That happened here. Carol's internal investigation turned up the pregnancy allegations against bailiff Steve Melinder and the resulting $300 monthly "hush" payments to lawyer Mehaffey. The last straw in this segment of the Mehaffey resume was the documented finding that Slug *knew* of this situation and encouraged the bailiff/process server to continue paying Mehaffey.

There was one other crucial factor in this scary scenario: *Mehaffey was not pregnant!*

Like I said, this episode cost Melinder his marriage. The record – detailed in heavy documentation by at least two newspapers and two network television documentaries – shows Mehaffey has confronted various lovers with accusations of pregnancy during her violent rants and accusations staged to get money, property, or both. Today she remains childless.

None of this fiasco was made public. James Lombardino left the DA's office in 1979. I guess you could say he went into "full-time" private law practice. Many years passed until 2010 when Lombardino, aka "Slug," became a successful Republican candidate for the 308th District Court, a family or "divorce" court. He got endorsements from the Republican kingmakers of Harris County despite midnight-hour information about his record in the DA's office. He won reelection in 2014 but was ousted in 2018 in the Democratic sweep of county officeholders in Harris County. At least Mehaffey's name wasn't among the list of supporters on his campaign letterhead.

HER WEB OF VIOLENCE

Mehaffey's issues continued to grow in the year 1979, forty-one years ago as of this writing. Shortly after the bailiff and "Slug" incidents, I got a phone call from Felix Mares, the chief investigator in the Galveston County DA's office, asking me if I knew a woman named Catherine Mehaffey and a man named Gary Taylor. Well, yes. I told him that Gary was a courthouse reporter for *The Houston Post* and that Mehaffey was a criminal defense attorney known in our books as "the kiss of death." He said that the previous night the Galveston police shined their lights on the two while they were partially clothed and in the middle of what appeared to be sexual intercourse on Stewart Beach.

Over the decades since this happened various legends have been voiced at the courthouse, in newsrooms and bars where reporters and the courthouse crew are known to frequent. One of them has the two of them buck naked on a Spiderman towel. Another said it was a Superman towel because, after all, Superman was (is) a newspaper reporter like Taylor.

Yet another legend has Taylor completing the task at hand before he would answer any questions from uniformed law enforcement officers. "Are we breaking a law," the laugh-filled legend reports have the always good-humored and self-deprecating Taylor as saying.

In reality, the couple was in an effective stage of unzipped jeans, discreet, yet in – shall we say – an enabling, facilitatory position. Suddenly, Taylor saw the headlights of an approaching vehicle. Then there was the guy with a flashlight. "We disengage," he remembered, "and are just sitting there by the time he reaches our spot."

To demonstrate the mindset of the Black Widow, Mehaffey admitted to her newest lover that she was fearful the intruder with the flashlight was a hit man hired by Tedesco's family. "It was my most memorable first date," the then-reporter recalled.

Mares was calling me to determine if law enforcement authorities in Galveston should file charges.

"That's up to you," I said. "But let me say that I hate to see Gary get into trouble. He's somewhat of a friend because he's interviewed me for several crime stories and has proven to be a trustworthy reporter."

After I got the call, I briefed my boss, Don Stricklin, the chief of Special Crimes, about the situation. Stricklin immediately took steps to summon Gary from the courthouse press room. He met with me, Stricklin and Jerry Carpenter, a Houston police detective assigned to the DA's office. We took turns warning him about her. He told us not to worry, that he could handle her. "She has two nicknames," I said to him, "the Black Widow" and "the Kiss of Death." He remained unfazed. Some reporters don't realize it when they're hearing wisdom from experts. When he left the office, I turned to Stricklin and said, "Don't worry. He'll be back in a few weeks or so."

I wish this was the end of the story. No way, I'm afraid.

In fact, it wasn't long before Gary came to our office scared to death. Catherine Hyde had emerged! He wanted help. I provided a tape recorder for his home phone to record her threats. I also gave a recorder to Jim Strong, a reporter with a radio show who was Taylor's good friend. Strong had a daily radio show dealing with the news of the day. He told us he also was getting threatening calls from Mehaffey. When it rained, it poured.

When she'd call Taylor, she would be screaming and hollering at the top of her lungs – like a banshee. In her calls to Strong, she sounded as meek as a lamb and complained about Taylor's treatment of her. She later couldn't afford rent for her own apartment and had taken up with Strong, as a friend, not one on her growing list of lovers. I followed Strong home one day for a search to determine if the Black Widow owned any firearms. We found only clothes and a Sony television. I took note of the serial number on the TV. Was it stolen?

Notwithstanding our quiet inspection, we got caught! She came home unexpectedly and immediately wanted to know who the hell I was and what I was doing there. I told her that I was a reporter friend of Jim's who had just stopped by for a visit. I could tell that she was suspicious and probably didn't believe a word of my story.

When I returned to the office, I ran a check on the Sony TV through the National Crime Information Center (NCIC) and learned that it was reported stolen in Rhode Island. Acting on this information, Stricklin called Mehaffey's attorney, Lloyd Oliver, to advise him of our finding. Later that afternoon, I drove to Oliver's office to take possession of the stolen property.

I was later looking at the offense report and saw that this TV set had a different model number, prompting me to call Sony to notify them of an apparent duplicated serial number with a different model number. Sony confirmed that this was common practice at the time. Same serial number on two different models! I had never heard of that before. This being the case, Stricklin called Oliver to let him know she could pick up her TV in our office. The Black Widow was off the hook.

Mehaffey in fact came to the office to retrieve the television. When I brought it out to her, she looked like she'd seen a ghost. She cussed me out and swore, "I'm coming back here with a hand grenade and blow up all you Special Crimes motherfuckers!"

"Okay," I said with the cool, "I guess I'll see you later."

This, we learned, was another Mehaffey tactic – threats of violent acts ranging from one-on-one confrontations to death, sometimes with arson mixed in.

When the doors opened on the elevator from our upper floor, Gary Taylor was standing there to help the woman I thought was his violent, erstwhile lover carry the television out to her car. Just a week before, he was afraid of her hurting him. Now he's with her to help her get her television back. I was on the path to believe this was a prime example of the kind of control that she had over men. But there was a key fact I didn't know at the time.

The man known as "Junkyard Dog" was no lovesick puppy, as I initially thought. I wasn't told at the time that Don Stricklin called him and pleaded for him to come up and help out Mehaffey. He meant help her out of our office. Neither Stricklin nor anyone else wanted to be in this temper-tantrum-plagued woman's presence for very long. We didn't realize that it wasn't really wise to place Taylor back in the company of Mehaffey when he was doing his best to break up with her without violence.

Like Mehaffey's first husband, Dr. Tedesco, and the law student/lover who lost his law books and papers in a fire, Taylor fell victim to what had become a routine Mehaffey ploy. Two weeks after helping the woman with her TV, he returned home to find that his house had been burglarized. He came to the quick realization that Mehaffey had something to do with it.

He fell into a web like those weaved by a real black widow spider. The real McCoys are known to eat their male companions after mating. Mehaffey was finished with any sexual acts with her familiar beach boy. She wanted to eat up his life.

Taylor went to her house to confront her about the burglary. He knew she was responsible, and she admitted it! The web began to squeeze its victim. She told Gary that his things were in the closet. When he opened the closet door, he found nothing but an empty space. Then he heard the sickening cock of the hammer of a loaded revolver. The Black Widow, likely feeling she was so close to the death of her victim that she could taste it, fired several rounds through the door.

Taylor's heart throbbed loudly. He knew he could either stay put and die or take a chance and run. He opened the closet door, picked up a chair as a shield, and ran out of the room as Mehaffey fired her pistol. One shot grazed him in the back of the head. He had enough adrenalin to fumble with the deadbolt and get out the front door. Mehaffey followed and shot him once more in the back. She had a gun in each hand like an old television cowboy or a femme fatale from the Old West or a film noir.

The twice-wounded Taylor fled to a small grocery store where he called for an ambulance. Once in treatment, a doctor told him that he shouldn't be alive because the bullet was only a centimeter from his heart.

A REAL CONVICTION... SORT OF

Taylor waited almost three decades to pen his true crime memoir, *Luggage by Kroger*, to detail his side of the Black Widow story. Arguably, as with most femme fatales documented in both fiction and non-fiction, the Mehaffey story largely centered around sex. The male victim in this case will tell you it was more than just frequent sexual intercourse, although he will admit that as a single, about-to-be-divorced thirty-two-year-old man about Houston, it was present in all three acts of the tragedy.

This episode in the life of a widely respected reporter began in September 1979 and lasted only until January 1980. Those like me, who have lived with the countless details surrounding Catherine Mehaffey's life, feel that this particular Black Widow has accounted for any number of years in our pursuit of ultimate justice. And, by the way, this is "justice" that we really haven't yet seen after this Teflon-enriched woman has prevailed for more than four decades, evading all but one or two criminal charges. That's forty-something years! Suffice it to say that the man his fellow reporters referred to as "Junkyard Dog" – a reference to the popular Jim Croce song which "kinda/sorta" reflected his approach to covering stories in the big city – was going through a divorce and ready for action.

Now by "action" I mean sexual exploits. Mehaffey would find the tiara of a beauty contest winner ill-fitting. But she could turn heads with the best of them with her above-average attractiveness and sometimes ribald personality. And I've already told you about her willingness to hike up her skirt to display her private parts. Put it this way: she tempted the Junkyard Dog enough to pull down her panties on a public beach that required all private parts to be covered.

The truth was that Taylor, the father of two young girls, sought a release from reality, which would include the child custody question. When such goals becomes the highest priority in a loose male's life, sex becomes the center of everyday operations. Mehaffey was the only blip on Junkyard's screen. He was available at her every beck and call to have sex. The beauteous blonde shared a law office with a male who made oral sex from "one of his whores" a regular amenity. Mehaffey wanted the same comfort and got it from Taylor. On more than one occasion she summoned him from his lair in the courthouse press room to her office just blocks away. "You're my whore," she told her couch mate as she stripped down to her blouse and engaged in various sex acts, all within earshot of her law partner.

So, Taylor fulfilled two major needs all in one. Not only was Mehaffey an entertaining "drinking buddy," she also was what proved to be a sex machine. "She was a clinical nymphomaniac," Gary would say years later in his book and in personal conversations. Today, he talks like he wishes it wasn't a case of a Black Widow seductress as much as a Sally that Harry was getting to meet with more often. Early in their relationship the two of them spent quality time laughing, often at Mehaffey's imitations of Harris County Courthouse regulars such as sitting judges and felony prosecutors.

But the laughing died and those shots rang out. Mehaffey, charged with attempted murder, went on trial in March 1980. Bert Graham, the chief of the Trial Bureau, prosecuted the case. Bert was a Houston native and graduate of Lamar High School. To this day, he holds the Harris County record for the longest sentence ever passed – one thousand years – for when he took the lead to try Henry Solomon, who along with two other defendants, kidnapped, and raped three coeds from a Rice University residential college and held them captive overnight. Solomon and his cohorts had a party in which their victims played along because they didn't want to be murdered. The next morning, the rapists dropped off the girls at their campus residence. The victims immediately called police, bravely coming forward to file a detailed report of the violence committed against them. At the trial, Graham said, "I asked for the one thousand years, in order to send a message to the parole board."

Bert Graham worked hard to earn this reputation for tough prosecutions. He had the distinction of having won convictions in fifty-four consecutive contested felony cases, twenty-eight of which were jury trials with twenty-six others that went before a judge without a jury. Then came this case. Alas, the jury deadlocked when defendant Mehaffey claimed that she fired in self-defense, stating that one of the two guns was the one that Taylor had brought to her house.

Jim Skelton, who represented Mehaffey in her trial for the attempted murder of Taylor, remembered one of his client's favorite stories about her formative years. She was barely a toddler when the local priest came to visit her family. Mehaffey didn't want to see the priest.

"So, she starts shouting 'doo-doo' and 'pee-pee' at him – the only nasty words she knew at that stage in life," Skelton said. "She was a real wampus kitty from the start. Catherine's always been that way."

Mehaffey was born in the Philadelphia area and moved with her family to Houston at age four. Befitting a movie script, her birthdates fluctuated over the years as did her birthplace, which could have been Chicago. She was born in 1948 – or was it 1943? Whatever her real age, she gained a youthful reputation as a rough-and-tumble tomboy, never afraid to take on other girls or boys in schoolyard fights. She was schooled at Houston's private Catholic Saint Agnes Academy. After graduation she enrolled at the University of Texas in Austin.

The strawberry blonde with the attractive, impish features of Sissy Spacek was a popular young woman, known for her quick wit and sometimes abrasive comments.

"She was the classic narcissistic personality," attorney Skelton said. "I've always said she had a misdemeanor brain and a felony mouth. She'd go to a Whataburger and demand to have what McDonald's was serving. Everything with her is eventually confrontational."

The State got a second trial. A jury found the shooter guilty and sentenced her to ten years in prison. But the Texas Court of Criminal Appeals reversed the verdict in the second trial. Taylor stressed to prosecutors that his highest priority was to see that she never practiced law again. He knew how important a bar card to use in all sorts of shady pursuits was the most important license in the would-be killer's life. Prosecutors knew by this time that the defense would likely agree to a plea bargain, and they did. In return for a guilty plea to the lesser charge of aggravated assault, Mehaffey would receive a ten-year probated sentence. Taylor consulted with Graham and the two concluded that if Mehaffey got ten years of hard time she could likely get out of prison on parole after serving one year. At this time in the Texas criminal justice system, it was very common for inmates to receive parole after serving one tenth of their sentence.

Graham believed at the time that the ten years' probation would cause her to be less likely to violate the law over that period than being on parole after having served only a year in prison. In other words, Mehaffey would be more concerned about going to prison, having never been there, than she would be on parole having already done one year of hard time.

She would be less likely to violate the law while on probation than she would be on parole.

The Black Widow was still on the law enforcement radar screen. Tommy Anthony Bell, age twenty-five, was not a stranger to the criminal justice system. Indeed, he had risen to the top of the short list of suspects in the Tedesco murder. Mehaffey owed Bell $10,000 and grew irritated when Bell kept pestering her about the unpaid debt. Bell was found shot to death in his apartment, a .357 Magnum pistol found nearby. The term Russian roulette was used in a medical examiner's ruling of suicide. Further implicating Bell was the fact authorities found items stolen from Taylor's residence, a burglary Mehaffey admitted to him she had arranged.

The Tedesco family filed a $10 million wrongful death damage suit against Mehaffey and Bell but the case never went to trial after Mehaffey's aggravated assault conviction in the Gary Taylor case. Over the years frustrated homicide detectives and prosecutors sarcastically suggest Tommy Bell might still be alive had he not ever associated with Catherine Mehaffey.

It would seem that everyone now had the Black Widow's number and she would be forever thwarted. Oh, but that Teflon came to the fore. She knew that the current Texas criminal justice system made it possible to petition the judge in your case to declare an end of your probation after just serving half of it. In 1988, after Mehaffey served five of the ten years' probation, a visiting judge granted the motion. Not only was she off probation, she got her law license back! The Black Widow was now free to roam without hindrance, an unbridled predator.

Just like a Harris County electorate foolish enough to elect "Slug" for a divorce court judge, the city of Dallas didn't know any better than to accept Mehaffey as an attorney with advertisements on the sides of Dallas Metro buses.

Down in Houston we were eagerly awaiting the time when we could say, "We told you so." Unfortunately, many lives were adversely affected and some lost before that happened.

An investigator's life sees many bad men – and women – hauled in and tried and convicted. I believe in these pages you will see justice administered but will sometimes share my frustration and disappointment hearing the details about how some of them got away or stopped short of getting what they really deserved.

The Black Widow stayed at the top of the list. You won't believe for how long.

Catherine Mehaffey

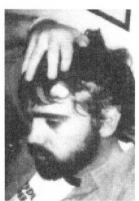

Gary Taylor   *Gary Taylor head wound*   *Tommy Bell*

Weapons found   *Bert Graham, ADA*

CHAPTER 2

"HERE COMES THE JUDGE"

On Friday, June 18, 1976, bureau chief Bob Bennett called me in his office late that afternoon and told me that he had a "super-secret assignment." As a young investigator, I always rose to the occasion when I realized the boss had that deep trust in my ability to keep secrets. Bennett placed the large 35mm camera case on his desk and said, "I need you to go take some pictures this afternoon and if they don't come out, don't bother coming back to this office on Monday."

I felt his trust and wasn't going to fail. My actual response: "Yes, sir, won't be a problem." I was confident but thought: *Holy shit, I've never even used a 35mm camera. What am I going to do?*

The boss then told me that if I ever told anyone about this investigation and he found out that he'd fire me on the spot. He said that only a handful of people knew about the investigation, which had started three months earlier. He said that the only person who knew about the case outside the bureau was Carol Vance, then district attorney who was everyone's boss, Houston Police Chief "Pappy" Bond, HPD Detectives Earl Musick and Sam Nuchia, and Sergeants Carl "Bob" Rees and Stanley Plaster of the HPD Vice Division.

I have to inform you at this point that Sam later became an assistant U. S. attorney in the Southern District of Texas, until he became the Chief of Police in Houston, under Mayor Bob Lanier. In 1997 he was elected judge of The First Court of Appeals in Houston.

I became an instant member of this elite crew. Hardly any of the others assigned to Special Crimes even knew about the investigation – only a select few.

He proceeded to tell me that we were investigating the duly elected state judge who sat on the bench of the 174th District Court. Judge Garth Bates was involved in a bribery scheme. Bates was a former Houston City Council member who had married into money and lived in a mansion near Rice University. He was known to rule in favor of the state most of the time, which induced Vance and most of the assistant DAs to like him.

One of Judge Bates' faults was that he liked to gamble, participating in gin rummy games with a bunch of crooks every afternoon in the bar located in the Sam Houston Hotel, near the Courthouse. One of the crooks usually at the table was Ed Ricklin, a local con man and gambler. Ricklin had become a friend of a "fence" named Nuckie "Frenchie" Fontenot, owner of a pawn shop, Northwest Jewelry and Loan, located at 9655 Hempstead Road, on the northwest side. Frenchie had a pending case in Bates' court for concealing and receiving stolen property that was taken in a robbery of a local jewelry salesman, Charlie Mize.

Ricklin made mention to Fontenot that he was a friend of the judge and could possibly help him on his case, but it might cost him some money. Special Crimes learned about the case when another local con man and gambler, Jerry Kottwitz, ran his mouth and it got back to the officers in the HPD Vice Division. The vice officers, in turn, went to Special Crimes and met with Bennett and Johnny Holmes.

During this same time, Musick and Nuchia had approached Frenchie about the investigation, and he agreed to cooperate in return for a possible deal on his pending case. Therefore, Bennett knew that Ricklin and the judge would be meeting at Ricklin's townhouse on McCue, in the Galleria area, that afternoon.

Bennett proceeded to tell me to take the film to a photo store that had no dealings or contracts with any law enforcement or government agencies, and to get the pictures developed as soon as possible. Hell, I was still thinking about what he said earlier if the photos didn't come out. He said that this would be the first meeting between the two that could be photographed. Yes, I was feeling the pressure. I went back to my office, worrying about my job. I opened the camera case hoping the operation manual was there. Fortunately, it was. I loaded the new tool with 35mm film and prayed that I wouldn't screw up.

I headed out to McCue and found a high-rise parking garage that overlooked Ricklin's townhouse. Here comes the judge! He went right up to Ricklin's house, well within the crosshairs of my new right-hand camera. I shot about twenty photos of his coming and going, praying the whole time the pictures would come out. I worried the whole weekend about the photos and on Monday morning I stopped by Floyd's Photo's Shop near downtown. I asked them if they had any government contracts or did any work for the government. They did not. So I left the film for development and told them I needed them later in the day. My work came out glossy and nice, and instantly I became the new Special Crimes photographer, undercover or in the open daylight. Shit, I couldn't even spell "photographer" then.

That week Bennett assigned me to assist Musick and Nuchia, in the investigation. Earl and I ended up working on hundreds of cases together when he was assigned to the bureau for over ten years. Earl is one of the best police officers that I ever worked with, as you'll read in this and some of my other chapters.

Basically, the investigation began when Charlie Mize the jewelry salesman sold some jewelry to Frenchie Fontenot, who learned Charlie kept these valuables in Houston's "high-dollar" Memorial area on the west side. Fontenot recruited career criminals Michael Ashley Nycum, Howard Pope, Steven Roy Clements, and professional wrestler Michael Gregory Todd, known as "Yukon Eric." Their job was to rob Mize and his family in their home.

THE KID AT HIS POST

Nycum got too high on drugs to participate in the robbery, which netted over $100,000 worth of jewelry. His absence effectively cut him out of the split, pissing him off to no end.

As a result, Nycum spilled the beans to Detective "Steve" Stevens of the Memorial Village Police Department. He snitched on the other robbers or "hijackers," as I call them. Stevens contacted Nuchia and Musick and provided the identities of the robbers. They wore stockings and pillowcases over their faces during the caper.

Because of the difficult identity of the suspects that Musick and Nuchia arrested, they went to Bennett in Special Crimes for help. He granted immunity to Pope, then got Todd and Clements charged with the robbery of the Mize family. The cases fell in Garth Bates' court, and they started working with Henry Onken, the court's chief prosecutor.

Immunized, Pope provided the details of the robbery plan under the direction of Frenchie, who ended up taking in all of the stolen jewelry. With this new information, Musick and Nuchia went back to Bennett to work with him and Oncken in trying to make a case on Frenchie. They were unsuccessful until Bennett shared further info about Frenchie that he had learned from vice officers.

Al Heath, a character who will appear in the next chapter, was working as a confidential informant with Harris County Sheriff's Deputy John Tanner. Heath told Tanner about the stolen jewelry. Tanner then worked with Musick and Nuchia and helped these great law enforcement officers set up a buy and busted Frenchie with the stolen jewelry.

Bennett and Oncken felt they had a very good case on Frenchie. Even though Frenchie was offering to try and snitch for help on his case, Musick and Nuchia told him no deal.

More good guys started to enter this already-complicated scenario. On March 3, 1976, police Sergeant Plaster along with Sergeant Rees met with Bennett and Holmes and advised them they had an informant who told them Frenchie Fontenot had been approached by Ed Ricklin, a gambler, and friend of Judge Bates, about having his case dismissed. As a result, Holmes initiated the case of bribery against the judge.

The next day, Musick and Nuchia went to Frenchie's store and taped him in the meeting where he finally admitted to his plan to buy his way out of the case. Fontenot said he'd been approached by Ricklin. Ricklin said he could "take care" of his case for $30,000. He also said that he didn't want to talk any more until he spoke to his attorney, Carl Ray.

This Musick-Nuchia operation prompted an early evening meeting that same day in Special Crimes, with an impressive cast in attendance: Bob Bennett, Carl Ray, Don Baker, Earl Musick, and Frenchie Fontenot. They formulated a plan for Fontenot to tape his conversations with Ricklin. At this meeting, Fontenot signed a consent to have an electronic device attached to his body so his conversations could be recorded. The problem was, Fontenot would have to go through Jerry Kottwitz in order to get in touch with Ricklin.

Kottwitz was out of town for several days, so it wasn't until March 9, 1976, that Fontenot and Ricklin spoke on the phone. During their conversation, there was no mention of money, only that Ricklin had received specific instructions on how the case would be handled, and if Fontenot didn't approve it wouldn't cost him a dime. Ricklin told Fontenot that he really didn't like talking on the phone because he felt there was always the chance somebody might be listening. They agreed to meet in a few days at the Denny's located on the Katy Freeway, a convenient location on the west side.

The next day Dr. George Hancock placed a cast on Frenchie's left arm in order to hide a wireless transmitter. The doctor crafted the cast to make it easy to turn it off and on, therefore saving the life of the batteries.

Their next face-to-face meeting wasn't until two weeks later. It took place at the El Chico Restaurant in Northwest Mall. Ricklin showed up in his 1975 two-toned blue and white Cadillac, wearing one of his leisure suits.

Ricklin was a person that many considered a high roller, someone who wanted you to think he was socially prominent and had lots of money. He was heavy set and wore an abbreviated Afro. He was always well-groomed and well-dressed.

Soon after the meeting, Special Crimes set up a plan in which Fontenot would leave the money in a safe deposit box and give the key to Ricklin when they decided on a price figure.

Fontenot and Ricklin only met once in April when Ricklin told him that he was busy working on a murder case with the judge. Ricklin also said that he was waiting for a report regarding Frenchie's case but that someone in the DA's office was putting pressure on this particular case. During a conversation in May, Ricklin said that Fontenot's case was going to be delayed for a year because the chief prosecutor, Oncken, was seeking serious punishment for Fontenot. In this context, Ricklin reminded Fontenot not ever to mention anything about Judge Bates.

In a meeting that took place at the Northwest Mall between Fontenot and Ricklin on June 1, Ricklin made a phone call to Harris County extension 486, which is the back line to Judge Bates' office, and they discussed a $30,000 figure to have Fontenot's case dismissed. Fontenot told Ricklin that he needed some insurance by talking to the judge himself.

Two days later, while Fontenot was conversing with Ricklin on the phone, a third person walked into Ricklin's apartment and Fontenot asked this person – thought to be Garth Bates – how many years they could get. "Ten years," the judge replied.

Ricklin told Fontenot that there was supposed to be someone from the Grand Jury Section of the DA's office with the judge, but they didn't show up.

Detective Nuchia drove to Ricklin's apartment during a Ricklin/Fontenot phone conversation and saw a black Cadillac with Texas District Judge license plates. The plates traced directly to Bates. The car was parked directly across the street from Ricklin's apartment. Later, Nuchia saw Judge Bates come out of the apartment and followed him to his residence located near Rice University.

On June 8, Fontenot learned from Ricklin that neither the judge nor the assistant DA would meet with him. The frustrated Fontenot called the judge on his back line. He told Bates that he had the money and was working with Ricklin but didn't think that Ricklin was "doing him right." Judge Bates said he couldn't get involved, that all he was interested in was that justice is done. Bates added that he was a good friend of Ed Ricklin and said he planned to transfer the case out of his court.

Later in the day, Ricklin called Fontenot and told him that it was wrong for him to call the judge, who was taking this risk as a favor to him, Ricklin. He also stated that if the case were transferred from the 174th that he could no longer help Fontenot. Furthermore, the price was now $60,000 to take care of his case.

On June 16, Fontenot, Ricklin, and Kottwitz met at 5400 Memorial and discussed the deal, but nothing was finalized. The next day, Jerry Kottwitz came to Fontenot's pawn shop and told him that he could take care of his pending cases for $100,000. Two days later Fontenot called Ricklin's home, and Judge Bates answered the phone. Bates said he was a friend from out of town, but Fontenot recognized the voice.

Later that afternoon, I drove to Ricklin's residence in my police junker, a light green metallic 1968 Ford station wagon, and set up an observation post in a parking garage on the fourth floor across the street. About half past four o'clock, I shot about fifteen pictures of Judge Garth Bates leaving the Ricklin abode and getting into his Cadillac.

Special Crimes Bureau soon called a meeting that included Fontenot, Bennett, Holmes, Nuchia, Hubbell, and me. We devised a plan entailing the $60,000 in cash being placed in a safe deposit box at Texas Commerce Bank, where Fontenot would take Ricklin and show him the money. Once this took place, Fontenot would ask for his insurance by speaking to the judge. In any event, we planned to arrest Ricklin once he got the money.

On this same day, Fontenot called Ricklin and told him that his attorney, Dan Ryan, wanted more money. Ricklin told him to fire his attorney and that he'd find him another. Ricklin called attorney Gerald Pate and left Fontenot on hold. Pate's secretary told Ricklin that the attorney was in court. Ricklin said he'd call back.

That afternoon Ricklin showed up at Frenchie's pawn shop and told him that he'd only talk to him while sitting in his car outside. Ricklin also drove a Cadillac. Once inside the car with Fontenot, he said he wanted the $60,000 up front and that if he went free, he'd want another $15,000 for his part getting the judge to cooperate. If he got probation, he wanted $10,000.

On July 14, we learned that Texas Commerce Bank didn't want us to exchange the money in their bank. Bennett, Holmes, and Baker went to Bank of the Southwest and found the same misgivings. We hatched another plan: exchange the money at Northwest National Bank, where Fontenot already had a safe deposit box.

The next day, Bennett and Baker went to Texas Commerce and got $60,000 in one-hundred-dollar bills. The money was immediately taken to Special Crimes where we recorded the serial numbers of each and every bill. It took a long time on our copy machine. It also required some protocol. Any time a law enforcement agency copied currency, it was required to contact the United States Secret Service for permission. We also had to provide the agency with its own copies.

During the noon hour that day, I sat in my favorite observation post overlooking Ricklin's home on McCue near the Galleria when I spotted Judge Bates drive by at a slow speed without stopping. Fifteen minutes later, Ricklin drove up in his Cadillac. He parked at the curb and got out with a flowered suitcase and went inside. It was less than half an hour when here comes the judge. I dutifully snap pictures of the judge entering Ricklin's house. Another half an hour passed before Bates and Ricklin came outside, shook hands, and parted company.

Special Crimes had to have another meeting – this time with the boss, District Attorney Carol Vance, in his office on the fifth floor of the Criminal Courts Building. Meeting with Vance were Holmes, Baker, and Hubbell. They advised the DA of the details of the plan in place. "It's a good idea," he said. "Let's go with it."

Later that evening another meeting was held at Hubbell's house. Bennett, Holmes, Hubbell, Baker, and Nuchia finalized the plan for the next day when the money would actually change hands – the very key needed to prove bribery against a sitting state district judge elected by Texans to preserve justice.

The final plan was to place the $60,000 in Fontenot's safe deposit box early the next morning and set up surveillance on the bank with DA investigators and HPD officers. We'd then wait for Ricklin to call Fontenot and meet him at the bank where he'd show him the money and call Judge Bates, who would be recorded when he talked to Frenchie. After the call, Ricklin would get the money and be arrested. We would take him to Special Crimes for questioning.

I got a call about nine that night. Hubbell told me my assignment on the big day: I was to go back to my observation post in the parking garage across from Ricklin's house and let them know when he left the premises. This really pissed me off because I thought I was going to miss all the action and not get to participate in the arrest of the distinguished-looking gray-haired jurist. On the other hand, I knew that I was just "the kid" in the bureau, so it wasn't that bad. I knew that not only were we a team, but a family as well, so I was just happy to be a part of this big story. I knew the news media would be going bonkers.

I had no idea that the next day, I was going to be right in the middle of the action.

THE STAGE IS SET!

Around seven the next morning, I parked at my usual post overlooking Ricklin's house. It wasn't long before I saw Ricklin, Bates, and an unknown white male, later identified as James Brown, come walking out of Ricklin's house. Judge Bates got into a white Oldsmobile. He wore a red baseball cap and blue overalls.

Ricklin got into his maroon Cadillac and was carrying a briefcase. He drove west with Judge Bates following him. Brown left in a green Buick but did not follow them.

I radioed the other investigators and officers who had the bank and Fontenot's pawn shop under surveillance. I advised them that our suspects were probably headed their way. Hubbell, parked near the pawn shop, observed Bates and Ricklin drive past the shop and park across the road near the Foley's Department Store at the Northwest Mall. It was just after 8 a.m. if you were keeping score – and I was along with my other teammates.

Fifteen minutes later, right on cue as planned, Bennett and Fontenot entered the Northwest Bank before it opened and placed the money in Frenchie's safe deposit box. So far, so good. Simultaneously, Debbie Burkhalter, Special Crimes secretary and radio dispatcher, discovered ten one-hundred-dollar bills in the copier. Holmes had accidentally left them there the night before.

Something had to be done *fast*. Fortunately, Bennett and Holmes ran a tight ship. Their people knew what to do in what amounted to an office emergency.

Assistant DA Ross Rommel took the crucial first step: "Base 300 to 301," he said into the two-way communicator.

"Go ahead," Holmes the airplane pilot responded, businesslike.

"Can you call the office, please."

Holmes, every bit the true "Sherlock," knew that something must be terribly wrong because Rommel knew not to bother any of the Special Crimes staff working this nerve-wracking operation. Rommel's move proved to be a game-changer. Events would underscore this move as being the case.

The mall fronted on Hempstead Highway, which ran past the pawn shop, located just across from Foley's. HPD Sgt. Rees and Officer Mont-gomery were parked near Hempstead to watch the traffic. HPD Detective Earl Musick was parked near the Penney's on the mall's north side. Nuchia, along with Bennett, were parked near the bank. Also in the bank parking lot were DA's investigators Baker and Emily Vasquez.

At 8:55 a.m. Musick spied Ricklin drive by the judge's car and give an affirmative nod as a signal for the judge to continue toward the bank. Baker then saw Fontenot pull in a parking spot near the bank's front door.

The stage was set!

Or was it?

Fontenot got out and made some motions to the investigators that the plan was changing and that there was a gun involved. Shortly after that, Ricklin went up to Fontenot and handed him a grey briefcase as they proceeded to the front door waiting for the bank to open at nine o'clock.

The doors opened, and Fontenot entered alone while Ricklin remained outside. Seconds later, Baker and Vasquez entered the bank to arrest Ricklin once the money changed hands. The problem was that Ricklin never came in because Fontenot had come out and given him the $59,000 in the parking lot. Yes, the agreed-on price was $1,000 short.

There were some miscommunications between the HPD officers and DA investigators. All the actors left with no one following them! We just lost $59,000 and no one arrested!

It wasn't a case of here comes the judge to jail. No. There *went* the judge!

I was listening to this "cluster fuck" go down while sitting helplessly on the fourth floor of a parking garage less than five miles away from the scene. One could tell by the radio traffic that there was panic in Bennett's voice, as well as those of the others.

I actually felt relief. At this moment I thought, *I'm glad I wasn't assigned to the bank and lost the money. Somebody's ass is going to be in trouble with the boss.*

I could hear on my HPD radio officers and investigators on the ground talking to the two HPD helicopters, known in local policing as "Fox units," advising them of the situation. The radio chatter was frantic: *We just lost a shit load of money that wasn't ours!*

Holmes realized that it was a good thing that he left a thousand dollars on the copier, so we had Fontenot make a call to the judge and tell him that he accidentally shorted him a thousand dollars. "Don't worry," the judge said, "I'll get it later."

Baker and Vasquez went to the judge's home around 10 a.m. and spotted him in the driveway, still wearing the same red cap and overalls. He eventually left about three hours later, driving toward the courthouse. Investigators and the HPD Fox unit lost sight of him about thirty minutes later.

I remained alone for several hours in the parking garage overlooking Ricklin's townhouse. Then other investigators and officers showed up there. Before their arrival, I saw Ricklin park in front and get out of his vehicle carrying a gray briefcase and chrome-plated sawed-off shotgun under his arm. I radioed Bennett and Holmes to give them the report. Bennett began drafting a search warrant for Ricklin's house in search of an illegal weapon.

At 2:40 p.m., I moved my "trash mobile" to the north side of McCue. By then, I had HPD Sgt. Bob Rees in my passenger seat. Nuchia and Texas Ranger Kelly Whitehead, a former classmate of mine at Sam Houston State, were parked behind Ricklin's townhouse.

At that same time, a City of Houston garbage truck with four city workers on board was headed north on McCue emptying the garbage cans into the back of their truck. A man later identified as "the maintenance man" went to Ricklin's front door and told him that there were some "strange people" parked around his house.

Ricklin came out of the townhouse to check on the situation. He was carrying his sawed-off shotgun. Rees and I got out of the county station wagon with guns. The garbage collectors quickly jumped under their garbage truck to take cover.

I lost sight of Ricklin, who was hidden behind the truck, and Rees pulled the trigger of his 9mm in Ricklin's direction because I heard the sound of his hammer striking the firing pin and nothing happened.

By that time Nuchia and Whitehead had rushed Ricklin and placed him under arrest and secured him in Nuchia's city ride.

While in front of Ricklin's apartment, Judge Bates drove up in his black Cadillac with that traditional white judicial license plates issued by the State of Texas: TX 326.

"Here comes the judge!" We almost hollered in unison, with Earl leading the chorus. Earl turned and pulled out his badge and flashed it as the judge started backing up. When Musick ran to the driver's side window, the judge asked him, "What's going on?"

Earl informed him that he was under arrest for bribery.

JUDICIAL AFTERMATH

"There must be some kind of mistake," Judge Bates retorted, sounding like a defendant in his court. Musick searched him and found $2,900 in the judge's right front coat pocket. The serial numbers matched those on the one-hundred-dollar bills we had copied earlier.

"I got those from Ricklin," Bates explained, already concocting a defense plea.

I'm standing by thinking, *"No shit, Sherlock; why do you think we're out here?"*

On the way to Special Crimes, HPD Officer Jimmy Sturdevant read the judge his legal warnings and listened to Bates tell him he well understood his Miranda rights, and he further stated that he'd get everything straightened out when he talked to Carol Vance. Sturdevant just smiled patiently.

Nuchia read Ricklin his rights and asked him if he'd sign a consent form for us to search his house, which he promptly did. After signing the form, Nuchia, Whitehead, and I entered the house with Ricklin in tow.

Nuchia asked Ricklin where he had the money, and he said: "I'll show you." He added, "I only have half the money, I gave the four other bundles to Garth and he had me give two of the bundles to Brown, his probation officer."

Nuchia asked Ricklin, "You mean you got six bundles, and Judge Bates got six bundles?" Ricklin said, "Yes, and the judge had me give two of his bundles to Brown." Ricklin added that they split the money at Brown's office on South Post Oak.

Ricklin then reached down and picked up a white fuzzy decorative pillow from the floor near the west wall of his den. He unzipped it and removed six bundles of hundred-dollar bills that were each held together by a rubber band. "This is all I have," he explained. "The judge and Brown have the rest."

We then took the money, as well as the $1,059 in Ricklin's pocket and tagged it for evidence. We also saw the flowered briefcase and tagged it as well.

While Nuchia and I were searching the bathroom, Nuchia bent over, and his HPD ID and small phone book fell from his shirt pocket into the toilet. That got a big-ass laugh from me. He started cursing and saying, "Oh shit, all my numbers are running."

Ricklin then took us to Brown's office on Post Oak, and Hubbell and I remained there awaiting his return.

Meanwhile, back in Special Crimes, Bates was told that he couldn't speak to Carol Vance, so he said that he would have to give Bob Bennett an explanation.

Bates went on to tell Bennett, Musick, and Sturdevant that he was letting Ricklin in on a good investment and that Ricklin was collecting a gambling debt that morning at the Northwest National Bank. Furthermore, Bates said he never knew where the money came from. He tried to explain that Ricklin owed him some money, so he and Brown went over and picked up $4,000 from his debtor.

By four o'clock Judge Stanley Kirk read State District Judge Garth Bates his legal warnings. Investigators then compared the serial numbers of the six bundles of one-hundred-dollar bills and what do you know – they learned that they perfectly matched the numbers copied and sent to the Secret Service. The $1,059 in Ricklin's pocket was not a match.

While this was happening, Hubbell and I entered the Executive Suites at 1200 South Post Oak and met the manager, A. B. Cass, who told us that James H. Brown had recently leased the office space using a check written on the Garth Bates Ranch Account. He also advised us that Mr. Brown wouldn't return until five o'clock, approximately one hour away.

Upon Brown's return, Hubbell and I identified ourselves and told him that Judge Bates and Ed Ricklin had been arrested for bribery and we wanted the money that had been given to him. Brown told us that Ricklin handed him $10,000 in one-hundred-dollar bills at the direction of Judge Bates and was told by Bates to make a $10,000 payment on some property.

Brown then produced a copy of a cashier's check from Dickinson State Bank in the amount of $10,000. Brown said that it was for some property that the judge had been negotiating to buy.

After we explained to Brown that the money was taken in a bribe, he told us that if we took him to the U. S. Life Title Company that he'd get the check back.

Brown told us that he was a Harris County Adult Probation officer assigned to Judge Bates' court. He said he'd known the judge for quite a few years and told us that he kept Judge Bates' business books on the judge's two ranches and had conducted financial transactions for him for several years. Brown said that the judge called him the night before to say that Ed Ricklin was going to give him some money for a long overdue gambling debt and wanted Brown there just in case there was any trouble.

Bennett and First Assistant DA Sam Robertson interviewed Brown at Special Crimes and saw to it that he was summoned to appear before a grand jury on Monday, July 19, 1976.

While Judge Kirk read Ricklin his statutory rights in our office, the defendant said he had been well treated by officers, but he thought he was having a heart attack. He said Nuchia had revived him when he passed out earlier in the day. I wondered if it happened when Holmes gave him the bullet that misfired from Rees's gun. As a precaution, we sent Ricklin to Ben Taub General Hospital, where he learned he had merely suffered from hyperventilation.

The following week we brought in Jerry Kottwitz for his interview. He had some bullshit story about the whole ordeal, so we let him go and told him that we were going to bring him back and have him listen to some tapes we had made of him.

We counted all of the money that we thought we were going to lose to discover we were still missing $16,100, which mysteriously reappeared in Vance's desk when he was gone one day. It seems Houston private investigator Clyde Wilson had stopped by and told Vance's secretary, Carolyn Limmer, that he needed to leave the DA a personal note on his desk.

Wisely, the state district judges in Harris County recused themselves from any court hearing or trial involving their colleague Garth Bates. The unprecedented predicament called for securing a visiting jurist, Judge John Barron from Brazos County. Judge Barron heard the Bates case in which a jury found the one-time judge guilty and sentenced him to eight years in the Texas Department of Corrections.

Sometime later, Judge Bates applied to receive shock probation from Thomas Routt, the sitting judge in the 209th District Court. Before the sentencing, Judge Routt met with a former co-worker of the Texas Attorney General's Office and a friend of mine, attorney Timothy Sloan (a female), and asked her for her opinion.

"Didn't he lose his law license and bench?" she asked.

"Yes," Judge Routt replied.

"Don't you think that's enough?"

The judge proceeded to grant shock probation to former Judge Bates. And there went the judge to Fayette County, where oil was discovered on his property there. He made a lot of money from the venture – probably a lot more than $59,000 in one-hundred-dollar bills.

Garth Bates and Ed Ricklin meeting on June 18, 1976

Judge Garth Bates   *Frenchy Fontenot*   *Ed Ricklin*

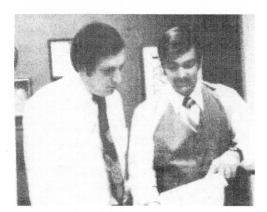

Earl Musick and Sam Nuchia

CHAPTER 3

BIG AL

In the tightly-knit law enforcement environs of the nation's fourth-largest city, Arnulfo Ordonez Heath, aka Al Heath, was well known as an informant, especially when the investigations involved organized crime cases. I had heard about him but never met him – until Bobby Blaylock and I arrested him shortly after the evidence in his pending delivery of cocaine case disappeared at trial. Al was about six feet tall or more and had some girth on him but wasn't too fat. Al was always smiling.

Specifically, he was being tried in July 1978 in the courtroom of colorful state District Judge "Wild Bill" Hatten. Judge Hatten was well known and respected around the Harris County Courthouse. You had to like him and respect him. He was practically the only judge in South Texas or, heck, the rest of the state who looked the part. Seeing was believing; Hatton had curly gray strands of hair that flowed to the shoulders. Was this the way Judge Roy Bean looked? Quite probably.

Funny things seemed to happen in the Hatton tribunal. In this case, some unknown individual(s) had used either a large screwdriver or tire tool to break into the court reporter's office and steal the evidence. We ultimately arrested Big Al's attorney, Ralph Chambers, along with former DA Investigator Lannie Phillips. To get enough evidence to prosecute Chambers and Phillips, we had to "cut a deal" with Big Al Heath. Part of his "deal" was that we would dismiss his case and in turn, revoke his federal probation involving counterfeit money. Plus, when he would be returned from his federal prison cell to Houston for the trial, he wouldn't be housed in the Harris County Jail.

On August 29, 1978, Big Al signed an agreement to cooperate with Special Crimes in the case against Chambers and Phillips. Later, Chambers came to our office to meet with his "client." Blaylock and I taped the meeting held in our conference room. We had carefully placed a hidden video camera and microphone in a bookshelf. During the meeting, Chambers told Heath that he needed to recover his portion of the stolen cocaine taken from Hatten's court reporter in order to sell it for money needed for his defense.

After their meeting, ADAs Henry Oncken and Don Stricklin, along with Blaylock and me, decided to put the cocaine in a tree on Big Al's property. Chambers could then pick it up, setting the stage for us to arrest him.

Detectives Earl Musick and Jerry Carpenter drove Big Al to San Antonio to recover Heath's portion of the stolen cocaine. The stash would be returned to the HPD Crime Lab, where chemist Martin Wuensche tested and marked the cocaine. We then placed it in a paper sack that looked like the same sack used when Chambers gave the stolen cocaine to Heath.

Blaylock and I went to the Heath residence and had Big Al's wife, Maria, or "Chuy," call Chambers and tell him that she had a package for him and that she'd call him later that night when he could pick it up. We made a recording of the conversation for evidence. Al's house was located in a small subdivision in the shadows of The Galleria, Houston's world-renowned shopping center. The house was located on a street off San Felipe at the dead end of a cul-de-sac, so there was only one way in and one way out.

Around ten o'clock that evening, Carpenter and I, along with Big Al, met at the Heath abode. Carpenter placed the paper bag containing the cocaine in a tree in the front yard. I directed Chuy to call Chambers and advise him that his package was in the tree and he could come get it at his convenience.

"I'll be right there," Chambers told her. Carpenter, Big Al, and I hid in a front bedroom, where we could observe the hidden package. The rest of our surveillance team, which consisted of Blaylock and Musick. were near the entrance of the street.

It wasn't long before Chambers and his son Mark showed up in front of the residence. Chambers knocked on the front door, and Chuy let him inside. We couldn't hear what was being said in the ensuing five minutes. Chambers came outside and headed straight to the designated tree and retrieved the cocaine. By then, Musick had radioed for an HPD patrol unit to assist in the arrest on San Felipe. The two uniformed officers were J. R. Swaim and L. L. Obenhaus. Swaim just happened to be one of my fraternity brothers at Sam Houston State, once again proving my lifelong adage that the good guys stick together.

We radioed Musick that Chambers was headed in his direction, effecting Chambers' arrest minutes later. Musick's pistol had fallen out of his waistband as he was getting out of his police vehicle. So, he improvised – he arrested Chambers with his pointed index finger, pointing the digit like it was a pistol. I can't tell you how many times when asking Earl to go with me to make an arrest I just had to ask, "Hey, Earl, be sure and bring your finger." I don't think I ever let Earl live that down. But I have to say in reflection that the pointed finger – the same "weapon" we used on the elementary school playground – got the job done. And no shots were fired!

MY EVER-PRESENT "PARTNER"

Once investigators returned to Special Crimes to meet with Henry Oncken, Don Stricklin, and two other prosecutors, Ted Wilson and Doug Shaver, we prepared a probable cause affidavit to effect the arrest of former DA Investigator Lannie Phillips. Blaylock and I drove to Phillips' house and waited until the warrant was signed by State District Judge Lee Duggan Jr., another great criminal judge (short hair). We now had the paperwork needed to make the arrest. It was 2 a.m. We arrested Phillips inside his house, sparking a seemingly endless barrage of cuss words from the mouth of Phillips' wife.

"Ma'am," I told her, "we're just doing our job. There's no reason for you to talk to us like this." What I really wanted to say, was, "Would you please shut the fuck up."

When we returned to Special Crimes an hour later, Carpenter and Musick questioned Phillips about the burglary, but he said that he wanted to talk to his lawyer first. He had been an investigator; he knew the routine.

I worked in the DA's office with Phillips while he was an investigator assigned to a district court. But I really didn't know him too well. I learned that Carol Vance hired him when he became district attorney. Lannie was a deputy district clerk in a court where Carol was assigned when he was an ADA. I didn't know much about Lannie's investigative skills, but he was one funny SOB. He and his brother, a clerk, worked in a comedy club on the weekends.

Once everybody was in custody and charged, Big Al was sent to a federal prison located at Eglin Air Force base near Panama City, Florida, to serve out his sentence in a counterfeiting scheme.

A few months later, Al returned to Houston. We would treat him as my guest. The U. S. Department of Federal Prisons placed him in my custody. I mean, I had volunteered to "babysit" him during his previous stay in our jurisdiction. We stayed in the Holiday Inn on Main Street, just a block from our office. I brought him to work with me every morning, so he could meet with the ADAs prosecuting Chambers and Phillips.

After two weeks, I decided that I could trust him because I'd gotten to know him pretty well. Plus, I was missing my family. I took him to his home after work and picked him up in the mornings and took him to work with me. I told Johnny Holmes, first assistant district attorney at the time, that I was taking him home at night. He covered his ears and said, "I don't want to know where he's staying or anyone else to know, as well. Just take care of him like you did Rothkopf. That's all I'm asking you to do, and I know you're good at doing that."

"Yes, sir that won't be a problem," I said, excited that he was still pleased with my protection of Bill Rothkopf, the star witness against Texas Supreme Court Justice Donald B. Yarbrough, another Special Crimes spectacular detailed in other chapters.

Big Al was a chef by profession and at one time was the head chef of the Balinese Room, which stood over the Gulf of Mexico and was a famous night club in Galveston during the 1940s and 1950s. It was operated by the Maceo Brothers – Sam and Rosario – and was a dance hall and illegal casino. Entertainers such as Frank Sinatra, Bob Hope, George Burns, and the Marx Brothers played the Balinese. Some of the famous patrons included Howard Hughes and Sophie Tucker. Al was a very likable and funny guy. By the end of his first six months of his "stay" at Special Crimes, everybody liked him. Some of the new guys thought he worked there as my partner because he went with me everywhere – like a shadow – except to the men's room, of course.

I took him along on investigations but never introduced him to the victim or witness as an investigator.

On one occasion, I took him with me when I was trying to find and arrest Kerry Crocker, who had jumped bail for Castration by Radiation on his own son, Kirk. In 1971, Crocker, a petroleum engineer, had put radioactive pellets in his son's headphones, under his bed, in his pillows, and other private places while he was going through a nasty divorce from Kirk's mom.

By 1972, Kirk knew something was weird about his dad, and he was beginning to feel the effects of the radiation poisoning. When he would stay with his dad on weekends, he felt as if his own father wanted to harm him for some unknown reason. He later said, "I could just sense it." On one occasion, Kerry Crocker went out to run some errands and told his son, "Be sure and wear your headphones. I don't want you to bother the neighbors." Once alone, Kirk found some silver pellets under some cotton in the earphones and called his mother. She told him not to worry. He also saw that his fingers were red and sore.

The next time he visited his dad, he found more pellets in his pillows and under his bed. He also had developed a rash, and his hair was falling out. This continued for about two years before he visited sixteen doctors and finally learned that the diagnosis was radiation poisoning.

A grand jury indicted Kerry Crocker in 1973 in connection with the chemical castration of his thirteen-year-old son. His case was pending in the 184th District Court, where I was the assigned investigator. A jury convicted him and sentenced him to ten years in prison. He appealed his case and was still out on bond until the Texas Court of Criminal Appeals could file its review. This process was in progress in 1978 when Crocker jumped bond and disappeared. I was in Special Crimes by this time. His bondsman wanted my help because he knew that I'd worked the case five years before. He wanted me to find Crocker because he didn't want to pay the civil fees for bond jumping.

It didn't take a rocket scientist to figure out that I deeply despised Crocker for what he did to his son. I wanted to find him. I grabbed Al and Crocker's file and went to Crocker's last known office located in the historic Millie Esperson Building on Travis Street in downtown Houston. When we arrived, I saw a security guard in the main lobby and showed him my police credentials.

"Have you ever seen this guy?"

"Yes," he replied. "He works on the ninth floor where the petroleum company is located."

The company occupied the entire ninth floor. We went there and I flashed my law enforcement identification and posed the obvious question.

"He's the owner of our company," she said as if I should have known. I asked her to fetch him for me, and she willingly complied.

We expected to see Kerry Crocker. The man the receptionist had summoned took us to his office, where I asked him, "Are you Kerry Crocker?"

"No!" he said, readily admitting that the photo I displayed resembled him. He insisted that he was not the individual in the picture.

When I told him he was going to have to accompany me to the sheriff's office to compare his fingerprints to make sure, he went "crazy" on me.

"We can do this the hard way or the easy way," I said to this crazed company owner. "The choice is yours. I can handcuff you, or we can just walk out of here like we're going to lunch. So, what do you want to do?"

We "went to lunch." We took him to the ID section of the sheriff's office where they compared his prints. He wasn't Crocker! We gave him a ride back to his workplace. He wasn't a happy camper.

Before Al and I returned to the office, the Crocker lookalike called Henry Oncken, the chief of Special Crimes, complaining about the "short fat white guy" and his "big Mexican partner" who'd arrested the wrong man.

When my "Mexican partner" and I reached Special Crimes, we had some explaining to do.

"This guy was the spitting image of Crocker," I insisted. "You'd have done the same thing, Henry. I never told him that he was under arrest, but I did tell him that he's going to have to be fingerprinted to confirm that he's not Crocker. I don't think that I had any other choice."

Henry was smart and sensible. He agreed that I handled the situation appropriately. I don't think that he was happy about Big Al being with me, but he knew that Holmes wanted me to take care of Al. If something "happened" to Al, we'd have no case against Chambers and Phillips.

Crocker was on the run a total of three years after the state's highest criminal appeals court upheld his ten-year conviction. He began serving his sentence in January 1981 and became a model prisoner in the Texas Department of Criminal Justice. Crocker was paroled in October 1986 despite his son's campaign to keep him behind bars as long as possible. He didn't return to Houston after being paroled to Tarrant County.

MEMORIAL PARK KEG STORY

My "partner" Big Al and I continued making all the rounds included in my list of duties and off-duty fun time. Soon after the ordeal with the Crocker lookalike, our DA softball team, the Indictments, had its annual weekend "challenge" softball game with the team from the misdemeanor division. I played second base for the Indictments and brought Big Al to the game and had him umpire behind home plate.

No one on the misdemeanor team knew who Al was and only a handful of guys on my team – those from Special Crimes – knew that Al was "on loan" from federal prison. After two games, which we won, we had a keg of beer for all the players. DA Carol Vance played on the misdemeanor team every year, so he could get to meet and know some of the new prosecutors.

Carol was a big stickler about knowing and learning all the office members by name. He was so adamant about this that he made a small booklet with pictures and personal information of all employees. While standing by the beer keg with Big Al, our star witness, Carol approached him and stuck out his hand.

"Carol Vance, how are you today?" the district attorney said. "What court are you assigned to?"

Big Al just looked at me, wanting to know what to say. I whispered in Carol's ear, "He's Al Heath, the witness in the Chambers Phillips case."

"Yes," the DA said, trying to recover. He turned to Al and said, "I knew that. Thanks for your help, Al. You did a great job of umpiring today. You're in good hands with Ken."

I was thinking to myself: Carol doesn't have the foggiest idea of who Al is, only that there was an informant that was going to testify against them. He probably didn't even know that Al was supposed to be in federal prison and on loan to us. But, hey, the busy DA had a lot on his plate.

A bunch of us on our team later went to Otto's, a well-known ham-burger and barbecue place on Memorial Drive and a favorite hangout of former President George H. W. Bush. We were still drinking our kegged beer and standing in the parking lot in front of the barbecue section of Otto's. I pulled Big Al aside and told him that we were going to play a joke on Don Stricklin, who was chief of the Narcotics and Organized Crime Division in Special Crimes. For some unknown reason, Stricklin nicknamed me Clouseau, after the fictional character in Blake Edwards's farcical The Pink Panther series.

Don was a "perfectionist," especially when it came to our cases and his hair – he had plenty of it. Don and I became good friends when we both were assigned to the 184th District Court in 1973. Don grew up in Baytown, east of Houston, and attended Lee High School, where he played on the football team and was very popular on the Lee High campus.

When his team had two-a-day football practices (morning and afternoon) before school actually started, his dad required him to bale hay. That had to be very hard work before the swelteringly hot afternoon practice sessions. In 1973, when Don, Sam Adamo Sr. and I were assigned to the 184th District Court, we were invited to play for the DA's softball team, the Indictments, because they needed some more players. Stricklin shows up wearing a train engineer's cap, and Adamo called him "Choo Choo," a name that would stick with him for quite a while. I don't remember anyone calling him that once he became a district court judge.

Don graduated from the University of Texas and later from Bates School of Law at the University of Houston. Don and I used to play practical jokes on each other quite often. My favorite antic was to stare at his well-coifed hair when we were in his office. He would eventually open the top middle drawer of his desk and get out a small mirror and examine his carefully sculptured appearance. He caught on and barked at me, "Cut it out!" Don was a great guy and very smart prosecutor. And I'm sure whoever did his hair was amply rewarded.

I gave Al my .357 Smith and Wesson revolver, which I had unloaded, and told him, "When I wink at you, take my pistol out of your pocket and say, 'Ken, here's your gun back.' "

Once the plan was laid, Big Al got back into our circle. A few minutes later, I winked at him, and he carefully pulled the gun out of his pants and said, "Here's your gun back, Kenny."

I thought Don was going to have a heart attack or dirty his britches.

"Don, it was a planned joke," I cautioned. "Relax."

We then decided to go to travel a few blocks down Memorial Drive to picturesque Memorial Park. We found the perfect place to finish off the keg: the jogging path by the tennis center. As you would expect as the rounds of beer reached an unsteady peak, we got a little rowdy. Understand, now, that we were law enforcement personnel and committed no crimes.

Investigator Joe Vara had Big Al get into a trash can to direct traffic in order to pull over attractive girls to meet the single guys. Somebody called HPD and complained. We look up and see an HPD patrol car coming around Memorial Circle with its red lights flashing. Remember, I've been telling you in these pages that law enforcement officials – the good guys – stick together. We were fortunate that the officers recognized some of us, put on the brakes, turned off the red lights, and backed away.

I retold this story with more details in 2008 when we had a softball team reunion at Otto's because they were closing the business in retirement to make way for a new bank and strip center.

Almost all of the old-timers in the keg crew showed up for the get-together along with Johnny Holmes. Johnny wasn't a former softball player, but we had all worked closely with him during this time. (You only worked closely with the dedicated crimefighter known as Johnny Holmes). Some of these special alumni were now criminal judges and defense attorneys. It was a great time seeing everyone again, and we all had a good time. (No, we didn't take in Memorial Park).

Not too much later after the reunion, Carol Vance had a book signing party for his book, Boomtown DA, at a friend's home in River Oaks. Most of the old softball players were there, including yours truly. We were all mentioned in his autobiography. Holmes, his trademark handlebar mustache well waxed, praised Carol, and told a few stories. He brought up about Carol being a stickler for remembering all the names of the employees and started telling my Memorial Park story.

I looked around at former players Don Stricklin, Jack Frels, Bob Moen, Mack Arnold, Joe Vara, and others. No, the umpire wasn't there. I'm sure I took the lead in looking for a place to hide. Holmes proceeded to tell the audience that it was my story that he'd recently heard at a softball team reunion. I thought that this couldn't be happening right now. We're going to sound like a bunch of idiots.

When Holmes got to the part about Carol meeting Big Al at the beer keg and asking him his name, he ended the story. I looked at the guys, and they were all relieved, as well as I was.

LIKE FAMILY TO ME

Before Big Al returned to federal prison, he wrote a letter to his cellmate, Orlando "Baby Bull" Cepeda, and told him that he couldn't wait to get back to prison because he needed a vacation. Cepeda was a former professional baseball player primarily for the San Francisco Giants and St. Louis Cardinals.

Cepeda was convicted for smuggling drugs from Colombia after conducting a baseball clinic. He served ten months of a five-year sentence before he was given probation. He was inducted into the Baseball Hall of Fame in 1999. Al remained friends with Cepeda and stayed in touch with each other until Al's death.

Al was well known in the Houston crime circles. He knew most of the major crooks in Houston, including the major Mexican drug leaders before they were called cartels. His street nickname was "Tio," which in Spanish means "uncle." Al also was a virtual walking crime encyclopedia. I could give him a name, and he would tell me the crook's history and what they were doing and where they lived.

The one thing about Big Al was that he never lied to me at any time in the thirty years that I knew him. I don't care what I asked him, he always spoke the truth. There was honor among informants. Big Al testified in the Chambers case that Holmes was prosecuting. Chambers was found guilty and received ten years in prison – and reported to TDC after all of his appeals failed.

When Big Al returned from his "country club" federal prison for the Phillips trial, I continued with taking him home every night and picking him up every morning for his trip to Special Crimes. By then everybody in the office knew and liked him. It almost seemed that he was part of our staff. We didn't include him in our weekly staff meetings or share any information on our cases with him – unless he knew the crook.

Some thirty years later, when I was retired, I received a phone call from one of my former interns from Sam Houston State. Steve Januhowski was then an HPD Narcotics investigator. He said, "Don't you have an informant who knew most of the major drug traffickers in Houston? I'm looking for a major offender that we've been looking for the past year and I need some help in trying to find this asshole."

"I usually talk to Big Al every week or so," I said. "If Al can't find him, nobody can. I'll give him a call and let you know."

I called Big Al and told him that my buddy from HPD was trying to arrest a crook wanted on some major drug deals and needed his help in locating this individual. He said that he played volleyball every day off of North Main with some members of a Mexican drug cartel and that he'd see what he could find out for me.

A few days later he called me and gave me the location of the crook. I asked him, "How in the world do you do what you do for me and haven't been killed yet?"

He laughed and said, "They trust me."

"Don't you think that eventually, they're going to figure it out that you're working with the police?"

"No way that's going to happen, I've been doing this too long to worry about it."

"Dude," I said, "I just worry about you and your family. I just don't want you guys to get hurt or killed." I ended the conversation by saying, "OK, man, just be safe."

I knew all of Al's family members very well since I was going to and from his house for almost a year during my "babysitting" duties during the Chambers and Phillips cases. His wife Chuy was a soldier to put up with all of Al's bullshit. She was a very nice and kind lady. Neither she nor any of their three kids had ever been involved with committing any type of illegal activities. His oldest son was the head chef for a fancy Los Angeles restaurant. His daughter was married to a heart surgeon in Galveston. His youngest son owned a bird hunting guide service near El Campo. He got to be good friends with my two sons because they were big into duck and goose hunting.

On several occasions, officers would ask me, "Do you trust that guy?"

"Are you kidding me?" I said, "I trust him with my life. He's never lied to me, and he has a good heart and soul. Plus, he gives me more information than you can imagine."

During the Phillips trial, Phillips' young son testified that his dad was watching the All-Star Game, which gave him an alibi in connection with a burglary at the Courthouse. The jury found Phillips not guilty.

Once Big Al was released from federal custody, I helped him get a job with a major oil company that had a large training facility near Beltway 8 and Bush Intercontinental Airport. The company had a large cafeteria and put Al in charge of it. I used to have a Special Crimes retreat at my beach house in Matagorda every year. I'd bring in Al to cook for us. One of the best things that Al did for me was to teach me how to make some "kick-ass" pico de gallo.

Big Al never got into any scraps with the law after his release from federal prison. I usually talked to him on the phone at least once a week. He spent the last sixteen years of his life fighting cancer. I went to lunch with him a couple of days before he died on January 25, 2010.

I delivered a eulogy at his funeral. I will always remember his contagious laugh, effervescent personality, and zest for life. I was glad to have known him and be his good friend. I miss him dearly and will never forget him. I loved the guy and I'm pretty sure that he felt the same for me.

Al Heath aka "Big Al"   *Ralph Chambers*   *Lannie Phillips*

Me and Dirty Mack Arnold   *Carol Vance and me at his book signing 40-plus years later*

Me telling the Big Al story for the first time at our softball team reunion in 2011. Left to right: Paul Schiffer, Me, Skip Cornelius, Kyle Rodgers (my son) Don Stricklin, and the back of "Dirty" Mack Arnold's head

Johnny Holmes saying something after he hears the Big Al story for the first time. Left to right: Holmes, Paul Schiffer, Me, Skip Cornelius, and the back of "Dirty Mack" Arnold's head.

Jack Frels telling his story about the Memorial Park Keg party

Don Stricklin and Ken Magidson   *Jack Frels*

CHAPTER 4

DR. FEEL GOOD

Sometime during 1977, Gwen Durrenburger, investigator for the Texas Medical Board, along with HPD Officers Sam Searcy and A. C. Alonso, assigned to the "Doctor Squad" in the Narcotics Division, met with me and Assistant District Attorney Don Stricklin in the Special Crimes office. Our subject was Dr. Robert Hennessy.

The doctor was writing more than just a few prescriptions for Dilaudid, also known as Hydromorphone, and other drugs – all without performing a physical examination of the so-called "patients." This practice clearly amounted to a serious violation of the Medical Board regulations, as well as state laws. All a person had to do was show up at the doctor's office and tell him what they wanted.

These patients had reported that Dr. Hennessy was usually bare-footed while working in his office. I refer to him in this story as "Dr. Feel Good." He enabled his "patients" to feel good with the illegal drugs he "prescribed."

I was good friends with both Searcy and Alonso because I went on almost all of their undercover operations in order to do the audio and video recordings of witnesses and suspects in their cases.

Often such duty is boring and dreadfully routine. These cases, however, were often very entertaining. The doctors were either intoxicated or high on some medication when the officers met them to ask for a prescription without a physical examination.

We learned that Hennessy was a graduate of Rice University, a very intelligent individual who had no respect for rules and laws. He was later stripped of his medical license.

On February 16, 1978, a mighty team of detectives mustered for an important task. The team consisted of Donny Schoenfelder and Ralph "Mouse" Reese, detectives from the Harris County Sheriff's Narcotics Division, and two HPD detectives assigned to Special Crimes, Earl Musick and Jerry Carpenter. These four were discussing a confidential informant, known as a "CI" in the law enforcement community.

At the time, Ralph and Donny were working on a major narcotics investigation and were unable to check out the CI's information. They needed the help of the Special Crimes investigators.

Ivey Urquhart, an ex-con living in a halfway house in the 3000 block of Austin, near downtown, was the CI. As the four detectives discussed their plan, Urquhart waited in the outer office. Since the county had never used Ivey, investigators needed to verify his information before committing resources and manpower to the case.

Musick and Carpenter promised Ralph and Donny that they would listen to the information and check on its validity, something that should always occur when using a first-time CI. After a while they brought Ivey into their office for an interview.

Ivey was a big man, whose face and body language clearly showed he had experienced a hard life. While in prison he was known as "an enforcer" or "building monitor." His job was to keep the other prisoners in line, which on many occasions required the use of physical violence. Although he was extremely respectful to investigators, he obviously was someone you would not want to mess with on the street. If you were in a fight or in prison, you would definitely want him on your side.

Ivey admitted that over the course of his hard life he had let other people talk him into doing things he knew were wrong. He told Musick and Carpenter that on this occasion he wanted to avoid being around people who would tempt him to violate the law. Avoiding bad influences was very difficult for Ivey, since the State of Texas required him to live in the halfway house with other parolees. So Ivey developed a plan to become a *"snitch,"* a person criminals despised and do not want to be around. Ivey's rationale – and every snitch had to have a rationale – was that once his crime buddies learned he was a snitch they would no longer try to convince him to get involved in their criminal episodes.

In the interview, Ivey went on to explain how two men who served time with him were planning to rob a Houston doctor in his home. These men were trying to talk Ivey into doing the robbery with them. Ivey identified the two as Harold Barnes and Steven Robertson. We easily determined that Barnes and Robertson were Ivey's fellow residents at the halfway house.

Musick ordered photographs of these two parolees as he listened to the CI provide more details. Unlike most informants, Ivey wanted to make sure everyone in the criminal community knew he had turned "snitch" and was responsible for the arrests. He almost appeared insulted when Musick showed some concern for his future safety if criminals knew he was an informant.

He assured Earl that he could take care of himself, that the "snitch rap" was exactly what he wanted. Earl hadn't encountered anybody quite like Ivey in his already long and impressive investigative career. Ivey had a sense of sincerity and appeared to be completely honest about his motives. More importantly, he seemed genuine in wanting to change his life. No one appreciates true rehabilitation more than a law enforcement officer.

But those of us commissioned to haul in lawbreakers become very cynical about come-to-Jesus experiences contrived to get lighter sentences. With Ivey we had hopes his plan would achieve his purpose with no serious physical harm involved. However, from the information he was providing, Musick was convinced Barnes was planning a dangerous home invasion robbery in which someone could be seriously hurt or killed.

Barnes was supposed to meet with Ivey. But Ivey didn't trust him, saying he was not that dependable due to his ongoing drug habit. After gathering all the information from Ivey, Musick and Carpenter drove him out to the Austin address and tried to locate Barnes, Robertson, or their vehicle. Ivey said Barnes was driving a Pontiac station wagon. There was no sign of it nearby. Earl and Jerry dropped off Ivey a block away from the halfway house after instructing him to call them once he had talked to Barnes and learned more specifics about the plan. They needed their snitch to find out exactly who the intended victim was and the location of the planned robbery.

From the information Ivey provided, Earl and Jerry believed the doctor involved was Robert Hennessy, who lived on Rutland in the Heights, northwest of downtown Houston. We had recently worked an investigation involving Dr. Hennessy with HPD Narcotics Officer Sam

Searcy, who was assigned to the "Doctor Squad." So we contacted Sam and briefed him on the information we had at this point. Sam arranged to have a surveillance team on standby to assist in the investigation.

The next morning Ivey called to confirm Dr. Hennessy was the target, along with his wife. The doctor had been supplying Dilaudid to Barnes, Ivey had learned.

Ivey provided us with the doctor's address and the license plate number of Barnes' 1968 station wagon. Earlier that morning Earl had observed Barnes in his vehicle at the Austin address. With this new information, Narcotics officers agreed to set up surveillance on the doctor's home. We also established surveillance on the Austin address and the station wagon.

Early in the afternoon Ivey called and told us Barnes changed the plans because Robertson had to make an unexpected trip to Dallas. This information was verified by Robertson's parole officer, Ms. Denton, in the Houston office. Denton told us Robertson requested and received a travel permit to go to Dallas. Barnes told Ivey he was getting the guns and would pick him up at the Austin address with Robertson's replacement, Frank Cornelius, aka Frankie Wayne Shirley.

Musick arranged for Ivey to meet with Carpenter and me. Well known as the office's wire expert, I placed a recorder and a transmitter on Ivey, who then returned to the Austin address to await Barnes and Cornelius. When the two arrived, we began to monitor and record their conversations with our CI.

Jerry and I heard them planning the robbery in detail. Barnes had witnessed some of the tactics Ivey used in enforcing order in their cell block and he encouraged Ivey to use those same tactics to force the residents to disclose where the drugs were located.

We could tell from the conversation that Barnes had provided two guns for them to use during the robbery. On tape, Barnes explained how he could not go inside the house with them because the doctor knew him. The plan was to drop both men off with guns about a block away from the house. Barnes would then wait in the station wagon for them to return with the money and Dilaudid.

At about 4:30 p.m. the three men headed to the Heights location. We alerted the narcs the three men were headed their direction and instructed them to hold their positions while we arrested the three robbery suspects. It was important for safety reasons to have us make the arrest since we knew the identities of Ivey and the other two suspects.

During the entire drive to the location Ivey was doing a good job of secretly transmitting information to us about the weapons and plan as it developed.

When they arrived in the area, Barnes parked on the corner of 14th Street and Rutland, about a block from the doctor's home. When we observed Ivey and Cornelius getting out of the vehicle and start walking toward the doctor's home, the arrest team moved in quickly and arrested all three men.

We recovered both guns and while Musick was handcuffing Barnes, he said, "If you had waited a few more minutes, you would have gotten the Dilaudid and had me for robbery."

Little did Barnes know that we had him for robbery and the later statements he provided were enough to draft a search warrant for the doctor's home, where we would recover the Dilaudid.

We took the suspects to Special Crimes where Musick obtained a confession from Barnes and immediately started typing a search warrant for the doctor's house. It was not unusual that prosecutors were in the Special Crimes office at all hours and they were always willing to help in any investigation. These prosecutors were brilliant lawyers who were dedicated to their job, coming to work early in the morning and leaving late at night. They also made themselves available for law enforcement twenty-four hours a day, seven days a week. There are many officers and ex-officers who can attest to the dedication of the prosecutors in Special Crimes.

Two in the office that evening were Don Stricklin and Johnny Holmes. When Johnny learned that Musick was typing a search warrant, he volunteered to type it. Johnny's typing skills were likely superior to those of the best stenographer or court reporter in the courthouse. None of us could say no to him if he volunteered to do this kind of grunt work.

Stricklin had already reviewed the information we developed. He felt we had sufficient probable cause to search the Hennessy residence. Stricklin had contacted a judge who was waiting for Musick to present the probable cause to him for his review. Yes. We needed the warrant typed quickly. We luckily had the fastest typist available. He was accurate, too.

While Musick was obtaining the search warrant, our surveillance team was concerned because neighbors had witnessed the arrest and were talking with each other about it. The officers were afraid someone might call the doctor's home. Because of their concern, Stricklin instructed the surveillance team to secure the house, but not to conduct any search until a magistrate signed the warrant.

With these instructions, we moved in, arrested Dr. Robert Hennessy and his wife, secured the residence, and waited for Musick to arrive with the warrant.

About the time Musick arrived with the search warrant, Dr. Hennessy and his wife, Christine Marie, an attractive woman with blondish brown hair, were both denying there were any drugs on the premises. The narcotics team had separated them and hadn't yet conducted any search. However, after Musick arrived, he showed the warrants to the doctor and then to his wife. After looking at the warrant, she made a statement about feeling embarrassed by what was happening. She again denied having any illegal drugs in the house, but Musick assured her that we would find the Hydromorphone.

After considering her options, Christine told Musick she had hidden the Dilaudid (Hydromorphone) in the master bedroom, whereupon she escorted Earl, Officer Tommy Wilcox, and me to the bedroom.

She pointed to a potted plant and told us she buried the Hydromorphone under the potting soil. Tommy checked the pot and recovered two unlabeled prescription bottles containing 179 Hydromorphone pills just under the soil.

Both Hennessy and his wife were arrested and charged with possession of a controlled substance with intent to deliver. On July 12, 1978, Dr. Hennessy was convicted of these charges. The judge took a thirty-minute break before the sentencing portion of the hearing. Dr. Hennessy, however, fled the courthouse. In absentia, Hennessy was sentenced to thirty years in TDC.

He was missing for several months and had been arrested and in custody twice in Los Angeles. He used a fictitious name on both occasions, so he was easily bonded out. Once Los Angeles law enforcement officials received his prints back from the FBI, they realized that they'd released a wanted felon. He was later arrested by Dallas PD, but he somehow escaped their clutches.

He was on a $50,000 bond when he absconded and became a fugitive. The bonding company offered a $5,000 cash reward for any information leading to his arrest. Since the bonding company was responsible for the full amount of his bond, it was willing to pay for information needed to nab him for keeps.

On September 13, 1978, a friend of mine from my days working at the Harris County Juvenile Probation Department and the Harris County Sheriff's Office called me late in the afternoon to ask if I were looking for Robert Hennessy.

I didn't hesitate.

"Hell, yes, I am," I replied. He then told me that Hennessy would be meeting his wife that night at some apartments located near the intersection of Buffalo Speedway and Westpark on the southwest side. He further advised me that Hennessy had returned to see his wife and he would be at a location only for a short period of time. I immediately went to this location and around ten o'clock that evening I observed the doctor coming out of an apartment. When he got close, I got out of my county car.

"Dr. Hennessey, you're under arrest," I stated firmly.

The dude took off running. He was eastbound on Westpark. I was in hot pursuit.

"Freeze or I'm going to blow the back of your head off!" I sounded serious, I have to admit.

He stopped and about that time, I tripped on a driveway and my gun slid across the pavement. I was lucky. It was out of the doctor's reach.

Scraped, mad, and determined, I quickly popped to my feet and gave chase.

"I'm not kidding you," I yelled at the fleeing doctor. "I'm going to blow the back of your head off."

Then I noticed out of the corner of my eye, an elderly man walking down the sidewalk across the street with a bag of groceries. When I said that, he threw the bag up in the air and put his hands up.

I felt pretty bad about that, but Hennessy had stopped, and I placed him under arrest and took him to HPD Narcotics so they could transfer him to the county jail.

The next morning after learning of Hennessy's arrest, Earl Musick said that he was very impressed with my tenacity and dedication. From that day forward, Earl started calling me "Rin Tin Ken," after the old TV show, *The Adventures of Rin Tin Tin*.

Dr. Robert Hennessy

Harold Barnes

Ivey Urquhart

Don Stricklin and Earl Musick

Stricklin waiting for warrant

Holmes and Jerry Carpenter

Hennessy memo

Hennessy poster

CHAPTER 5

THE SCOUNDREL

In 1973, Paul Skalnik was an Austin police officer who bought untold thousands of dollars of items while in Florida writing hot checks. He got caught and received ten years' felony probation. No police force wants a hot check writer; he got fired. He later returned to Texas and his old habit. Again, he got caught and saw his probation revoked in Florida. When he was arrested in Texas, he was incarcerated in the Harris County Jail without bail.

The county had him in an isolation cell next to Claude Lee Wilkerson, who was awaiting trial for masterminding the kidnapping and murder of Houston radiologist William S. Fitzpatrick, jeweler and suspected fence/drug dealer Don Fantich, and his office manager, Georgina Rose. Wilkerson was a former employee of Fantich. Others charged in the case were Bobby Avila, David Roeder, and Mark Cass.

The latter three kidnapped Fitzpatrick, Fantich, and Rose during a $200,000 robbery at Fantich's Spring Branch jewelry store on January 23, 1978, and drove to a farm near Shiner, southeast of San Antonio, and forced to kneel in freshly-dug graves before being shot to death.

Roeder and Cass fled Texas to the State of Colorado. Colorado state police later arrested them for capital murder. They were extradited back to Harris County and HPD Detective Walter Burkham and ADA Don Stricklin picked them up from the Colorado authorities. Meanwhile, Wilkerson confessed to HPD Detective Earl Musick about the murders.

Musick taped the confession session in Special Crimes prior to the capture of Roeder and Cass in Colorado. Wilkerson said he wanted an attorney but kept on talking anyway.

In May 1983, Wilkerson was released from Death Row, where he was sentenced for the triple murder. The U. S. Supreme Court ruled that the confession was not admissible nor were the "fruits" of the confession – the names of the co-defendants, where the bodies were buried, and all the other incriminating evidence. All of these "fruits" were the only evidence we had in the state's case. Wilkerson walked free.

In a jail cell on the other side of Skalnik was Travis Morales, a local Hispanic activist and member of the People United to Fight Police Brutality. Morales was charged with instigating a felony riot that took place Sunday, May 7, 1978, during the annual Cinco de Mayo celebration in Moody Park.

The incident became known as the Moody Park Riot. Two KPRC newsmen – Jack Cato and Phil Archer – were stabbed during the riot, which protested the death of Joe Campos Torres, who was beaten and thrown into Buffalo Bayou by Houston officers the previous May.

While sitting in the Special Crimes conference room one day working on a case, I got a phone call from Paul Skalnik.

"Hey, Kenny, it's Paul."

"Where in the hell are you, in jail?"

I was just joking because I thought he was still a police officer in Austin.

"Yes, they've got me in isolation because of me being a former police officer. I need you to come and get me because I've got something to tell you, something that will interest you regarding a couple bad guys that are in isolation with me."

I immediately went to the jail, "checked him out" and brought him to the office. After talking with him for a while, I called Assistant District Attorney Andy Tobias, the prosecutor in the Morales case, and told him that I had a college buddy who was in a cell next to Morales. I asked Tobias if he was interested in knowing what Morales was saying about his case.

Andy wasn't known to mince words: "Hell, yes, I am."

Tobias grew up in Marlin, south of Waco in Central Texas, and later graduated from Texas State University, where he played football and was named honorable mention All-American. Andy always had a lot of "get up and go." When he was the chief of Division D in the late eighties, I was the lieutenant in charge of the investigators in the same division. I used to play a lot of jokes on some of the prosecutors. I left Tobias a "pink pad" message from a Mr. L. E. Fant, with the phone number of the Houston Zoo. Some of the other investigators and I were outside his office listening to his return call.

"Yes, ma'am," we heard him say. "This is Andy Tobias with the Harris County District Attorney's Office. I'm returning a call from Mr. L. E. Fant."

You could hear the lady say, "Sir, this is the Houston Zoo. Mr. L. E. Fant, really?"

"Ma'am, I'm just calling Mr. Fant back, that's all."

"Zoo, L. E. Fant."

Andy hesitated a second, mumbled something and said, "I'm sorry." He hung up while we were laughing our asses off.

You play jokes on colleagues you like and admire. Andy was a dedicated prosecutor for decades. He made many friends all around the Courthouse. He was very willing to working with Don Stricklin of Special Crimes, the prosecutor in the ill-fated Wilkerson case. I knew Don would be highly interested in what Paul Skalnik had to say.

So, Paul became our jail snitch.

I'd pick him up at the jail every morning and bring him over so we could get his notes and talk to him about what the two inmates were saying about their cases.

You might want to laugh and suggest that it's always important to know the right people. I met Paul Skalnik my first day of my "rat year" at New Mexico Military Institute while in line to have our heads shaved. This was part of the tradition for first-year cadets, aka "rats." I immediately felt I was getting to know a con man. He told me that he had just graduated from a military high school in the "valley."

I got the message: he was a pain in the ass for his parents. No one I knew would attend an all-male military high school because he wanted to.

I went to NMMI to play football and baseball because I was nominated by my congressman, George H. W. Bush. I met the U. S. Naval Academy football coach in Houston and took him a copy of my transcript. The coach looked at it, shook his head, and said, "Have you heard of New Mexico Military Institute?"

"No sir, I haven't," I replied.

"That's where Roger Staubach went for a year before attending the Naval Academy." So, there I was on my first day, hearing the con. Skalnik proceeded to tell me that he already knew what to do because of his experience in high school. He told me that "I'll be running NMMI in no time."

I thought to myself: *This idiot is a bullshit artist and con man.* While at NMMI, I was the one of the few persons able to get his number. Yet Paul became one of the highest-ranking two-year cadets in the history of the Institute. He was a big-time suck-ass with the brass and staff as well as the cadet officers. He was also appointed to be on the NMMI Honor Board, which made decisions regarding a cadet who was accused of an honor offense, being it lying, stealing, or cheating.

To be on the Honor Board, you had to display honesty, and integrity, and character that must be rock solid. He was the first cadet in the school to sign a contract with the U. S. Marine Corps, which meant that he'd go to two Marine summer camps and be a lieutenant upon graduation from NMMI. I knew this guy would never complete his obligation with them because I knew that he was a "sissy," or as they say in the Marines and many other all-male corps, "he was a real pussy."

When he returned from his first summer camp, he showed up at the Institute wearing a neck brace. I could see what was coming next. He was getting out of his contract due to medical reasons. When I saw him alone one day I said, "Paul, you're nothing but a big ol' pussy." We both laughed.

He did have a really rough and tough look about him, however. He looked like one "bad ass" Marine first sergeant. If you saw him in a dark alley, you'd not want to cross him or challenge him to a fight. He was a thick-necked, stout man who could grow a thick beard in less than a day or two. Yet he stood only five-feet-eight-inches tall.

I didn't dislike him even though I was the enlightened one who knew he was pulling the wool over the eyes of people who should know better. He also knew that I knew he was nothing more than a bullshit artist and con man. I actually liked him because he was so goofy. I always treated him with respect, but when we were alone it was a different story. He knew that I knew the real deal.

After graduation from NMMI, he attended the University of Texas in Austin, where he was elected president of his fraternity. I'm thinking, *Are people really that stupid? Must be Phi Lambda Dumb Asses.*

After UT, he became an Austin police officer. Now that was a real joke. This is when he got caught writing bad checks in Florida and got fired. Finally, his true colors were coming out. The right people were getting his number.

He hooked up with this rich girl from Pearland whose family owned a string of funeral parlors in Southeast Texas. The family disowned her because of her relationship with Paul the con man.

SCOUNDREL'S REPUTATION ENHANCED

After Paul helped us out on both the Wilkerson and Morales cases, I checked him out of jail because we weren't going to send him back to Florida until he gave testimony. Once I checked Skalnik out of jail, I told him to call me every day and let me know his location and status.

About this time, I met Aron Frank, a jeweler and owner of Amco Jewelry. To this day Aron remains a good friend of mine. The first time we met he learned that I was an investigator for the DA's office, prompting him to ask me if I could help him with a hot check that he took on a $15,000 diamond ring. He said some crook who had a name that sounded like "scoundrel" was the culprit. He was totally pissed off about losing the beautiful diamond-banded ring.

My eyebrows went up in the air. I laughed and said, "If it's Paul Skalnik, I went to school with that con. I'll get your ring back."

Aron's eyes lit up. "That's the name," he yelled. "That's the name!"

I told him I'd have the ring back to him within a week or two. I could tell that he thought I was the con. He didn't believe me.

At first, I couldn't find Paul. I began to skin the cat another way. I called his dad in the Houston suburb of League City and told him to tell Paul that I was going to put his ass back in jail if he didn't call me. I didn't usually talk to a father figure like this. But I was pretty frustrated since I was responsible for him being out of jail. Paul knew that he was going to eventually have to go back to Florida and face the judge who originally sentenced him.

I'd learned from the sheriff's office that the Florida judge had called and was pissed about Skalnik being out of jail. He hated Skalnik and was going to send him to prison, so he wanted him back. Back in those days, you could check a prisoner out of jail and keep him for as long as you wanted.

Paul called me the next day.

"Hey, Kenny, what's wrong?"

"Where have you been and where's the diamond ring you stole?"

"What ring?" What a dumb ass.

I hesitated a few seconds and said, "I'm the wrong guy to fuck with.

I'd better have that ring back in my hands within days or I'm going to put your ass back in jail. Then I'll be sending you back to Florida where that judge is going to put you in a cell under the prison."

This time he took his marching orders more seriously. About a week later, a package came in the mail to me. It contained Aron's diamond ring. The idiot had wrapped it in newspaper and packaged it in a shoe box.

Later, he testified against Travis Morales. I told him that I needed someone to go to Matagorda and do some work for me. I would pay him for his time and labor. He agreed and I gave him a key to my house.

The next weekend, I went to my place and saw that he'd cut the grass and completed the work assigned to him. I figured he'd call and let me know how much I owed him, but he never did so.

Several weeks passed before I returned to Matagorda and notice that my stuff was disappearing little by little. I figured that the idiot was coming down during the week while I was back at work in Houston. I didn't have a phone at the beach house, so I had no way to get in touch with him. I left a legal-sized page note taped to the front of the fridge, which basically said that if he didn't put the shit back in the beach house that I was personally going to drive him back to the Florida prison. I also told him to leave behind the house key I had entrusted to him.

Any trust I had in Paul had disappeared. On Monday, I called Buster Oliver, the eighty-year-old Matagorda County constable and told him my story. I made it clear that I didn't want Paul arrested, I just wanted my lawn chairs and other things back in my house. I asked Buster to please get my key back.

Ten minutes later, I get a call from Buster. Paul was at his side and wanted to talk to me. He put Skalnik on the phone and he proceeded to tell me some bullshit story about him working on a shrimp boat during the week, etc., etc., etc.

I told him to give Buster my key and to put my stuff back. He put Buster back on the phone and I tell him not to arrest Paul and hung up.

Two hours later I got a phone call from a guy who told me he was a fraternity brother of Skalnik's at UT and that he let him stay with him when he testified in the Morales case. While there, Skalnik stole a credit card from the mail and went out and bought a new TV at Western Auto. He said the funny thing was that Skalnik signed his own name on the invoice.

I hung up and called my buddy Jim Sparks, the chief of the Matagorda

County Sheriff's Office warrant division, and told him that there'd be a guy at my house who was wanted out of Florida. I told him he could verify the charges if he ran a check through the National Crime Information Center.

I knew that Skalnik had no plans to leave my house and that he'd still be there.

Sparks called me an hour later. "He's in jail," he told me. I told him I'd be there as soon as I could get loose. My partner, Bobby Blaylock, and I drove to Bay City, where the jail is located. When the jailers brought him down to release him to my custody, he's wearing my cap, shirt, belt and shorts. He was even toting one of my paperback police books.

I jerked the cap off his head and the book out of his hand. I promptly handcuffed him when he said, "Why the handcuffs, Kenny?" I said, "Are you kidding me? You can't be trusted, and I can't believe that I gave you as many privileges as I did."

We drove to my house, which was about twenty miles away. All the way he made all these excuses. I told him to shut up. I didn't want to hear another word from him. I also learned that Skalnik had kept my key and gave Buster one of his old keys.

When Paul and I arrived at the beach house, I discovered the messy condition of the place, where Paul and his girlfriend had been living free of charge. His girlfriend – the one from the well-to-do Pearland family – had a physical problem. The woman had only one kidney and experienced problems with urination. She often needed assistance getting to a toilet. I soon learned that in an emergency she had to urinate in my rather large crab pot, which normally rested on a stool in the kitchen. She had placed the pot in the living room, I guess for her convenience. It had not been emptied.

Man, there were lots of messes that needed to be cleaned up. This was only one of them. Paul's dog, a little brown terrier, had done his business all over my house. I took off the cuffs and told Paul to perform the neces-sary housework.

It took him an hour. I cuffed him again when he finished. He didn't like it. I told him I couldn't trust him two feet. Bobby and I placed him in my county car, and we headed back to Houston with Bobby driving his girlfriend's Cadillac.

We drove her to her parents' mansion in Pearland. The parents wouldn't have anything to do with her. We drove her to a motel with the terrier and left her there. We left Paul at the Harris County Jail. I haven't seen him since. I looked up his criminal record and learned that he served one term in the Florida prison system and served time in the Texas Department of Corrections on one other occasion.

BENNIE THE BOA AND OTHER STORIES

When I attended my twenty-year reunion at NMMI in 1990, I related this story to my classmates. Everyone was shocked because they figured I'd be the "crook" and Skalnik the policeman, not the other way around.

When at NMMI, I was the school "bootlegger." I had made up a phony Texas Driver License for myself in order to buy beer because I was not yet twenty-one. I was the "Radar O'Riley" of the school – far from the "model" cadet like Paul Skalnik.

On most Friday and Saturday afternoons, you'd see a line of cadets in my dorm placing their beer orders. My roommate, Tom Rogers, and I would charge $1.50 for a six pack, which provided us with just enough profit to pay for our own beer. Funny thing, before NMMI, I never had a drop to drink.

Twenty years later, I arrested Jack Henderson King, an old man who manufactured phony Texas Driver Licenses for thieves. These crooks, in turn, used them with stolen credit cards. King had all the equipment needed to make these fake IDs.

We seized the equipment and I started making TDLs for all the undercover officers from HPD and DPS narcotics units. This was more efficient than the six months it took DPS to provide one for an officer's undercover alias. This didn't make any sense to me – I could make a TDL in less than thirty minutes. I told the undercover narcs I'd learned how to do this in college.

At New Mexico Military, everyone thought that my roommate, Tom Rogers, and I were brothers even though our last names were spelled differently. He was from New Jersey and had the strong "Jersey accent." We didn't even look alike. Tom was a scrawny little Yankee-looking guy and I was a well-built Texan. The TAC Officer of the college barracks, Captain Robert "Bob" Terry, called us "the Gold Dust Twins."

We'd go to one of our favorite liquor stores in Roswell dressed in our khakis and a white t-shirts because we didn't have access to any civilian clothes. We'd usually buy so much beer that the owner, knowing we were cadets, would have to help us load the cases on a dolly and carefully roll them to the trunk of my 1968 yellow Chevrolet Nova. We'd then beer into guitar cases and smuggle it into our barracks.

On one occasion, while Tom and I carried several guitar cases under our arms, Captain Terry stopped us and asked what we were doing with all those guitars. I made up some cock-and-bull story about us having a "hootenanny." He said, "You guys don't play guitars." I just mumbled something under my breath and kept walking with two or three cases of beer under my arm until we reached our room in Saunders Barracks.

Captain Terry wasn't stupid. He had to know what was going on. The captain was a tall and slim man who stood over six feet tall and had the overpowering voice of a typical drill sergeant. Most cadets were terrified of him. I, on the other hand, felt some kind of special bond with him.

Several months after my arrival at the Institute, my cousin shipped Bennie, my pet boa constrictor, to me. I had purchased Bennie for ten bucks that summer while visiting my friend and 1963 Little League World Series teammate, Rudi Strickland, in West Palm Beach, Florida. I bought an aquarium for Bennie the boa and put him on an old sawed-off stump I found on the grounds of NMMI. I kept these private quarters next to my desk in our room.

Every morning for two years the TAC officer on duty conducted room inspections. This was usually Captain Terry. Bennie's introduction to the captain was memorable.

"*RODGERS!*" the captain screamed. "What in the hell is that?"

"My pet snake, Sir," I answered, dutifully.

"Get that goddamned snake out of your room right now."

"Yes sir, Sir. Right away, Sir."

For the next two years, Captain Terry would ask me when I was going to get rid of Bennie the boa. "Right away, Sir," I'd reply. I never did. I would only move Bennie when the U. S. Army would come to NMMI and do inspections once a year.

During our rat year most of the old cadets would have you shine their shoes and brass. They'd make you run errands for them all over the place. They didn't mess with Tom and me very much, however. I assumed it was because they thought that anyone who kept a big-ass snake in his room must be nuts. Tom and I also played on the college baseball team. Upperclassmen shied away from messing with athletes. By the end of my first year most of the cadets called me "Snake Man."

During Homecoming 1969, our First-Class Year (the last year of junior college), while in our favorite liquor store, Major Cameron Bradley, another TAC officer, entered the store and saw Tom and me. We hauled ass out of there! Cadets could be expelled for using alcohol or drugs. We knew we were in big trouble and returned to our room during the Homecoming festivities held on the campus. We anxiously awaited the dressing-down from Major Bradley. It was just a matter of time.

The major was a small man, a career U. S. Army officer and alumnus of the Institute, just like Captain Terry, when it was a four-year college. Bradley had a shrill voice. He was a pretty nice and understanding guy. He also was head of our school ski team. He knew me personally since I was a team member. He also knew that I drank because one time while skiing, I fell and the cap to my sheepskin wine flask fell off, covering me in sangria. When we got on the bus in Ruidoso to return to Roswell, the major asked me what happened. I told him some crazy story about a lady spilling wine on me at lunch. He had to smell the alcohol, but he didn't say any more about it.

Thirty minutes later after our exit from the liquor store, Bradley showed up at our room wanting an explanation. He had obviously been drinking himself. He had the smell of Jack Daniel's. I told Major Bradley that it was our last Homecoming at the Institute and that Tom and I were homesick and lonely. I also told him that we didn't have any of our family members attending, nor did we have dates to the dance. We just wanted to get a couple of beers to help us cope.

"You know I could have both of you boys tossed out of here, don't you?" He hesitated after a few seconds and added, "I'm not going to write you up for that, but I'm going to report you for being out of uniform. Just don't go into any more liquor stores or drink while you're here."

"Yes, Sir," we said in unison. "That's fine with us. Thanks!"

The next afternoon we went back to our liquor store dressed in our khakis and white t-shirts. The owner said to us, "That man told me last night that you boys are cadets at the Institute and not to sell you any more alcohol."

I told him that Bradley was our uncle and a janitor at the "toot farm," a name that the locals called the school. I also told him he didn't like for us to drink and that's why he said what he said.

I knew that we had to be his best customers because of the amount of beer that we bought on a regular basis, so he said, "Okay, what'll you boys have tonight?" We loaded up his dolly with our usual order and headed back to the Institute.

Years later, when heading to visit Greg Bishop, my very good friend and former classmate at St. Pius X High School, at the very top of Sampson Mountain, outside of Denver, I stopped by NMMI, and got to visit with Captain Terry, who was then retired as a colonel.

When I asked him why he never "busted" Tom and me for all of our misdeeds, he said, "I liked you guys. I used to do the same thing when I was a cadet. You guys reminded me of my days at the Institute."

He proceeded to tell things that Tom and I did that I didn't even remember. Captain – I mean Colonel – Terry graduated from NMMI in 1955 when it was a four-year college. I wished it was a four-year institution when I was there because I would have stayed there. I loved that place. Colonel Bob Terry died two years after my visit.

One of the things I did learn at the Institute was how to study. We had study hall from 6 p.m. until 10 p.m. Sunday through Thursday. It made my last two years at Sam Houston State so easy.

One final word about NMMI's "prize cadet." As I have said, Paul Skalnik went to prisons in both Florida and Texas. In Texas he did time for Sexual Abuse of a Child in 1989. He's currently a registered sex offender in the State of Texas and on parole in Texas. It's safe to say they don't mention him around my alma mater in New Mexico.

Cadet Skalnik, P. E.   *Cadet Rodgers, K. K.*   *Cadet Rogers, T. E.*

Bennie and me

Captain Terry and me in 2012

NMMI Captain Terry and Major Bradley

NMMI College Baseball Team

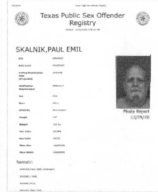
Skalnik sex offender

CHAPTER 6

THE FENCE

Hunter Carruth had the reputation with law enforcement officials in Harris County as one of the major criminal "fences" in the Houston metro area. A fence is a person who buys and sells stolen property and makes a profit from it.

I first met Hunter and his wife, Carole, in 1978, when Johnny Holmes radioed me to meet him and Henry Oncken at the Brownstone Gallery on the corner of Westheimer and Virginia. When I knocked on the back door, I was met by Carole Carruth, who was wearing a "see-through" gown with nothing underneath. Needless to say, I was speechless. I entered and saw Johnny and Henry. I was dumbfounded. I was thinking: *"What the hell is this all about?"*

I'd heard talk about Hunter from HPD Burglary and Theft detectives but had never met him or his wife before this occasion. I later learned that Carole was a former model for Justin Boots, whose ads were in *Playboy* with her modeling their latest products for ladies. I could completely understand why. The scantily clad woman was gorgeous. I guess it was unfortunate that, remaining a professional, I refrained from closely examining the gifts with which the Good Lord blessed her with, even though I could see right through the gown.

Despite the fact that this was in the early days of Special Crimes, Johnny, Henry, and I had already been through more than just a few significant cases. This episode reminded me of a time when the three of us interviewed a witness regarding Don Yarbrough, the Texas Supreme Court justice whose case is detailed in latter chapters. This witness was a well-respected professional, but he was always very rude to almost everyone. We were sitting at his kitchen table in his expensive home near Rice University. His wife was very attractive. He was "butt-ugly" and very rich. He asked me while we were all sitting at the table, "Why are you staring at my wife?"

"I was just wondering how such a beautiful woman could be married to such an ugly SOB like you," I quipped. I had never been anything but honest, maybe too honest. I thought Johnny and Henry were going to fall out of their chairs. I was just tired of listening to this man's bullshit. And another thing: I was working on a Saturday, my normal day off.

Let me get back to Hunter and Carole. Hunter told us that he could get his hands on some documents that were locked in a safe. The papers could implicate some "wrong doings" by a couple of very high-ranking officials at City Hall and HPD. After our meeting, we never heard from him again. I actually think he was trying to confirm that the "alleged" documents actually existed. The fact was we didn't know. All we had were the rumors that had floated around for several years. That's exactly what they were, vicious rumors. Now we had some shady character trying to shake us down.

A few months later, on Friday, July 21, 1978, Don Stricklin called Blaylock and me into his office. He directed us to interview a young man who'd been caught stealing gold from his employer, Balfour Jewelry, a major company well known for making class rings for high schools and colleges, as well as World Series Championship rings. He was stealing gold and trading it to Hunter Carruth for cocaine.

We took a statement from him after he agreed to cooperate. We then got a search and arrest warrant for Carruth and went to his residence at 3611 Montrose Boulevard. I remembered the two-story house because it was a beautiful structure that had created a lasting impression when I saw it as a five-year-old kid. My pediatrician's office wasn't too far from the house. I dreaded going because I was usually going to get a shot, which I absolutely hated. The sight of the house helped take the pain away.

At about 5:45 p.m., Bobby and I were met at the residence by HPD detectives from the Fence Detail. There were also some SWAT officers with us to assist in executing the warrant. Bobby and I went to the front door, while HPD covered the rear entries. Bobby was kicking in the front door while wearing his brand-new black dress shoes. In the process the heel on one of his new shoes came off. I couldn't help but laugh, and so did he.

We gained entry with Bobby limping around like a crippled "Herman Munster" about the same time as the other officers came through from the back. The HPD officers arrested a male who was on the first floor with cocaine in his possession. Bobby and I proceeded (Bobby limped) up the stairs.

While making our way to the master bedroom, we heard a revolver being cocked.

"Hunter," the limping Bobby firmly instructed, "drop the gun or we're going to kill you. We better hear it hit the floor or you're going to be one dead SOB."

Seconds later, we heard a big thud when the gun hit the floor.

As we entered the room, Hunter and Carole were lying in bed and Carole had a needle stuck in a vein in her head "shooting up" what we later learned to be cocaine. She looked so bad that I didn't even recognize her as the same woman that I'd met six months earlier. She was charged with possession of cocaine, Hunter with theft and possession of stolen property. A court sentenced Hunter to three years in prison. Carole received seven years' probation for the possession of stolen property and seventy-five days in jail for possession of the controlled substance.

As of this writing in 2020, Hunter is deceased and Carole's whereabouts are unknown.

Hunter Carruth

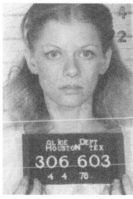

Carole Carruth

Bobby after the arrest (You can't see the broken heel on one of his new shoes).

CHAPTER 7

THE KING OF HARASSMENT

During December of 1979, I received a phone call from Assistant DA Randy McDonald, who worked at the complaint desk at DA Intake, along with another ADA, Brad Beers. The call was in reference to an individual known as Ronald Eugene Rossi.

At this juncture in the DA's office, a person could walk into Intake and file a complaint against someone. The ADA would in turn send a letter to the object of the complaint in order to get his or her side of the story.

Both McDonald and Beers had spoken with the complainant and the suspect in this case on several occasions. The ADAs described the situation as a "he-said-she-said" predicament. They needed my help. McDonald said that right after the events between these two individuals began that something strange started happening. The two prosecutors started getting more than one hundred magazines in the mail at their homes, none of which they ordered.

Furthermore, McDonald reported to me that even their friends were getting the same magazines. Both he and Beers suspected the potential defendant in this ongoing fiasco. This individual, Ronald Eugene Rossi, "seemed kind of weird." Every time Rossi would come to Intake, he'd bring along his own witness, Dora Santamaria. The witness seemed to go along with everything Rossi said, causing McDonald and Beers to become even more suspicious.

I soon learned that the complainant, Laurie Hall, was a flight attendant with Texas International Airlines. She was as nice as your typical flight attendant. She appeared to be honest enough to cause the prosecutors to believe her over Rossi. She was a beautiful strawberry blonde that would cause any guy to turn his head when she passed by.

Soon after this experience, both McDonald and Beers were transferred to Special Crimes. It wasn't the end of this story.

Several weeks later, on January 24, 1980, Laurie Hall and her mother, Julie Anders, came to my office for a meeting. McDonald was present along with ADA Bill Eggleston. (In 2020, Eggleston and Beers were attorneys in private practice in Harris County).

Laurie told us that she had dated Rossi for a short period in 1979 but decided that she didn't want to have anything further to do with him. He kept wanting to get back with her. He kept calling her and sending her cards.

She said that Rossi would call her in different cities when she was traveling with the airline. Strangely, only the airline knew the specific city where she would be staying, as well as her hotel.

You might say that Laurie "got the creeps." For example, at approximately 4 a.m. the morning of October 1, 1979, Laurie awoke with Rossi standing over her bed in Houston. She screamed for the intruder to get out of her house, a commotion that woke up her roommate. Rossi asked for his house key back. But Laurie said she never had it.

Rossi went to the living room and made a phone call. Lauri picked up the extension in her room and told him to get out, which he did. She noticed after he left that he'd pilfered all of her keys. Around 5 a.m. Dora Santamaria called her looking for Rossi. Laurie told her that Rossi had taken her keys and she wanted them back.

Three days later Laurie flew to Vermont after parking her car in the employee parking lot at the airport. When she returned later in the week, her car had disappeared.

The next mysterious incident unfurled two weeks later when she began receiving numerous phone calls with no one on the other end of the line. As she tried to talk to the caller, someone threw a large cinder block through her bedroom window. About 6 a.m. Laurie and her roommate learned that their apartment door and Laurie's mother's car door had been super-glued shut.

At wit's end, Laurie turned to a friend, FBI Agent Phil Armand in New Orleans. Armand, who also happened to be a friend of mine, had received a copy of Laurie's DWI conviction record in the mail with the return address of the FBI in Houston. Someone also sent the DWI conviction papers to her employer, as well as others.

Laurie further stated that on November 10, 1979, around 4 a.m., which was the day of her mother's wedding, that someone had slashed the tires on the cars owned by her roommate and her stepfather.

Two days later Laurie returned from a trip and found a single long-stemmed rose with a note signed by Ron Rossi. Her roommate also received a Happy Birthday card from Ron on November 18.

The harassment intensified. A few days later someone followed Laurie to the Sakowitz store located in the Galleria. The culprits were Rossi and his "girlfriend" Santamaria. Rossi tried to get into Laurie's vehicle, but when he saw that her mother and stepfather were with her, he took off. That night Laurie's roommate found her stolen car parked in front of their apartment with the ignition keys hanging by a string on the doorknob.

Less than a month later, Laurie learned that while moving to a new residence, someone broke into her old apartment in the Memorial area and stole some of her expensive clothing and her airline uniforms. To her horror, she was entering her new apartment on Houston's west side one day and found a note on her door, which said, "Be good and be on time." When leaving to go to work, she learned that her car wouldn't start. She called her mother for a ride, and her car wouldn't start either. They later learned that someone had put water in their gas tanks.

When a determined individual wants to harass you, they often use the telephone. Less than a month after the water-in-the-gas-tanks episode, at 1:25 in the morning, Laurie received a phone call from someone who wouldn't speak from the other end of the line. She then heard a knock at her door, prompting her to call the apartment security. When they arrived, they found a Christmas present and card to Laurie from Rossi. On the same day, when Laurie was taking out her trash, she noticed that her car had been moved. When she got into her car, she learned that someone had stolen the card used to enter the apartment complex.

Two days before the end of 1979, Laurie drove up to the entrance to her apartment complex when she noticed Rossi trying to gain entry by using some kind of law enforcement badge. She advised the security guard that he was the person that had been harassing her.

"Please don't let him in!" she urged the guard. Rossi left immediately.

I later learned that Rossi was a "reserve deputy" with the Harris County Precinct 5 Constable's Office. He was actually serving as a karate and/or judo teacher there.

The new year began with further harassment. On January 22 Laurie learned that someone entered her car and set the back seat on fire, but the flames faded out and didn't cause the car to burn or explode completely. Laurie also reported to us that on two occasions that the Post Office had received a change of address from her current address to that of Rossi in the 2300 block of Haldane.

Apparently, the same person also called her bank and told a banker he (or she) never received the new checks. The bank mailed the caller some new checks to Rossi's address. Someone (Rossi?) began forging Laurie's name to pay Laurie's bills. Her phone bill was around $28, and they would send the phone company a check for $300 or more. Eventually, she had "bad checks" floating around.

I went to the Post Office in late January to retrieve the two original change-of-address cards and took them to the Document Examination Laboratory at the Houston Police Department. An analysis of the cards reflected that both were being forwarded to Rossi's home address.

A. D. Queen, the document examiner at HPD, advised me that the handwriting and the signature on one of the cards matched the signature of Dora Santamaria. I had provided him with a copy of the DA Intake complaint form that Santamaria had filed on October 4, 1979.

I returned to Special Crimes and had three grand jury subpoenas issued for Ron Rossi, Dora Santamaria, and Kathleen Van Keuren, Rossi's stepsister. Rossi and Santamaria showed up at Special Crimes with Rossi displaying a cast on his writing hand. He claimed he suffered the injury when he defended himself from a burglar at his home. We told Rossi and Santamaria that we only wanted handwriting exemplars from each of them. Both took the Fifth Amendment against self-incrimination on the advice of their attorney.

Later, I checked with police and learned that Rossi had made so many burglary complaints that it ceased to be funny. He'd reported the same Rolex watch was stolen on numerous occasions.

Document examiner Queen was there to investigate and conducted the handwriting exemplar. He made Rossi write with his non-writing hand. Queen determined that Santamaria did forge several documents. At that time, I told Rossi that he could leave. I further advised Santamaria that if she would cooperate as a witness against Rossi that the DA would grant her immunity from prosecution. She agreed to cooperate.

She broke down crying. She told me that Rossi had threatened her with bodily harm if she failed to follow his directions. She was scared to death of him, detailing for me that Rossi had handcuffed her on many occasions. She would be glad to cooperate in return for immunity, which was granted by ADA Eggleston.

Dora Santamaria swore in an affidavit that she had met Rossi in March 1979. She broke up with him but would get back together with him, always because he harassed her. Rossi also told her that if she wouldn't get back with him that he'd do harm to her family.

She corroborated Laurie Hall's harassment case against Rossi. As Rossi planned and carried out his harassment of Laurie, he handcuffed Santamaria and inflicted pain by "spanking" her. The victimized woman became so depressed that she tried to commit suicide by taking a handful of Rossi's sleeping pills. But he rushed her to the hospital where she survived when doctors pumped her stomach.

She supplied us with countless details of criminal events that we used against this king of harassment. He even set up the "theft" of his car and boat in order to collect insurance. And this was just one of the alleged thefts he reported to authorities.

THE MONKEY AND THE ELEPHANT

When Rossi left Special Crimes that day, we had Private Investigator P. M. Clinton follow him along with ADA Brad Beers. Investigators Hubbell and Horn were set up on Rossi's residence because ADA Eggleston said that he would probably have to draft a search warrant for his house.

Once Rossi arrived at his house, he began loading boxes in the trunk of his 1976 Cadillac. While this was happening, Santamaria told us those boxes contained Laurie's clothes and uniforms that were taken in the burglary of her home.

Investigators then followed as Rossi drove the loaded trunk to the corner of Long Point and Wirt Road on the westside. He parked his car next to a Goodwill box. Investigator Hubbell communicated with ADA Eggleston via radio.

From the office, Eggleston instructed Hubbell to place Rossi under arrest before he removed the boxes from his trunk and placed them in the larger Goodwill donation box. We needed to preserve this evidence!

Meanwhile, we processed a search warrant for Rossi's vehicle and residence. As Hubbell arrested him, Rossi closed his trunk. Following protocol, Rossi was allowed to make a phone call to his attorney, Victor Blaine.

Just more than two hours later Eggleston and I arrived at the location with the search warrant. I also had Laurie's mom and stepfather meet us there in order to identify Laurie's clothing and uniforms.

We then proceeded to Rossi's residence. We were met by the Harris County Precinct 5 Constable Tracy Maxon and one of his captains. They promptly took away Rossi's badge and ID.

We found other evidence along with various weapons and narcotics, which were tagged and placed in our Special Crimes Property Room. Rossi refused to open his safe. I didn't have on my kid gloves. I told him I would have someone come out to open the safe with a cutting torch. He decided to open it. Lo and behold it contained numerous Rolex watches and other valuables that he had previously reported stolen. Rossi was insufferable. He alleged that one of us had pocketed one of his valuable watches.

"Are you kidding me?" I said to him. "No one took anything that wasn't evidence." I was actually starting to get frustrated with this hopeless hooligan.

We took him to where the case all began – DA Intake. This time we had charges – two counts of burglary and one count of auto theft. I then had the pleasure of escorting him to the Harris County Jail. I was careful with the accusatory asshole. You could never imagine what he would accuse you of. I made sure ADA McDonald accompanied me.

I then did something that I had never done before. I pulled my county ride to the side of the street before we got to the jail. I turned to Rossi.

"Have you ever heard of the law of the jungle?" I asked him. I looked sideways at McDonald, who must have thought I was going to shoot the prisoner.

Rossi said not a word.

"Monkeys don't fuck with elephants," I stated, "and I'm an elephant, and you are a monkey. If one assistant DA, one of my family members, or a friend of mine gets a magazine that they didn't order, I'll be coming for you, and you can count on it."

I was dead serious. I let my words sink into Rossi's noggin.

"Do you understand?"

Not a word.

I stayed relentless. I told him we would sit outside the jail until he acknowledged what I said. He finally said yes, and we proceeded to the jail for processing.

I believe in my heart, my soul, and my gut that experience in law enforcement conditions that part of your brain that stirs up intuition. *You know what you know!*

I knew right then what would likely happen. Some would call it clairvoyance. I call it pure investigator's instinct – I knew at that very moment that I would one day be a target of Ron Rossi. Even so, I took great delight in "just doing my job" – putting a clever evildoer behind bars out of free society.

McDonald and I returned to my car. I sensed correctly what was coming.

"You scared the holy shit out of me!" said the prosecutor, who later became a judge in Chambers County.

"You know the thing he did to that poor girl, innocent and never hurting anyone. And he caused her family great pains. And her roommate! This was a crying shame! They didn't deserve all that harassment over the fact that she didn't want to date the son of a bitch anymore."

I did find a Louisiana truck license plate in Rossi's safe and tracked down the owner who told me that it was on his truck parked at a garage in Aspen, Colorado, where his condo was located. He was worried about his truck, so, I told him that only the plate was probably stolen and not the truck. He called and confirmed that the truck was still there. I knew that Rossi was friends with a City of Houston prosecutor, Matthew Talty, who had recently been to Aspen. I called Talty and he confirmed that he and Rossi had recently been to Aspen.

"With friends like Rossi," I told him, "you don't need enemies."

On February 4, 1980, while searching some of the papers taken from Rossi's house, I discovered several blank credit applications, one of which was partially filled out in the name of Candy L. Rossi. I also found an American Express credit card in the name of Candy L. Prather and the bill of Ronald G. Prather, along with a bank statement in the name of Ronald G. Prather and Candy L. Prather.

It was determined from Laurie Hall that Ron Prather was a flight attendant with her at Texas International Airlines. Rossi had been to a party with her at their house during the summer of 1979. We also learned that Rossi had filed a change of address with the Post Office from their address to Rossi's. We saw some of their mail in his house but didn't know about that of the Prather's.

However, we did have Rossi's briefcase, which was found in the trunk of his vehicle. It had some of their mail in it, as well. I then contacted U. S. Postal Inspector Willie Williams about the violation.

I also learned that Rossi had applied for and received a Diners Club credit card in the name of Laurie A. Rossi. I advised the security division of both Diners Club and American Express of the case and asked that they send me the original application in order to do a handwriting exemplar.

The investigation continued. I spoke with Karel Lorehn, who at one time was Rossi's girlfriend and roommate. She advised me that she was taking a judo class Rossi was teaching. The class proved to be the prelude to a relationship. She tried to break up with him in the late part of 1978. What do you know? Rossi started harassing Karel by telephone. Things got so bad that she tried to commit suicide by slashing her wrists. She later became friends with him and even lived in his house for a while when he and Dora Santamaria were harassing Laurie Hall – and other females! *Go figure!*

The complex saga started to unravel even more. I learned of still another young woman Rossi dated. Robin Smuts, a nurse, was another victim. I was unable to contact her, but Dora Santamaria came by my office and brought me a tape of Rossi and Robin Smuts along with a book, *Techniques of Harassment,* that Smuts left in Dora's car.

ADA Bill Eggleston spoke with yet another one of Rossi's former girlfriends, Millie Thibodeaux. She said that she had a pending lawsuit against Rossi for defrauding her out of $20,000 worth of stock. During their relationship, he was arrested at the Sharpstown Foley's Department Store in 1975 in possession of several counterfeit one-hundred-dollar bills.

That same year when she returned from a trip, she found several stolen auto parts in her garage. Rossi told her that he'd gotten them from a car that he had stolen. She also said that either July of 1975 or 1976, Rossi reported to his insurance company that his house had been burglarized. Valuable pieces of furniture were stolen. Millie later saw the furniture in Rossi's lake house near Hempstead. Rossi told her if she ever told anyone about any of these shenanigans that he'd hurt her children. He'd make numerous trips to Mexico and bring back large quantities of drugs, particularly Valium.

Sometime after I filed the case, I had several female ADAs come by the office and tell me that they knew Rossi because he was passing himself off as a private investigator. They saw him hanging around the Criminal Courts Building. They described him as "weird," and on several occasions, they thought he might be stalking them.

I'd found several photos of female attorneys that Rossi had taken around the courthouse, some of which included assistant district attorneys and defense attorneys. One picture was a posed photo of ADA Kris Moore that appeared to have been taken in a house. I called her to question her about the photo.

"I used to date him," she said.

"You've got to be kidding me," I replied and added, "How long did you date this weirdo?"

"A while," she said.

"You've got to be kidding me. It only took me a few minutes to figure out that there's something mentally wrong with this guy and it took you 'a while'?"

The first Rossi trial ended in a hung jury, probably because his attorney, Vic Blaine, who said in his final argument that I was only involved in this case because Laurie was my girlfriend.

What a crock! This was absolutely untrue – the typical poppycock a defense attorney conjures up when he has a scheming, lying client like Ron Rossi. I was involved because it was my job to dislike crooks and get them off the streets, especially those who sneak around in darkness harassing innocent women.

Blaine should've come up with a better argument because the verdict in the second trial – on March 23, 1982 – Ron Rossi was convicted and sentenced to a "light" sentence of ten years' probation.

In his pre-sentence investigation interview, he denied doing anything wrong. He took no responsibility for anything he'd done. His stepfather told an investigator that he thought his step-son had some emotional problems." *No kidding. Who has the time to spend harassing someone for as long as he did?*

Shortly after the trial, I started to get late-night phone calls. Guess what? The person at the other end of the line never said anything. I usually hung up. The last one I got, I said, "Hey Ron, remember you're a monkey, and I'm an elephant." I can't prove or know for sure it was him, but he would be my first suspect.

The calls stopped. There was no more monkeying around.

I also later received other complaints about him from other women. I always referred them to the U. S. Secret Service. The Secret Service was now dealing with a new crime trend – identity theft. You could actually spend your entire career following Rossi around watching him commit crimes.

Years passed. On September 13, 1991, I received a phone call from the FBI. The agents wanted to talk to me about Rossi. They suspected that he shot an airliner that his wife, a flight attendant, was on.

"That really doesn't surprise me," I said to them. One agent had heard I had investigated Rossi before and thought that I might have some information the Bureau could use. He told me that Rossi and his wife were going through a divorce and that he has been harassing her. I told him that our search warrant had resulted in us finding a few weapons.

This had been eleven years earlier. Rossi could not be stopped! I told the agent no one wanted to stop Rossi more than I did. I forwarded him all the files we had on him.

On October 2, 1991, I received a phone call from Lisa Rossi, Rossi's wife at the time. Well, what do you know: She wanted to talk to me about Rossi harassing her. She told me that he just flew overseas using false ticket information. He also forged the notary's signature to obtain a flight ticket. He was taking a lot of "medication" and still owned many firearms. She advised me that Rossi was always telling her he was "going hunting" when he would leave their house "with a bunch of guns."

I never heard any more about this ongoing investigation after this meeting with Rossi's estranged wife.

I have been a police officer in the State of Texas for more than forty years and have never seen such a harasser as Rossi. Can you imagine your daughter getting involved with someone like this crook? I couldn't understand how such beautiful women could enter into relationships with someone like him. He used fear and intimidation in order to control women or keep a former girlfriend. If my daughter had been involved with someone like this, there'd be a "come to Jesus" meeting sooner or later. Probably sooner.

I believe I know what you're thinking at this point in my memoir: This guy Rossi is much akin to the Black Widow, Catherine Mehaffey Shelton. And like Mehaffey, Rossi has yet to serve any measurable time locked behind bars. As I have said, some people have a great talent for skirting the law and the justice they should be served.

Since his conviction, in this case, disposed in 1982, Rossi received five years' probation for obtaining drugs by fraud in 1992. Ron Rossi keeps getting probation instead of hard time. He's that silent evil that lurks in the shadows of Southeast Texas. In my estimation, he's still the criminal monkey.

And I'm still the elephant!

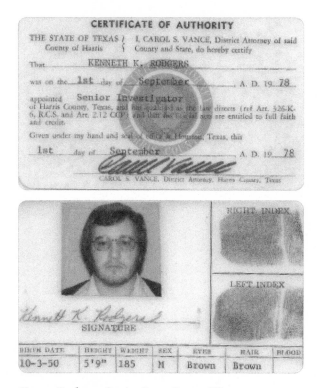

Kenny Rodgers, Senior Investigator ID
September 1978

CHAPTER 8

HITMEN FOR HIRE

On May 1, 1980, Harris County Fire Marshal J. J. Pruett contacted Assistant District Attorney Don Stricklin to discuss an individual who'd been hanging out at an icehouse/lounge on the Old Beaumont Highway and told the owner, Lonnie Earl Taylor, that he would burn his business or any other business if the price was right. I can tell that any person reading this account would not set foot in this sleazy east Houston establishment. Most patrons were local hoodlums, unemployed longshoremen, or just plain riffraff. I'm not going to supply you with the name of the place and its address.

Pruett, along with two other deputy fire marshals, Sheldon Lawson and W. B. Anders, came to Special Crimes with a cassette tape of a phone conversation between Taylor and the suspect in this case, Jerry Edward Vaughn. The tape was made the day before. It basically confirmed what Taylor had told Pruett and his investigators.

Taylor told Vaughn that he knew of a guy who would be interested in using his services to burn some apartments he owned. Taylor arranged for Vaughn to meet with Special Crimes Detective Jerry Carpenter, who could look pretty "seedy" himself.

The next day Bobby Blaylock and I "wired up" Jerry for the meeting set up at 11 a.m. at the lounge. Jerry drove a DA investigator's undercover vehicle and Blaylock and I, along with Pruett and Anders, were in the Special Crimes surveillance van. Upon arrival, Carpenter went inside.

Minutes later Anders and I followed, bought a round of beers and started playing pool in order to back up Carpenter in case there was a problem.

After Taylor introduced Carpenter to Vaughn, they went to Carpenter's vehicle where Vaughn immediately started talking about arson. He said he wanted five percent of the insurance proceeds.

Carpenter told him that he had a partner and Vaughn volunteered to eliminate the partner. For about fifteen minutes they discussed in detail the crimes of murder and arson. They finally reached an agreement that Vaughn would kill the partner for $2,500 with a $1,250 down payment. Carpenter gave him the physical description of Bobby Blaylock but didn't name him.

Vaughn also wanted his partner's address along with his vehicle information, which included his license plate number. Vaughn said that he would pick his own time and place of the event. As they ended the meeting, they agreed to meet again at noon a few days later. At that time Carpenter would provide the $1,250 down payment along with a photograph and address of his partner.

On May 5, Hubbell, Blaylock and I, along with HPD Criminal Intelligence Officers Danny Wendt and Eddie Fowler and fire marshals Pruett and Anders went to the lounge about an hour prior to the scheduled meeting time. Once we arrived, Anders, Wendt, and I went inside and started drinking beer and shooting pool.

At noon, we observed Vaughn entering the lounge. According to plan, Carpenter showed up minutes later. Vaughn and Carpenter immediately went outside to Jerry's car in order to complete their transaction. Once in the car Vaughn told Carpenter that he thought there were three undercover officers in the lounge. He became very nervous. He asked Carpenter to show him his wallet to see if he had a police badge. He saw none so he relaxed a bit and took the down payment of $1,250 in cash. Bingo! We arrested Vaughn as he returned to his vehicle.

After his arrest, I asked for consent to search his vehicle, which he agreed to. After he signed a consent form, Hubbell and I searched and found two 12-gauge shotgun shells. He also gave us consent to search the trailer where he lived, but he said his ten-year-old son was there and he didn't want a bunch of officers rummaging through the place. I told him that only two officers would search and that I would remove the handcuffs we had placed on his wrists while in the presence of his son. "That's fine," he said, "but I want you to know that I do have an illegal shotgun there because I got drunk one night and sawed off the barrel." Blaylock and I found it under his bed.

I then took him to State District Judge Frank Price, where he was given his magistrates warning and was appointed Mike Hinton, former Special Crimes prosecutor, as his attorney.

Mike told us later that Vaughn was planning on "ripping off" Carpenter and "blowing smoke" about the fires that he set. I told Mike that Vaughn had five prior convictions, two of which were federal charges, and was currently wanted out of Manatee County, Florida for a felony escape.

On January 20, 1981, a district court sentenced Vaughn to ten years in the Texas Department of Corrections.

ROUTINE SOLICITATIONS

In the early spring of 1982 Texas attorney William A. Chanslor, 50, who was formerly the president of the Houston Trial Lawyers Association, placed ads in two paramilitary journals, *Soldier of Fortune* and *Gung Ho*. He used a fictitious name when he placed the ad. The ad read:

WANTED: EXPERTS IN POISONS AND
CHEMICAL AGENTS WITH ACCESS TO SAME.

His mission was to kill his wife, Sue Sanders Chanslor, who was confined to a wheelchair after a stroke in 1979 at the age of 39. The stroke left her paralyzed, with some brain damage and recurring bouts of headaches. Before the stroke, she was a very athletic and active woman. She later testified during the trial that she wanted to end her own life.

Chanslor received a few replies from his ads, but nothing that meant much. He then ran across a five-volume set of books entitled *How to Kill*, by John Minnery, a Canadian weapons expert.

Chanslor eventually called Minnery, whom he refers to as Dr. Death, and asked him about poisons that are undiscoverable.

They had several more detailed conversations over the next few months regarding this topic. In one of their talks Chanslor mentioned a drug known as DDVP, which he could purchase for $750. Minnery told him that is the same thing used in Shell No-Pest insecticide strips. You could get these over the counter for only $10.

Chanslor decided not to go the No-Pest route. He wanted to meet Dr. Death at the airport in Toronto at a later date in order to discuss another poison, ricin, which is found in castor beans. Doctors were finding it hard to trace ricin.

Minnery decided that something "just wasn't right about this" and contacted the Ontario Provincial Police to let them know what was going on. He eventually spoke to Detective Keith Symonds of the OPP.

On April 8, 1982, Symonds met Chanslor, posing as an associate of Minnery, at the airport in Toronto, and told Symonds that he wanted to kill his wife by poisoning her with ricin. Chanslor also paid Symonds $500 in cash in order for him to deliver ricin to him in Houston.

The next day, Symonds contacted our office and advised us of their investigation. I spoke with him and arranged to pick him up at Houston Intercontinental Airport the following day.

My partner, Bobby Blaylock, and I met Symonds and took him to the Host Hotel, which is located adjacent to the airport. We got two adjoining rooms at the hotel in order to video the meeting, which had been scheduled with Chanslor. Bobby and I spent little time in setting up a video camera and microphone in the AC vent connecting the two rooms. I have to say that we had become very adept at set-ups like these.

The next day, April 21, 1982, Chanslor met with Symonds in his room. Symonds put on some surgical gloves and a mask, then proceeded to give him a substance purported to be ricin. At that time Chanslor gave Symonds $2,500 in cash. When Chanslor was leaving the room, we arrested him for Conspiracy to Commit Murder.

A state district court found Chanslor guilty and sentenced him to three years in TDC and fined him $5,000.

The Texas Court of Criminal Appeals reversed the decision in 1985.

One of the reasons that Special Crimes was so successful in doing these cases in such a prompt manner was due to our experience.

We had done so many solicitation cases – let's face it, some people in Houston want to kill somebody – that we had developed some type of plan to proceed with these types of offenses, right down to planting wires in AC vents. For all I know, those wires are still in that hotel right where we put them.

Jerry Vaughn

CHAPTER 9

SCOTLAND YARD

One day while sitting in my office, I greeted a visitor, Martin Knights, a Scotland Yard fraud detective visiting the United States for the first time. He was here to visit a flight attendant, Fran Swedberg, whom he met in London during one of her overseas flights.

Knights originally went to HPD to learn about their fraud division, but the officers there sent him to our office because they told him that we did almost all of the major fraud cases in Harris County.

While I was explaining to him about Special Crimes and the kind of cases we handled, I received a phone call from a former assistant district attorney, "Dirty Mack" Arnold, now a criminal defense attorney.

Dirty Mack was calling about a person trying to sell him a Rolex watch he thought was either stolen or a fake. Arnold got the nickname of "Dirty Mack" because he was the catcher on our softball team, the Indictments, and was always covered in dirt and dust from the game action.

He said that he'd set up a meeting in order to look at the watch and asked me if I was interested in going with him, which I did. I grabbed Earl Musick, our HPD detective assigned to Special Crimes, and took the Scotland Yard detective along so he could see exactly how we work and do things in Houston USA.

The meeting took place in the southwest part of Houston in a fairly nice neighborhood. Mack came to our office prior to the meeting and

I put our Nagra recorder and a wireless transmitter on him in order to monitor and tape the meeting.

Shortly after we arrived and got situated for the meeting, a carload of guys showed up to meet Mack. We were only expecting one person, not a small army of suspects. Earl was in his unmarked city police car and I was in my county undercover vehicle with the British detective.

After a short meeting, Mack told them it wasn't an authentic Rolex and wasn't interested in paying what they were asking for a fake. Actually they weren't too smart because the dial of the watch said "Rodex."

Earl and I decided to arrest them. When I pulled out my .357 Smith and Wesson with a two-and-a-half-inch barrel from my ankle holster, Scotland Yard Detective Knights said, "What in the world are you doing with a gun?"

I replied the way most people around me would expect. "You're in Texas, man, we don't make an arrest without a gun in our hand."

"We don't even have access to guns except in certain situations," he said.

"Not here, man," I said.

We rolled up to the suspects' vehicle and arrested them. We didn't realize these guys were football players from a local college out trying to scam an unknown victim. These guys were huge, all over six feet tall. There were so many of them that we ran out of handcuffs.

While Earl and I went to search their vehicle, I asked Knights to keep an eye on the one uncuffed suspect. He immediately pointed his index finger like a barrel of a gun at the suspect. I almost fell down laughing.

After HPD "harness bulls" (uniformed patrol officers) transported the suspects to jail, I gave Knights a ride to a British pub (The Ale House and/ or Ron's Pub) across from where he was staying and noticed that he was still visibly shaken.

"Are you going to be okay?" I asked.

"That just scared me to death. We don't carry guns and that just made me very nervous."

"I can see that, but that's just the norm for us."

Knights became one of my very good friends and spent Christmas with my family one year. It was funny that when we were eating our Christmas meal Martin passed gas right there at the table. It made my kids laugh like crazy.

"Are you kidding me, Martin?"

"In England," Martin said, "it's normal and meant as a way of thanking your host and a compliment for providing such a good meal."

"I'm glad no one was smoking at the table or you'd have blown us all up."

He later moved to Houston permanently when he decided to move in with girlfriend, Fran. She had a massive heart attack on her couch one day and died while her parents were visiting.

Years later we became roommates for about a year or more. He didn't have a phone in his apartment, and I told him that I had to get a phone installed because of my job. He later complained that no one ever called him, so I later walked across the street to a pay phone and called him.

"What are you doing?" he said.

"Well, you were complaining about not getting any phone calls, so I'm calling you."

It turned out that the apartment manager was Katherine McMaster, a former secretary in Special Crimes. She asked me if I would like to work security at the apartments and get free rent. Of course! Then she advised me that the security manager will be calling me and would want to meet with me. She advised me that he had a speech impediment and didn't want for me to think that someone was playing a joke on me.

A few days later, the security manager called the apartment and Martin answered the phone. The man asked to speak to me, and Martin said, "Come on Ken, I know this is you, quit playing around."

He soon realized that it wasn't me at the other end of the line and felt like an idiot.

Martin still lives in Houston and works as a travel agent. I gave him the nickname of "Fartin' Martin."

Me and Fartin' Martin

CHAPTER 10

WHAM BAM THANK YOU MA'AM

During March of 1981, I received a call from Larry Kincaid, an undercover sheriff's detective, asking me for help with an HPD murder suspect currently held in the Harris County Jail. His name was Keith Pharoah Johnson, also known as David Lynn Simpson. He was being held for a misdemeanor charge of an assault on a minor and for a parole violation out of the state of Maryland.

HPD Homicide received a tip from Crime Stoppers that Johnson was the killer of David Eugene Dixon in February 1981. Dixon, twenty-six, was an occasional construction worker friend of Johnson's. His body was found near the San Jacinto River in east Harris County. Evidence showed he'd been shot twice in the back of the head. There also was strong indications that someone attempted to strangle him before wrapping his body in a discarded carpet.

Detective Kincaid and I went to the jail to interview Johnson about the case. Johnson told us that he'd been arrested about thirty times since he was seventeen years old.

He confessed to killing Dixon because Dixon's ex-wife, Linda Dorma Long, thirty years old at the time, promised that she would give him a house in San Marcos if he killed her husband.

"She used sex to get me to do things for her," Johnson said, echoing a common refrain of male criminals. He said that he met Long when he and Dixon "swapped women" one night. He later moved in with Long.

He told us, "She said that she wanted him killed because he wouldn't give her a divorce and she didn't want to pay for it."

Johnson went on to tell us that Long lured Dixon to her house using sexual innuendo. Long and Dixon had some drinks and smoked marijuana while Johnson hid in a nearby closet. He waited there until Long gave him the cue – when she got out of bed to go to the bathroom. Then he was to come out of the closet and kill Dixon.

"I went out and hit him in the head with a .22-caliber pistol," so the confession went, "and then shot him in the back of the head twice. He didn't die, so I rolled him over and with the blunt end of an axe I hit him on the head a couple of more times."

Johnson said that he got a friend to help him load the body in the trunk of his car, covered it with bed springs, took it near the San Jacinto River and placed it in a hole.

Long was unaware of the fact that Johnson was being held in the county jail, so we had him call her and set up a meeting for later that day.

We checked Johnson out of jail and took him to Long's house in the far east end of Houston. I was wired with our Special Crimes Nagra recorder. I also took HPD chemist James "Jim" Boling with us just in case Long said enough to implicate herself. We could then arrest her and search the house for any evidence of the crime scene. It was Boling's very first day on the job. He was scared to death about going out with officers and possibly arresting someone in connection with a murder. When we arrived at the house, Boling was visibly nervous and began to sweat like a "whore in church."

"Relax, Jim," I said to him, "you'll be in the car if we arrest her. I'll come out and get you. You'll be okay. You're HPD now."

"I'm just a chemist, man, not a police officer," he pleaded. "I didn't know I'd be doing anything like this when I signed on. Especially on my very first day."

"Don't worry, everything'll be fine, just try to relax."

Johnson introduced us to Long as two good friends trying to help him in the case. We needed all the details in order to assist him in a possible defense and/or alibi. Linda Long was in her late twenties like I was and fairly nice looking. She had a prior charge of burglary of a habitation with intent to commit theft in 1975. She had received eight years' probation.

Long told us that a "trap" was set for Dixon when she asked him to come to her house. She said that Dixon was wanting to have sex with her, so it was easy to get him to come over. Dixon moved to Atlanta, Georgia, after the couple's divorce but occasionally came back to Houston. One reason was to have sex with this woman. Long proceeded to explain to us all the details of how Dixon was killed and more details of how the body was discarded near the San Jacinto River.

After we had enough on tape to file charges against Long, we arrested her and brought Boling in to search for any possible evidence of blood. Boling was still a nervous wreck who was sweating profusely when I went to get him to come inside. We transported Long to HPD Homicide so detectives could interrogate her and file charges after I provided them with a copy of our conversation. Boling said when we arrived at HPD, "I'll never forget this day as long as I live."

After this experience, whenever I saw Jim Boling in the courthouse or at investigator association meetings, I'd always ask him, "Hey Jim, been on any big arrests lately?"

He always smiles and said, "I will never forget that day as long as I live."

In October 1981, a court sentenced Linda Dorma Long to sixteen years in the Texas Department of Corrections after a jury trial. She was paroled in 1985 and hasn't been arrested since. In 2020, Larry Kincaid was serving as Chief of Police in Granger, Texas.

Keith P. Johnson   *Linda Long*

CHAPTER 11

A JOURNEY TO DEATH

Steve German followed his brother to Houston looking for work in the late summer of 1981. Instead of landing a job in the Bayou City, however, German ended up in the jungles of Peru. His body was found a short time after his arrival alongside a dirt road with two bullets in his head and face. His hands were burned with acid beyond fingerprint recognition. It appeared that someone was trying to cover up or hide his identity.

German had problems finding a job in Houston until he met a Deer Park man, Carlton Wilkes, who offered him a job making $15 an hour working in a warehouse located in Lima, Peru.

The weird thing about the job was that German had to fit a specific physical description of height and weight in order to stock the shelves in this medical warehouse. He stood six feet tall and weighed one hundred and forty pounds. The prospective jobholder was originally told that he was going to be a consultant of sorts for an import and export company. Either way he thought it was better than being a day laborer in Houston or the industrial suburb of Deer Park.

Carlton Wilkes claimed to be an engineer of some type. Wilkes also claimed that he never met German until he arrived in Peru, but German's family said that Wilkes took him to San Antonio on a business trip prior to traveling to the South American country. While there, he took him to a dentist and had X-rays taken of his teeth. Wilkes told him it was required to travel outside of the USA.

Wilkes told German's family that Steve quit the job after arriving and said that he paid him $1,400 in back wages, which didn't make any sense to the German family, since he'd only been there for a couple of days. Wilkes claimed that the last time he saw him was when he dropped him off at a travel agency and he met with a "greasy looking Mexican guy."

The German family couldn't get any straight answers from Wilkes, plus his story didn't make any sense to them.

On October 3, 1981, Steve German called his brother Mike from the Miami airport right before he was to depart for Lima. Mike told him, "Just cash in your ticket and come home." Mike said that about that time Wilkes showed up and Steve said, "Goodbye."

In the early morning hours of October 7, 1981, Steve's body was found about thirty-seven miles from Lima. Later his mother, Dixie German, received a phone call from a spokesman, Steve Seche, from the U. S. Embassy in Lima, saying, "It's with profound regret that we must inform you that your son's body has been found in Lima, Peru, and we think he was murdered."

It took seventeen days and $2,000 for the Germans to get Steve's remains back to Missouri. They never viewed the body because the Boone County medical examiner, Dr. Jay Dix, told them that the sight was terrible to view. Dix also told them that the dental X-rays taken after his death in Peru "certainly looked similar."

The family was still hoping that it might be a mistake. The question still remained as to who killed him and why.

A short time later the German family contacted the FBI, DEA, and the U. S. State Department and still got no answers. They eventually hired a Houston attorney, Doug O'Brien, in order to get the attention of the authorities. O'Brien was formerly a Harris County assistant district attorney and spent some time as a prosecutor in the Special Crimes Bureau. Doing his duty as the family's attorney, O'Brien gave Mrs. German my name, office address, and phone number.

Soon after that, she mailed me a letter along with a story from a Missouri newspaper about her son's murder.

I called her immediately after I read her letter and the newspaper story.

"I can't get any government agency to investigate my son's murder," the victim's bereaved mother told me. "I'm so frustrated. Thank you so much for calling me."

"I completely understand," I assured her, "and I will do whatever it takes to get to the bottom of this. If someone killed one of my kids, there'd be hell to pay for whoever did it."

Then I said, "The first thing I'm going to do is find out who the hell is this Carlton Wilkes character. I'm going to pay this guy a visit and get you some answers. I promise."

A few days later, before I even got out to find Wilkes, I got a phone call from a lady who was frantic about her daughter.

"My daughter and some of her friends who were in a beauty contest together are at the airport to get on a plane heading to work in a warehouse in South America. I can't stop her, and she won't listen to me."

"Ma'am, please calm down and give me your daughter's name right now," I said, knowing time was of the essence. "I need your phone number. I promise that I'll call you right back. I have to hang up and see what I can do to stop her."

I called an HPD officer assigned to the Houston Intercontinental Airport on the dayshift.

"I have somewhat of an emergency," I told him, "and don't have time now to tell you what's going on, but I need this girl paged on the intercom system. I need to talk to her right now and stop her and her friends from getting on a plane."

I gave him her name and he put me on hold. Every second seemed like forever to me.

Eventually, I heard the voice of a young girl. I said who I was and where I worked. I told her, "You and your friends can not get on that plane under any circumstances. The last person that went to work for Carlton Wilkes in South America at a warehouse was murdered. That's what's going to happen to you guys if you get on that plane."

She agreed and thanked me. She said, "We didn't know anything about that."

I called her mom back and she was totally relieved. And extremely grateful.

I later learned that Wilkes required the girls to take out $250,000 worth of life insurance, in which his company was the beneficiary. Wilkes later told a grand jury that that was prompted by the $60,000 that he incurred from German's death, which I knew was total bullshit. The girls told me that Wilkes said the insurance was required by the Peruvian government.

Over the next few weeks, I made several visits to Wilkes' "shit hole" office located in Deer Park. He would never give me any details and was very evasive every time I asked him a question. He even accused me of harassing him at one point.

"You haven't seen nothing yet," I told him. "I'm just doing my job by asking questions and trying to find out the truth about what's going on here?" I told myself, *This guy is a lying, crooked asshole.*

After being exasperated by Wilkes, I met with my boss, Henry Oncken, then chief of the Special Crimes Bureau. Henry grew up in Houston and attended Lutheran High School. He graduated from the University of Houston and its law school, as well. He joined the DA's office in 1969 and was the chief prosecutor in Judge Garth Bates' court at the time of Bates' arrest for bribery. Henry transferred to Special Crimes and later became the first assistant district attorney under Johnny Holmes. Following that he served as a criminal district judge and the U. S. attorney for the Southern District of Texas. I also have to say that I found Henry and his wife, Jackie, to be two of the nicest people in the world.

I already knew that we had no jurisdiction in this matter, but I hated to see this guy get away with doing something like this. There also was a good possibility that he would probably do it again with murderous results. It was obvious to me that this prick had something to do with German's murder and we couldn't do a thing about it. It was just very frustrating to me.

THE *REAL* CARLTON WILKES?

The last time that I saw Wilkes was when I served him with a grand jury subpoena. Oncken took him in front of the grand jurors and he told them some cock-and-bull story about writing a book on how to steal someone's identity. *Really? No wonder the German kid's fingertips were burned with acid.*

Of course, they didn't return an indictment because we had no jurisdiction. Henry and I just wanted some straight answers and the truth, which we didn't get.

Shortly after Wilkes' grand jury appearance, he disappeared from Houston to parts unknown.

I was saddened and frustrated for the fact that I didn't have any answers for the German family. I was very happy that we might have saved some lives by keeping the girls from working for that idiot. I had to admit that this has been one of the strangest cases that I had ever worked on in my forty-nine years as an investigator.

But hang on, the story gets better.

Approximately two years later, I learned from Sgt. Howard Burger of the Alaska State Police that Wilkes showed up in Seattle, Washington, after he sold his Deer Park house and divorced his wife. He was then using the name, Don Edward Manning. He'd put an ad in the local Seattle newspaper wanting truck drivers to work for a new company in Alaska. He hired Richard Quien and sent him to Alaska, where they shared a cabin in the wilderness near Palmer, Alaska.

Wilkes had tried to take out two life insurance policies on Quien totaling $500,000, which was later denied.

Quien was later found dead in this remote Alaskan cabin after the Alaska State Police received a letter from a person who claimed to be an eyewitness to the murder, claiming to have seen the suspect kill both Quien and Wilkes, aka Don Manning. The letter said that the killer ground up the body of Wilkes and placed the remains in a nearby river.

On August 3, 1983, when the Palmer Police Department and the Alaska State Police arrived at the cabin, they found that Quien had been shot in the head. Police thought it might have been done with a .44-caliber Ruger. They also found that Quien's leg had been badly burned with acid. Police also found Wilkes' diary, which was later compared to the anonymous letter sent to the police, by FBI technicians. They said they had a match.

The letter also had a postmark from Los Angeles. The Alaska state police and Palmer PD later learned that Wilkes boarded a plane in LA on the same day of the postmark and that he flew to Singapore. This latest murder was very much similar to the murder of Steve German. *Gee, I wonder who wrote that letter?*

Alaskan authorities said that it was an attempted insurance swindle. Alaskan prosecutor Michael White wrote an affidavit using the information provided by the police in order to support a murder charge against Wilkes.

While in Singapore, Wilkes filed a claim with American Express stating that his Travelers Cheques were stolen. They issued him new checks after he swore in an affidavit to the claim. Upon his return to the United States, he opened a bank account with the "stolen" checks and charges were later filed against him for bank fraud.

After Wilkes learned of the charges, he fled to Laredo. While trying to cross over into Mexico he was arrested for the bank fraud warrant and placed in the Webb County Jail, his bond set at $5 million.

About this same time Wilkes was charged with the murder of Richard Quien in Alaska. Also found when Wilkes tried crossing the border were sixteen different forms of false identities in his possession, one being that of Don Edward Manning, who died in 1947 in San Antonio at the age of five. Wilkes and Manning were born a year apart.

Wilkes had obtained Manning's birth certificate and was able to get an Alaska State ID, as well as credit cards and bank accounts using his name. Wilkes also had the names and other information on fifteen other children who died in Texas during the late 1940s.

Authorities also seized from Wilkes lists of sources for machine guns, silencers, blow guns and darts, tear gas, and other firearms and rifles. He also had a list of women that he'd had sex with and rated them from A to F. *I bet that was a short list.*

Since the murder in Peru, Wilkes was linked by U. S. authorities to illegal activities in the United States, Mexico, South America, and Southeast Asia. They also learned from the Mexican authorities that Wilkes had earlier met with some women in Mexico and told them that he had a large ranch near Houston and offered them jobs taking care of his children. They all declined.

Several people in Texas, Arkansas, and Colorado answered ads that Wilkes had placed in newspapers offering jobs operating heavy equipment. He charged them $350 apiece for an "application fee" and they never heard from him again.

Wilkes always played the role of a rich Texas oilman and rancher, but he was just a "poor broke dick" who lived in a middle-class neighborhood in Deer Park. He drove a "clunker" car. He had a glorified and exaggerated impression of himself and his lifestyle.

While in custody in Laredo, Wilkes had a heart attack while masturbating and died. When I heard that, I thought to myself, *Well, Wilkes always thought that he had a good grasp of things.*

Most of the cases that I mention in this book contain information that I have in my possession or obtained from other sources by doing research. As a former police officer and now a private investigator, I have access to databases that most people don't. Since Wilkes was never indicted and I misplaced a box of my old files, there are no official Harris County records.

I know that I'd done some research on him when I investigated this case, so I used my databases and other sources of research and can't find any records of Carlton Wilkes. There are records on a Carlton Wilkes, but not the evil one identified in this chapter. I searched some of the aliases that he used and can only find the date of their deaths in the 1940s. It's like he never existed.

Who was the real Carlton Wilkes?

CHAPTER 12

WHAT A GREAT EXTRA JOB

As I placed my Smith and Wesson pocket knife in the shirt pocket of HRH Prince Abdullah Bin Saud, I said, "Just keep the knife since you ruined it."

The prince would come in my room every night and use my knife to carve on the wooded cap of his cheap stinking-ass cologne. On this night near the end of my stay in the Hyatt Waikiki working as a bodyguard for the sixteen-year-old prince, I looked at the blade and saw that it was ruined – or as some of my fellow Texans say, *ruint*.

Once the knife was snug in his shirt pocket, the prince said in his thick Arabic accent, "Ken, you give to me?"

In a pissed-off tone of voice, I said, "Hell, yes, you fucked it up, so you can just keep it."

I know what you're thinking. But that's just the way I talked to him, just like he was a dumb ass teenager like I used to be – and not a prince of the royal family of Saudi Arabia. Please understand: He liked the way I spoke to him and he liked me a lot – so much in fact that he later wanted me to quit my job in the states and serve as his full-time bodyguard.

He then took off his new gold and stainless Presidential Rolex that he recently got in Paris and handed it to me and said, "Here, this is a gift from me to you."

I felt bad about the way that I spoke to him, but quickly tried to find something else that I could give him, so I took my State of Texas belt buckle and handed it to him. Who knows? He probably still has it.

The gift exchange continued. He went in his room next to mine on the twenty-first floor and came out with his "boom box" stereo and said, "Here, Ken, this is yours now, too."

I reported to Dan, the man in charge. I called Dan to ask him if I could take gifts from the kid and learned that you never refuse a gift from a Saudi because it's like a slap in their face.

A few months earlier, while I was fishing in Matagorda in the summer of 1981, my neighbor came over and said that someone named Dan called me on his phone from Paris, France, and said that he wanted me to call him collect as soon as I could because it was very important.

Dan Pursley was a friend of mine I met at Sam Houston State University. He also had been a Harris County sheriff's deputy assigned as the process server in State District Judge Lee Duggan's court while Johnny Holmes was the chief prosecutor.

While filling in for off-duty HPD officer Michael D. "Mad Dog" Harrison at the plush Warwick Hotel near Hermann Park and the Texas Medical Center, Dan met the sister of the King of Saudi Arabia, HH Princess Alanoud bint Abdul Aziz, and became her chauffeur while she was in Houston having some medical tests done down Fannin from the Warwick at the world-renowned TMC.

After several days, she liked Dan so much that she offered him a full-time job as her chief of security. He quit the sheriff's office and dropped out of law school during his last semester at South Texas School of Law.

I called Dan and he told me that he needed me to come to Hawaii and work for him as a bodyguard for the royal family of Saudi Arabia while they were on vacation. I told him that I only had two weeks of vacation left, but that sounded good to me. He said all expenses would be paid and that I'd get $150 a day paid in cash. That sounded even better since the family I was supporting needed the big payday.

Dan later sent me the pre-paid ticket and I flew to Honolulu with a short stopover in Los Angeles on my thirty-first birthday on October 3, 1981.

When I arrived in Hawaii, I took a cab to the Hyatt and met up with Dan. I remember that it was only eight in the morning but the time zone difference meant he had an NFL game on the TV in his room. He told me that I'd be working for a sixteen-year-old prince named Abdullah and that he was a pretty good kid. He said that while the prince was awake, I would leave the door to my next-door room wide open in case the prince needed the man responsible for his safety at all times.

Dan said that the prince's aged nanny was in the room on the other side of mine. He warned me to be careful of the nosy old bitch because she could cause some problems. He said that she was part of the entourage only because she'd worked for the family for more than thirty years, which meant that "she's part of the family."

She was one of the more than one hundred Arabs that we were tasked with protecting. Dan provided me the layout of how things worked and took the time to detail the family history and about Abdullah's mother, Princess Mudhawi, who was the sister of King Fahd bin Abdul Aziz Al Saud. From what he told me about the mother, I concluded that she sounded like a cold-hearted bitch, a factor that made me nervous. I also learned that Abdullah had four brothers and two sisters staying in the same hotel.

He said that they left Riyadh, Saudi Arabia in August and flew to Paris, where Pierre Cardin measured each member of the royal family for their new clothes before they left for the Seychelles Islands in the Pacific Ocean.

I learned that Dan was mainly responsible for the youngest prince, Aziz, who was thirteen years old. I later found out that he was a "handful" to tend to. While in the Seychelles, the family went offshore fishing and caught a large marlin which they took to the hotel. Aziz put the fish in the swimming pool!

Now, I'm thinking: *These are my kind of people. They're crazy like me.* I learned different later.

After settling into my room, I went down to the restaurant where I was just fixing to take a bite of the steak and lobster that I ordered and Dan walked up to me and said, "We got to go play soccer."

"Are you kidding me?" I pleaded. "I just sat down to eat and haven't even taken a bite and not only that, I can't even spell it, much less play it."

"We're watching them, not playing, stupid."

We both laughed as I still didn't know what to expect.

We loaded up on one of the three buses that we had and stopped by a small sporting goods store located in a small strip shopping center near the park. The family must've spent a couple thousand dollars on soccer equipment, which included shoes, socks, shirts, shorts, and balls. The owner was one happy soccer camper when we left. I think they bought out the store by the time they finished. I remember watching this proprietor as we pulled away from the curb outside – he had one big-ass grin on his face.

The kids played soccer for less than an hour. At this juncture, I'd still had not met Prince Abdullah and was kind of anxious about how the first encounter would work out. Once they were finished playing, they took off their shoes, socks, shirts, shorts, and even the soccer balls and put them in the trash cans near the public field where they had played.

"Are they crazy?" I said to Dan. "What's up with that?"

"You haven't seen anything yet," Dan replied.

I was totally astounded that they'd just thrown away all that expensive equipment as if it were a used kitchen towel or, heck, toilet paper. I really wanted to grab the gear and donate it to a youth group or charity, but they'd drive off without me. I thought it was very thoughtless. I was actually pissed about it. As I would later learn, they were like that about everything. They had no idea about the value of things or people. It kind of made me sad and angry at the same time knowing that I was working for thoughtless people. They'd throw around one-hundred-dollar bills like I would a penny.

I finally got to meet Prince Abdullah once we were back at the hotel. He was a nice-looking kid who stood about five-feet-ten and was built fairly well for someone who lived the life of leisure. His skin was brown and hair black. I thought that he looked just like I pictured an Arab prince should.

Abdullah had his servant, Khalid, who was identified as "a companion." The companion stayed in the prince's room. All of Mudhawi's children had their companions along for the trip. Khalid was the spitting image of Sammy Davis Jr. I couldn't believe how much they looked alike – so much, in fact, that I nicknamed him "Sammy Davis." I wondered if the real Sammy Davis Jr. ever traveled to the Middle East for any special gigs because this eighteen-year-old companion looked like his twin.

By the time I left two weeks later nearly all of the Arabs were referring to Khalid as "Sammy Davis." I bet most of them didn't even know who Sammy Davis Jr. was or looked like, but they all really enjoyed calling Khalid that.

Abdullah came into my room wearing a lime-green shirt with black parachute pants and told me that he wanted to rent some bicycles and go riding. I said, "You look like an idiot. You can't see that?" He went to the mirror and stood and stared at himself for a minute or so. I explained to him that the colors didn't match, and he'd look like a fool riding a bicycle in downtown. He decided that he didn't want to ride that night.

Thank God. Sometime later in the week, he told me that he wanted to go bowling. I really didn't feel like bowling that night, so I told him, "We can't go because it's not allowed for Arabs to bowl in Hawaii."

He didn't know any better – he bought my bowling bullshit. I realized that the poor kid had been patronized all these years and had no social skills about how to dress or act. The kid had no "street smarts" about him.

When the prince went back to his room, I went down to the restaurant to get something to eat. I ordered a steak and lobster again because Dan told me that I could eat anything that I wanted from the menu.

The hotel restaurant had a display case where you could select the steak and the lobster that you actually wanted to eat, so I did just that.

While cutting into my medium rare filet with a lobster tail on the side, Dan came up and said, "We have to go right now."

"No way, man," I said. "I just got my food."

"Just get another one when you get back. Mudhawi wants to eat while on a boat trip tonight."

As we walked away, my mouth was still watering with the thought of that steak and lobster. I just couldn't believe it.

We ended up on some all-night cruise restaurant with one hundred Arabs and the food looked nasty and probably tasted like shit.

■ ■ ■

Once I saw Princess Mudhawi, I realized that she was one scary-looking bitch. She told Dan that she didn't like me because I never smiled. I told Dan that she scared the hell out of me because she had this mean-ass look about her.

She had dark skin, black hair, and this evil look about her. I thought she looked like a witch. I'm glad she didn't put a hex on me, or maybe she did, and I didn't know it. The only reason that I was still there was because her son, Abdullah, loved me. No one ever spoke to him the way that I did. That made for a long night, knowing that this evil-looking woman didn't really like me, but I really didn't care at that point.

While on the cruise I didn't eat anything because my mouth was still watering as I thought about the steak and lobster waiting for me at the Hyatt. Once back at the hotel, I called room service and got another steak and lobster dinner. I think while there for the two weeks, I'd eaten quite a few great menu items. After all, I gained ten pounds.

The next day, Abdullah and I sat around and just shot the bull. Dan asked me to see if I could call the Honolulu Police Department and find an officer to work for us, which I did. His name was Glenn Furukawa, a criminal intelligence officer. He was of Japanese descent, a short, husky guy who spoke with a thick Japanese and Hawaiian accent. Glenn was a really nice guy who was dedicated to his job and family. We remain friends to this day. We made him responsible for the safety of the eighteen-year-old Princess Sara, a pretty girl – attractive enough that Dan and I worried about the other security personnel hitting on her.

I can only imagine what Princess Mudhawi would do if she caught an off-duty police officer or deputy constable in the sack with Princess Sara.

One of the security officers – an off-duty deputy constable – was showing too much interest in Sara. Dan and I knew that there was something odd about the guy.

When I returned to Houston, I checked him out and learned that he was in the U. S. Marshal's Witness Protection Program involving organized crime in New Orleans. As soon as I let Dan know about these facts, he sent this man packing. Back in those days just about anyone could get a reserve commission, especially at Precinct 5 in Harris County.

Back to the bull session. About six o'clock that day, Abdullah told me that he wanted "a date," so I called Dan and asked him what he meant by that. I wanted to stay culturally sound with the Saudis. Abdullah informed Dan that on his sixteenth birthday, while in Orlando, Florida, that his brothers got him a prostitute as a present.

"Are you telling me that he wants me to get him a hooker?" I asked incredulously. "No way, man. I'm not a pimp. I put those kinds of people in jail."

"Look, just go downstairs and watch him," Dan replied. "You don't have to actually get him a girl. Just keep an eye on him and make sure no one messes with him."

I accompanied Prince Abdullah, Sammy Davis, and Prince Aziz's forty-something companion, Turki, to the hotel lobby. We then headed outside to the street, where we were literally attacked by young girls asking us if we "wanted dates for the night." I couldn't take two steps without being asked about "a date." I just couldn't believe it. To my knowledge, date-seeking "ladies" weren't this blatant in Houston, Texas.

I later learned that there were more prostitutes in Hawaii than any other place in the world. College-aged girls would come to Hawaii to live and had a hard time finding jobs. As a result, they would turn to prostitution in order to remain on the island frequently referred to as "Paradise."

I'm thinking, *I can't believe that I'm in Hawaii and watching an Arab prince trying to find a "date."* I tried to remember that I was just here for the kid Prince's safety – that's my primary job description and I should stick to it.

It didn't take Abdullah too long to find a date. She was a shapely young girl probably in her early twenties with long black hair, brown skin, and standing about five-foot-four. Then we headed up to our rooms. I was thinking while going up the elevator with the group: *What in the hell am I doing?* I realized once off the elevator that we now have to get by the old nanny's room and tell everyone to be super quiet and crawl on the carpet once we get next to the nanny's door. We didn't want her to hear us. Or see the "invited guest" of the young prince.

Once we got inside Abdullah's room at the very end of the hall, there's an immediate knock on his door. I looked through the peep hole and see the old heavy-set nanny standing there.

Now, I'm thinking that I haven't been there for forty-eight hours and it looked like I'll be on the next plane headed back to Houston. There goes $150 per day down the depths of the Pacific Ocean.

I quickly told Sammy Davis and Abdullah's date to get in the shower and turn it on. Once they are safely concealed there, I opened the door and let the old nanny in the room. She was old but she had sharp eyes. She surveyed the room with panoramic precision. "What's going on?" she pointedly asked.

I told her in a somewhat nervous voice that Sammy was taking a shower and that was about it. The whole while, she was going into all the other rooms like a detective with a search warrant. Surely, she must have heard my loud sigh of relief when she finally left the room.

I immediately called Dan.

"What in the hell have you got me into?"

He explained to me that everything would be fine and that the old nanny was just real protective of all the kids because she'd raised them all since birth. He further explained that she had nothing to do all day, so she was always nosing around.

The good-looking Hawaiian girl spent the night with the prince, and I had to stay up all night, with my door open until she left the next morning.

I had no idea of what it cost him, but I really didn't want to know anyway. I didn't really like the entire situation.

A few days later, he asked me about having a real date with a female and I tried to explain to him that you have to meet someone in school or wherever, learn about them, and get to know them. I said, "You just don't go down to the street and buy someone. It doesn't work that way." I don't think he understood. He just couldn't "get it." If I had had more time with him and had worked for him full time, I could've taught him to do what's right.

The next day Dan and I leased a couple of cars for the "kids." Aziz wanted and got a 1981 Ford Mustang convertible and Abdullah just had to have a Pontiac Firebird convertible. Even in Hawaii it took a while to find rental cars like these. It's a good thing that they couldn't drive because there's no telling what would have happened to them.

Later, all the security men loaded up on one of our buses and headed to a house that Abdullah's older brother, Prince Bander, had rented on the beach near Diamond Head. The house was immaculate, fronting to one of the most beautiful beaches on God's green earth. I was told that golfer Arnold Palmer owned the house, but he kept it rented most of the time to wealthy people who didn't want to stay in a hotel. Bander was paying Arnie's people $1,500 a day. It was used only once or twice during the royal family's three-week stay.

In Saudi Arabia members of the royal family didn't drink alcohol. But once off the continent, they would start sucking down alcohol like it was Kool-Aid. I watched those guys suck down some Heinekens during my stay. Every time that I saw an older prince, he'd have a beer or mixed drink in his hand. Funny thing is that I never saw any of the family members or their companions intoxicated. I learned that if any of their companions got out of line, Princess Mudhawi would send them back to Riyadh.

After several days, the kids would stay up all night playing an Arabic card game and sleep all day. Ah, yes, this allowed Dan and I to have some time to look around Honolulu. I took some hand-held Motorola portable radios so we could communicate between the rooms of the hotel. In my business you need all the buddies you can get. I hit up my buddy, Don McClendon, who'd previously sold me the Nagra recorder we used in Special Crimes years earlier.

One day, Dan and I had these special two-ways on and heard a director or somebody on the radio while the filming *Magnum P. I.* was taking place. We were sure that's who it was because the frequencies in the radios were set for the filming industry. I got on the radio and said, "Let's shoot that again."

"Who said that?" some voice uttered.

Dan and I laughed our asses off. We never did that again and realized that we'd better change to another channel on the radio – for security reasons.

■ ■ ■

Toward the end of my two-week extra job, Abdullah and Aziz wanted to go fishing. We hired a yacht to take us off shore so we could catch a marlin or yellow fin tuna. Dan and I stopped by the liquor store and got us a bottle of Canadian Club, so we could enjoy ourselves watching Sammy Davis and others try to catch a fish. I remembered about their last fishing trip in the Seychelle Islands when Prince Aziz caught a large marlin, brought it back to the hotel, and threw it into the swimming pool. I hoped that this wouldn't happen again.

Abdullah hooked up with something big but never got the fish close enough to see what it was.

After Dan and I killed our bottle, we started working on the *captain's* bottle, so we were feeling pretty good once we got back on shore. We decided we were going to race back to the hotel five miles away, which excited the boys. To this day I can't believe we didn't get stopped by Honolulu police because we were going over seventy miles per hour at five o'clock in the afternoon racing down Waikiki Boulevard.

Once back at the hotel, Abdullah wasn't feeling well, so I called the front desk and told the hotel manager on duty that we needed the house doctor. The manager and the doc came to my room to examine the princely patient. I don't think they had any clue about an accurate diagnosis. Sometime after they left, I got a call from Dan. He was laughing loudly and reported to me that the "prick" of a hotel manager stopped by his room and ventured to say that he thought I'd been drinking. Then it was my turn to laugh even louder than Dan since we both knew he had had more to drink than I had and smelled like a distillery.

The next night about a third of the royal family decided that they wanted to go eat at Benihana's and that they wanted to walk instead of taking a bus or limousine. I thought that it was only a few blocks away, so it didn't seem to be that big of a deal. Glenn and I escorted the group, but we were weary because it had been a long day.

After about half a mile with a Smith and Wesson .357-caliber revolver tucked in my left boot, I was tired and aggravated. The good thing was that the entire group pretty much felt the same way. Another good thing was that once we got to the restaurant, we knew we could order anything we wanted from the menu. First thing Glenn and I did was order some sake. Hey, the Arabs were driving us crazy.

After an hour or so we went outside, and I told them Glenn and I weren't walking. If they wanted security and protection, they'd better go with us. It must have been a relief to them because they were as tired as we were. Prince Turki decided that it'd be neat for all of us to ride in horse-drawn carriages back to the hotel. While standing there waiting to get enough carriages to accommodate our entourage, Abdullah spotted a good-looking Hawaiian girl and told me he liked her.

I'm thinking: *Does this kid ever get tired?*

Something told me that it was strange that she didn't approach us. I no sooner finished this thought than Glenn came over and told me that this potential date was probably a Honolulu PD vice officer! So, I grabbed the prince and told him no and to stay away from her and that we needed to head back to the hotel. I think Glenn told her that he was working an extra job for the Saudi Royal Family. We loaded up the "Royals" in two large horse carriages and headed back to the Hyatt.

"Damn!" I said to Glenn, "Can you see the headlines tomorrow? Houston DA Investigator and Prince Abdullah of the Saudi Royal Family Arrested for Soliciting Undercover Vice Officer."

The following day, Princess Mudhawi decided that she wanted us to move to another hotel on the far side of Oahu, which was about fifty or sixty miles away. We loaded up the three buses with all the Arabs and headed to the Presidential Hotel. We had to leave our luggage at the Hyatt just in case she didn't like the new hotel. If she did, the hotel staff would have to pack our stuff and bring it to us.

You just don't know how much trouble it was loading up all these Saudi royal family members and staff on the three buses and now you had to worry about these idiots from the hotel loading up all your things.

Once at the new location, the princess looked around for a few minutes and decided it wasn't a place for them. So, we loaded back up and headed back to Honolulu.

A few days later, I got on the plane wearing my new Rolex watch while carrying my "boom box" gift. *What a great extra job.*

■ ■ ■

I later worked several other extra jobs for different branches of the royal family when they'd have medical check-ups at the Texas Medical Center. When they'd travel, they wouldn't just bring themselves; they came with an army of Saudis. I don't know how many would be in the group, but no matter how many there were, they'd rent all the rooms on the same floor. Usually they stayed at the Guest Quarters.

I have a different story for each one, but one of the most memorable was when one of the Saudis' twelve-year-old kids took out his bow and shot an arrow down the long hallway of the Guest Quarters Hotel in the Galleria area on the fifth floor. The arrow barely missed an off-duty HPD officer who was doing guard duty by the elevator. I thought he was going to have a heart attack.

On another visit by the same group, they bought a young donkey or jackass after going out to eat and brought it back to the hotel. They tied it to a table by the elevators on their floor. Later, the hotel manager called Dan in my room and said, "Somebody come get that goddamn donkey out of this hotel. He's shit all over the place."

I don't remember who came and got it for us, probably because I was laughing so hard.

Another group that I worked for was made up of all males. The sixtyish prince was having a medical examination in the medical center and brought all of his sons and their friends.

One of his sons lived in Houston and was attending Lee College in Baytown. He was what you might call "Americanized."

I got to know him and thought to myself that I could've made Prince Abdullah like him. This prince "got it." He had a nice girlfriend and didn't go "throwing" money around. He acted like a "normal" twenty-year-old American kid.

They invited me to eat with them one night in a meeting room on the same floor where their rooms were located. I walked into the room and there was a huge roasted lamb which included the head and the legs. The legs pointed straight up in the air. The chest was cut open. Plus, the lamb was still covered with its wool.

The Saudis would just reach in with their right hand and yank out a piece of the lamb's meat and eat it. They supposedly used their left hand to wipe their ass. I damn sure wasn't going to ask them about that. They wanted to know why I wasn't eating, and I told them that I ate before I got there.

All things considered, I really didn't have much of an appetite.

Me and Prince Abdullah

CHAPTER 13

REACH OUT
AND TOUCH SOMEONE

During the month of October 1982, I was contacted by an aide to Harris County Commissioner Bob Eckels. Mary Frances Steward sounded like a concerned, law-abiding citizen and dutifully reported to me that something was dreadfully amiss in a detailed review of her long-distance telephone log.

It entailed the use of a remote-access feature in the county's complex phone system. Always trying to put in a light-hearted spin whenever possible in my work as a criminal investigator, I immediately paraphrased Ma Bell's jingle when I said to myself that "somebody is reaching out to touch someone" on the county's dime.

Mary Frances, a long-time Eckels aide who knew the ins and outs of Harris County, got to the point: She said that she didn't make any long-distance calls from her home and that records reflected that she had made more than one hundred and fifty phone calls from outside her office. "I make all county-related business calls while I'm at the office," she explained.

Furthermore, she said, every month each county employee with the authority to make long-distance calls is required to sign his or her long-distant log sheets, to be held accountable that the calls were made on county business only.

In order to make a long-distance call from outside your office, you were required to implement the remote access phone number and then enter a four-digit code. This code, like today's password, identified who made the call. At this juncture in the nation's third-largest county, most county employees outside of law enforcement didn't even know that they had this privilege, much less realize they needed the four-digit access.

I handled most of the harassing phone cases under the authority of Special Crimes. This made me the DA's office liaison with the security personnel of Southwestern Bell. Many citizens might not realize that the best way to handle harassment calls is through the use of "a phone trap" placed on the victim's phone in order to trace it back to the harassing caller.

Once I had worked through the process with the phone company's security personnel, getting a trap became easier. I also had assisted Southwestern Bell on several "sting" cases involving persons making fraudulent long-distant calls overseas. I would get some of our investigators and my HPD buddies to volunteer to help since we needed a large group of officers to catch these crooks in the act of making fraudulent calls. The county had it as a priority; it was costing them a lot of money.

Following up on Mary Frances' findings, I poured over the long-distance records of all county employees for about three weeks. I limited the scope, of course, to those who had an access code. I contacted those with more than a few remote-access calls. I soon determined that the remote-access number had spread out to non-county workers, so blue-collar workers, insurance company office workers and others were making more calls than county employees. I even began calling the numbers of the persons called trying to find out who was calling them. Most people wouldn't tell me or said that they didn't remember. I found more than six hundred fraudulent calls made in a two-year period.

Unlike the quick-action investigations you see portrayed in a three-minute scene on TV, these findings came after a long and tedious process of trying to track down the parties in this large number of phone calls. These fraudulent calls were costing the taxpayers thousands of dollars of what the politicians would label costly wastes of money.

I decided that if we did our own "sting" operation, we could identify some of the major abusers. Trusted sources – like any case involving a DA's investigation – were a crucial factor for success. I called Tom Suter, my good friend and former football teammate at St. Pius X High School in

Houston. Tom was part of the Southwestern Bell security team and we had worked together on several "sting" phone operations in the past.

I got most of our Special Crimes investigators and other HPD Criminal Intelligence officers to play roles in the sting. It would take place on a Saturday. Once someone dialed the remote-access phone number, the phone company would trace the number to the address where the call was originated from. Yes, it was "a trap."

Suter would in turn advise us of the details over the police radio that I provided him. Officers positioned closest to the suspect's address would go there and interview him or her. Most of the people we trapped said that someone told them that it was a free service available to them or they saw a sign in a phone booth that read, "Free LD call service," that included instructions on how to use this service.

A typical suspect said he or she could use this number and four-digit code, and so on and so forth. Our investigators gave the suspects two choices: go to jail or go to Special Crimes and make restitution. Of course, all decided on restitution.

The ones that wouldn't come to the door or had left their residence for some reason required a few extra steps. I'd call them on the phone and advise them of their situation. One of these people had made an illegal LD phone call from his office at a major oil company. I called him and he said that he didn't know anything about such a call. Then I called the number that was called from his office and spoke to the lady on the other end. I told her what was going on and she said that it was her son that called from the oil company. She told me she hoped that he wasn't in any trouble.

"Not yet," I said.

I called the guy back and played the tape of the phone call that I'd made to his mother. He confessed.

"I should come over and arrest your ass for lying to me," I told him, "so you come over to my office right now and bring your checkbook. You can pay for what you owe Harris County. We call this restitution."

He came to see me and, of course, was very apologetic.

We ended up catching about fifteen people in that Saturday sting operation. Most had been using the county system for quite a while and were our biggest offenders. A county employee who was a clerk in one constable's office was charged with Official Misconduct, a felony punishable up to ten years in prison and a $5,000 fine for using the service.

In addition, we collected thousands of dollars in restitution over the next month or two.

I recommended to our county communications people to change the remote access number and go to a six- or seven-digit code. I also strongly suggested that they reach out to the employees with codes and make sure they knew they would be "touched" to pay any inappropriate LD phone bills.

A few months later I was awarded the Houston 100 Club Officer of the Year honor. I was the first DA investigator to ever receive this high honor. I received a nice plaque along with a stainless-steel Rolex watch with the 100 Club logo on the face of the watch. I bet I was the poorest man in the United States to own two Rolex watches.

100 Club Award

CHAPTER 14

KARLA FAYE

Karla Faye Tucker had spent the weekend prior to June 13, 1983 with her current boyfriend, Danny Garrett, doing drugs and alcohol. At around three o'clock in the morning of Monday the thirteenth, Karla Faye, Garrett, and James Liebrandt went to Jerry Dean's apartment. There was premeditation involved here. They planned to kill Dean and steal the motorcycle he was meticulously restoring as it sat in the living room of his apartment.

After Tucker and Garrett entered Dean's apartment, Liebrandt went looking for Dean's El Camino located somewhere in the complex parking lot. He was going to steal it, as well. Tucker and Garrett had a set of Dean's keys that Tucker had either found or stolen sometime earlier.

When Tucker and Garrett entered the apartment, they found a pickaxe leaning next to the front door. It was a tool Dean used in his construction job. The duo, armed with Dean's work tool, eased into the bedroom to find Dean and a woman neither of them knew. Both were nude, obviously having engaged in sexual pleasures prior to falling into deep sleep, deep enough not to hear the entry of the dangerous intruders.

Garrett took possession of a ball peen hammer that he'd found lying on the floor in Dean's bedroom. Without warning, he began violently striking Dean in the back of the head. Surely, he was dead in a matter of seconds, his brains effectively bashed in and spread out over the sheet.

His task accomplished, Garrett calmly gathered up motorcycle parts to carry out to his truck.

Karla Faye Tucker remained in the bedroom, drug-crazed and armed with the pickaxe she found in the living room. She didn't like what she was hearing – the gasping gurgling from Dean's mouth. She wanted the irritating sound to stop. She took the axe, arched over Dean's head and chest, and began steady up-and-down chopping motions into the man's chest – non-stop for more than twenty deadly chops.

The chopping noise awakened Dean's unknown female lover. We don't know but when she opened her eyes she must have been horrified. Karla Faye was seeing Deborah Ruth Thornton for the first time. The bloody axe still in her hands, she told Deborah to keep her head under the covers; she was not going to harm her.

Then, in what must have been nanoseconds, Deborah Thornton made a fatal mistake – she peeked.

Karla Faye went back to chopping, this time into the chest of her unknown victim. Again, she struck more than twenty blows.

But the woman wouldn't die!

"Please finish me," the victim pleaded, reaching that immeasurable degree of pain that causes a human being to make such a dying request.

Karla Faye watched as her boyfriend reentered the bedroom after loading the motorcycle parts in the getaway vehicle. Garrett took the axe by its handle and dealt Deborah one final blow to the chest. It was the only time that Garrett hit any victim with the pickaxe.

Deborah Thornton was only on the premises because she and her husband had gotten into an argument the day before. Like too many individuals in such a situation, she took refuge in a bar. She met Dean there and went to spend the night with him.

It was not the only way sexual adventures would play a role in this tragic capital murder story.

Karla Faye would later tell people and testify in open court that she experienced intense multiple orgasms with each blow of the pickaxe to her naked victim.

The next morning one of Dean's co-workers – who had been waiting for Dean to pick him up – discovered the gruesome sight of two bodies, with chopped up torsos and heads. HPD Homicide detectives were immediately summoned and the now-famous investigation began.

Homicide Division wasn't an environment for rookie officers. The division had a well-established reputation for solving cases, whether small-time whodunits or celebrated cases that made Page One. To be an HPD Homicide detective you could be considered nothing but top notch.

Newspaper files were loaded with their names, for they usually lasted many years, even decades, wrestling with the clues that produced charges, indictments, and guilty verdicts. These men – and a few women during this period in history – were almost always hand-picked. Certainly, the captains were. Homicide captains always lasted decades, becoming storied newspaper and television characters. Lt. Breck Porter even had a building named for him. It's the Breck Porter Building on the property of the Houston Police Officers Union. Porter was a founding member of the association which later became the union.

I would put any Houston Homicide detective in this era up against any counterpart from any big-city police department in the nation. Every DA investigator knew each one of these plain clothes individuals. The District Attorney's Office prosecuted tons of homicides. Each one of them entailed close work with the detectives. They'd come to Special Crimes almost every day for one reason or another. Important reasons. They might need legal advice. Or they might need me to wire up one of their informants or witnesses.

We considered them the "Special Crimes Unit" of the Houston Police Department. I also would see them socially because all of the DA investigators and the homicide detectives around Harris County belonged to an organization known as the Southeast Texas Association of Investigators and Identification Officers. We would visit with HPD detectives and those from other policing agencies and spent quality time talking shop. We met monthly.

We also worked closely with the technical and crime lab personnel almost on a daily basis. The latent fingerprint personnel, which consisted of Herbert Foster, Norbert LeBlanc, and Peggy James, were the best at this important task. Charlie Anderson, the firearms examiner, and A. D. Queen, the document and handwriting expert, also were excellent. The rapport we developed hand in hand with their expertise and cooperation helped to thwart many evil doers.

Prior to the Harris County DA's office having its own investigators in the early 1960s, the DA used HPD Homicide detectives on an "as-needed basis." State legislation enabled district attorneys to hire their own investigators after officially qualifying them as Texas peace officers.

It shouldn't surprise anyone to realize that most of those hired were retired or even current HPD Homicide detectives. It wasn't difficult to convince the mayor and police chief of the benefit of having a few of the brightest and best HPD had to offer to work regularly with the district attorney.

■ ■ ■

Karla Faye Tucker was born and raised in Houston, the youngest of three sisters. Her father Larry was a longshoreman known to have had "a very rocky relationship." By the time Karla was eight years old she was smoking cigarettes, just one of those childhood vices almost always loosely identified as "things that she shouldn't be doing" at such a young age. When her parents divorced, she learned that her birth was the result of an extramarital affair, or a "had-to-marry" case.

By age twelve she was taking drugs and having sex. She later dropped out of school and became a prostitute. At sixteen she was briefly married to a mechanic, Stephen Griffith. That didn't last. Once in her early twenties, she steered down the biker route, hanging out with bikers during most of her waking hours. She met a woman named Shawn Dean and her husband, Jerry Lynn Dean, in this often-lawless environment. In 1981, the Deans introduced Karla Faye to a man named Daniel Ryan "Danny" Garrett. Karla Faye was just turning twenty-one and Garrett was fourteen years her senior.

Tucker and Garrett would be linked for life for their roles in the two murders.

Within days of the heinous crimes, Homicide detectives were getting leads in the case. HPD Detectives Teddy Thomas and Jim Ladd took on the roles of lead investigators. They and other detectives interviewed several witnesses who "hung out" or lived at 2205 McKean, where Danny Garrett and Karla Faye Tucker lived together. The house was located in the Spring Branch area on Houston's westside, on the opposite side of the Katy Freeway from the more exclusive Memorial area. The witnesses told investigators that they'd heard "talk" from Danny and Karla Faye about the murders but didn't take them seriously – until they saw the two with items taken from the scene – such as Dean's El Camino and the "restored" motorcycle that included stolen parts. Karla Faye also had Jerry Dean's black Harley Davidson wallet that had a chain attached to it. She was seen keeping it with the deceased Dean's Texas driver license.

This wasn't all. Karla Faye also possessed Deborah Thornton's wallet. She also flashed this evidence to her sister, Kari Burrell, and Danny's brother, Doug.

Soon after seeing these incriminating items, Doug Garrett went to his childhood friend, Homicide Detective J. C. Mosier, and told him everything he knew about the case. Doug was accompanied by Kari Burrell, who also was a witness to the conversations and the evidence waved in front of them by Danny and Karla. Kari also lived at the house on McKean with her sister and her boyfriend.

Thomas and Ladd had been meeting with Assistant District Attorney Ted Wilson of Special Crimes on a daily basis to keep him updated on the case. Once charges were filed, Ted would be the lead prosecutor. He was one of the brightest and smartest ADAs in District Attorney Carol Vance's office.

An expert on search and arrest warrants, he traveled all over the United States to give speeches at legal and law enforcement seminars. Ted began his legal career as a clerk in the office of Justice of the Peace Larry Wayne in Precinct 1 in downtown Houston, the county's busiest precinct for serving papers and trying misdemeanors – not to mention performing civil weddings.

From this post Ted was able to do as many up-and-coming would-be courthouse lawyers – serve as a clerk or legal assistant while going to night school at the nearby South Texas School of Law. While serving under Judge Wayne, probably the sharpest of all JPs in the county, Ted was learning from the best.

Ted was raised in Houston and graduated from Marion High School, which is now Episcopal High School. It didn't take Ted long to "move up the ranks" in the DA's office and end up in Special Crimes because of his special skills. His wife, Roe Wilson, served many years as head of the DA's Appellate Division before her retirement, which took place right about the same time as Ted's.

Ted presided at the meeting with the detectives right after they had interviewed Doug and Kari. The always-decisive Ted Wilson stated his belief that the state had probable cause. He promptly issued a warrant for the arrest of Karla Faye Tucker and Danny Garrett.

This paperwork also authorized a search of the residence of the two suspects. Judge Doug Shaver of the 262nd District Court signed the warrant. I would like to say at this point that the good guys always stick together. Judge Shaver was a former prosecutor in the Special Crimes Bureau.

Wanting to leave no prosecutorial stone unturned, Ted thought it would be a good idea to get the two suspects talking on tape about the murder. The warrants were enough but in Special Crimes you learned that the more incriminating evidence you had, the better your chances of nailing down a conviction that would be hard to overturn during the long-lasting appeals process in the State of Texas.

So, Detective Mosier brought Doug Garrett to my office where I placed a wireless transmitter in his boot and a Nagra recorder in the small of his back in order to record Karla Faye and Danny. Doug was to meet with his brother and his girlfriend that very afternoon. Doug told us that his usual mode of transportation to the McKean house was on his motorcycle.

We hatched the appropriate plan. Detectives Ladd and Mosier, ADA Wilson, DA Investigator Dann Fisher and I met Doug on the corner of Hollister and Kempwood, a major intersection in Spring Branch. I turned on both the transmitter and recorder for Doug. We then loaded up in our Special Crimes surveillance van and parked near the house on McKean. In the van were ADA Wilson, Detectives Ladd and Mosier, and me. Lt. Guy Mason and Dann Fisher were in Fisher's county car parked nearby.

Needless to say, we were all on the edge of our seats, prepared for the worst. We were parked in front of a house, where it was easy to figure that the typical resident in a quiet neighborhood would be curious about unusual activity.

"Can I help you with something?" the resident of the home closest to our van came up to ask.

I flashed my badge.

"Thank you, sir, but we're on the job. Please go back inside. We don't want to draw any attention."

"Sorry, I didn't know."

"No problem, I understand."

The encounter with this solid citizen reminded me of the time when Joe Vara and I were waiting for a crook to come home so we could arrest him with a warrant on one of our cases. He lived on that Memorial side of the freeway I just referenced. Woodway near Chimney Rock was known for its heavy traffic at practically any hour of the day. We parked on a side street where we could still see the house in question.

A young man came out to our car and said, "I'm Marvin Zindler's son and I want to know why you're watching my house?"

We all knew Marvin. Before he became one of the star personalities on Houston television, specifically KTRK-TV (Channel 13), he was a publicity-seeking Harris County sheriff's sergeant. Marvin was assigned to the Consumer Fraud Division of Special Crimes. We showed his son our IDs.

"We're not watching you or your house," I said to him. "So please go back inside and not draw any attention to us sitting here."

Undeterred, Marvin's son kept coming out every few minutes to ask us the same question. I had to take a firm stand or our cover would be blown.

"Look, man," I stated to him. "We really don't care if you're Marvin's son or not. My partner and I used to work with your dad. Please go call him and tell him that we're trying to arrest someone a couple of houses down from yours. Tell him we are going to arrest you for interfering with a police investigation if you keep coming out to our car."

We never saw Marvin's son again.

My firm tactic worked with Marvin's son. It didn't have to be as firm in Spring Branch as it was in Memorial to work just as well. I have to say our Spring Branch suspects were far more important, too.

The transmitter on Doug's person worked well. This "wiring" was my specialty. I felt very proud that we could hear everything that was being said. It was like taking a confession from both Karla Faye and Danny.

Karla Faye spoke of the use of the pickaxe, saying, "I came with every stroke."

Like I said, Ted Wilson was decisive. He heard the right words.

"That's enough," Ted said. "Go arrest them."

We converged on the house with Newman and Thomas, along with Fisher, going through the back door. Ladd, Owen, Mason, HPD officer R.J. Mikulec, Ted Wilson, and yours truly went through the front door, which was already partially open.

When I went to enter the house, a hand came out with a gun and stuck it in my chest.

"Whoa!" I cautioned. "It's me!" It was Dann Fisher with the gun.

I understood his confusion. There were people jumping out of the windows, trying to head for the hills. One guy who had been in the shower tried to escape naked. I wish that I'd hadn't seen that.

Karla Faye was standing in the hallway that led to the living room.

Danny had just left for work, setting up the need for us to call an HPD patrol car to arrest him a few blocks away.

I lost count of how many people were in the house, but it was quite a few folks. They were all transported to Special Crimes, where detectives and investigators interviewed all of them. Many of them became witnesses in the trials of Tucker and Garrett. (The naked guy had on clothes.)

There was a small hitch at Tucker's pretrial hearing in Judge Pat Lykos' court regarding my recordings made on the day of her arrest. Texas laws regarding recordings are based on the case of *Edwards vs. The State of Texas,* which contains the following in order for it to be admissible: *(1) a showing that the recording device was capable of taking testimony, (2) a showing that the operator of the device was competent, (3) establishment of the authenticity and correctness of the recording, (4) a showing that changes, additions, or deletions have not been made, (5) a showing of the manner of the preservation of the recording, (6) identification of the speakers, and (7) a showing that the testimony elicited was voluntarily made without any kind of inducement.*

And no, it wasn't the competency of the operator; it was the fact of the identification of the speakers.

The Edwards appellate ruling in the State's favor was regarding a Special Crimes case in connection with a tape recording made by Investigator Bill Hubbell. Johnny Holmes represented Harris County in the appeal.

When I originally turned on the recorder, there were so many officers and investigators talking simultaneously that I couldn't tell who was speaking. I couldn't rely on Doug Garrett to properly turn the recorder and transmitter on because he was so nervous. So, I did it to ensure that the equipment was on.

Judge Lykos wanted me to fast forward the tape of the segment when Doug entered the house. I explained to her that the recorder didn't have a meter like most recorders and that it would take me a while in order to find that starting point of the segment in question.

She just couldn't understand what I was talking about and was arguing with me about it. So, defense attorney Henry Oncken stepped in and agreed to the admissibility of the tape because he knew that it would eventually be admitted due to his experiences as a prosecutor. Plus, he didn't want to waste time dealing with Judge Lykos over an issue that she'd probably never dealt with before.

As has been well documented by the news media, the state tried and convicted Karla Faye Tucker and Danny Garrett for capital murder and sentenced them both to die for their crimes. Garrett died of liver disease in 1993 while in prison.

That same year Karla Faye became a born-again Christian. She was the first woman to be executed since the Civil War and had one of the largest group of followers ever assembled outside the Walls Unit at the time of her execution.

Most were protesting her death sentence. Texas Governor George W. Bush, the man who would become president of the United States, denied Karla Faye's request to delay the execution.

One of the people in attendance to witness Karla Faye's demise was Jackie Oncken, wife of former Special Crimes prosecutor and Karla Faye's defense attorney, Henry Oncken. It so happened that Karla Faye's other defense attorney was Mack Arnold, also another former Harris County assistant district attorney.

Danny Garrett

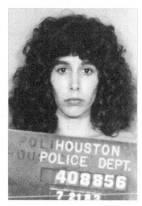

Karla Faye Tucker

Karla in Court

Karla Faye Tucker

Tape Affidavit

Search Warrant

CHAPTER 15

A LONG-DISTANCE MURDER PLOT

On February 13, 1984, Assistant DA Ted Wilson received a telephone call from the HPD Homicide Division about a possible solicitation of capital murder case. Ted took the information and made plans for us to meet with Richard Ray Sisk at the Whataburger on the west side.

Ted and I learned that Sisk was an ex-con who'd been incarcerated for burglary. Sisk was a thin, very frail man with long hair. He told us that four days earlier he had met an individual named Ronnie Roberts at Gab's Club, where Roberts was a part owner. His brother, Jimmy "Rusty" Roberts, also was a part owner, along with Ken Carpenter, a close friend of Rusty's. Sisk also said that he used to work at Gab's for quite a while.

Sisk went on to tell us that Ronnie Roberts said that he had a pending civil lawsuit against Carpenter for more than $100,000. Sisk quoted Ronnie as saying he couldn't believe that Carpenter hadn't been killed yet. Then Sisk made it clear to Ronnie that he was available for the job if there was money in it. Ronnie gave him $200.

Sisk went to eat with Ronnie at a restaurant on Highway 290. They talked more about killing Carpenter by compiling information about Carpenter's home address, among other details. Ronnie also gave Sisk his phone number, in order for Sisk to call him and keep him posted on what was going on. The next day Sisk and his brother, Joseph, went to a pawn shop and purchased a Winchester 12-gauge shotgun. It was a dramatic step like this that caused Sisk to have second thoughts – he just could not take a human life. So he called Homicide to tell detectives about the ongoing plan.

Now the ball was on our side of the court. Joseph Sisk provided us a copy of the receipt for the shotgun. We also retrieved the shotgun from his apartment.

Once back at Special Crimes, the job of breaking the news to Carpenter that there was a contract on his life rose to the top of my list of responsibilities. I should have known it wouldn't be a surprise. Carpenter said one of his bartenders told him about the alleged plan.

We had to talk in person, so Carpenter met me at my office the next day. He told me someone had shot at him the past September, leaving several bullet holes in the driver's side of his vehicle. Harris County officers were investigating the shooting but had turned up no clues. And obviously, they had no clues about the motive of such an attempt.

Carpenter provided me with Ronnie's phone number and address in Oklahoma City. I told him that he might want to disappear for the next few days while we developed a more intense investigation. Carpenter said that he couldn't believe that Ronnie wanted to kill him but added that there was a company life insurance policy for $500,000 on him with Ronnie as the beneficiary. Ronnie was well fixed but had sunk a lot of money on a car rental business. Carpenter ventured to say Roberts might be hurting for money.

I got information about the insurance company involved and learned it had a double indemnity clause involving "accidental death." Carpenter also told me Roberts' brother, Rusty, had been like a brother to him over the last ten years. At this juncture in the case, I told Carpenter I needed his word that he would keep this investigation a secret. If word leaked out, we were destined to fail. He complied and provided more details. He said he knew about a meeting between Ronnie and Sisk at the club the week before. An HPD officer, J.J. Henderson, who worked security at the club told him about it. I contacted the officer and got verification. Carpenter said that Ronnie told him later that he was talking to Sisk about the pending civil lawsuit.

Later in our meeting at Special Crimes I recorded a phone conversation between Sisk and Ronnie. Sisk told Roberts that things were looking good and that he had purchased a 12-gauge shotgun. According to plan, the "hit" was going to take place the following evening. Sisk said he would leave town immediately.

There was one more crucial element: Sisk needed some "hit money" to help pay his traveling expenses. Ronnie promised a $1,500 payment but said he needed to figure out how to get the money to him.

Next day – the day after Valentine's Day – Roberts called our recorded undercover phone line to speak to Sisk. He instructed Sisk to pick up the money at Hobby Airport at the Southwest Airlines air cargo terminal. Bear in mind that in solicitation cases like this one recorded evidence played an important part in the development of evidence.

Ronnie also advised Sisk that the shipping name on the package would be from a Jim Dunn. He gave Sisk the air bill number that would be required to claim the package containing the $1,500. Another $5,000 would be sent to Sisk a few days later.

"Just give me a few days," Ronnie said. "Let me know where to send the second package."

Sisk told Ronnie the murder caper would enable him to get out of Houston well before the body would be found.

Within minutes, Sgts. Dan McAnulty and Earl Musick of Special Crimes headed to the airport. My fellow investigator, Joe Vara, and I headed in the same direction. McAnulty observed Sisk retrieving the $1,500 package. As ordered, Sisk brought it out to the parking lot and turned it over to McAnulty. I took it and placed it in a clear plastic bag. Following a well-established routine, I put my initials and date on the outside of the bag.

Vara and I returned to the office with the package and met with another investigator, Dave Perry, a fingerprint expert. Perry soon got a fingerprint analysis. Meanwhile, McAnulty and Musick interviewed the employees at the cargo terminal who had dealt with the package.

We opened the package to find a *Sports Illustrated* magazine with fifteen $100 bills paperclipped inside. We noted the serial numbers and took photos. I called Carpenter and advised him of what happened. I told him he was going to have to find a place to "hide" for a few days. He was to provide me with his address since I planned to send out a couple of HPD undercover officers to stay with him until we got Ronnie arrested and charged.

The very next day we learned that Ronnie was sending $5,000 to Sisk at the Southwest Airlines cargo terminal in Harlingen in the Rio Grande Valley. He believed this to be the appropriate locale since Sisk was supposedly headed to Mexico.

The next morning, I readily got help from the Oklahoma Bureau of Investigation. I advised Deputy Inspector Daryl Wilkins of our investigation of Ronnie Ray Roberts. He was more than happy to assist our office. This type of cooperation is one of the most rewarding parts of the job: the good guys worked together to get the bad guys.

I advised Wilkins that Roberts had sent additional funds to our "hit man" in Harlingen. We discussed Wilkins' role. He was to send an agent to the airport in Oklahoma City to verify that the package had been sent to Harlingen. Once we knew the money was in route, we would file charges against Ronnie. We wanted to verify the evidentiary trail. I gave Wilkins a physical description of Ronnie as well as his address and telephone number. We planned to arrest Ronnie at the airport.

Sgt. McAnulty confirmed that there was a package for Sisk on a Southwest flight from Oklahoma City to Harlingen by way of Dallas/Austin. I immediately went to DA Intake to file charges for Solicitation of Capital Murder against Ronnie.

Shortly thereafter, I teletyped the warrant number along with other pertinent information regarding Ronnie to Daryl Wilkins, while McAnulty contacted Texas Ranger Bruce Castell and asked him to have the package in Harlingen forwarded to me.

Wilkins later called me to advise that Ronnie Roberts was in custody. They prepared to interview witnesses and help us in every possible way. Wilkens also said that he was going to send me a set of Roberts' fingerprints that included his palm prints, so we could do a comparison of the prints on the first package that we recovered.

Later, I went to Southwest Airlines and picked up the package from Harlingen. Once back at the office, I opened it and found an *Esquire* magazine with $1,000 on the inside. There was a note included that said, "This is all I could get, call me tonight at this phone number at 8 p.m."

I knew that none of that was going to happen. Ronnie Roberts was tucked behind bars.

On March 4, 1986, Ronnie pled guilty to the charges and was sentenced to ten years in the state penitentiary, probated. We got him convicted, but – like too many of his kind – he stayed on the streets.

CHAPTER 16

BLOWN OUT THE WINDOW

During an early Friday morning in May of 1984, my friend Terrell Newberry, who was the security director of Conn's, paid me a visit. Terrell showed up along with about seven other vendors regarding theft of property from their businesses. They were sent by HPD Burglary and Theft division because they knew it was going to require a search warrant and they usually had a lot of their detectives "take off" on Friday.

I had originally met Terrell when he needed a warrant to recover a new stove from a woman who wrote Conn's a hot check for the purchase. Investigator Wally Zeringue and I got a search warrant and promptly went out and recovered the stove. Newberry was thrilled. " Kenny," he told me, "I've been doing this for Conn's for a while and this was one of the fastest recoveries that I've ever seen."

"Terrell," I said. "this is Special Crimes and that's how we work. Welcome to Special Crimes."

Newberry was one of the nicest guys I'd ever met. He seemed like he had a meek and mild disposition and spoke with a lisp, but he used to tell me stories about going to a person's house on Thanksgiving Day and repossessing their TV while they were eating their turkey dinner and watching football.

"That sounds kind of heartless to me," I said.

"I loved doing that. They're stealing from my company, so I feel justified."

I thought: *I'll always pay my Conn's bill on time.*

I took Terrell and the other venders into our conference room and learned that their two suspects had come to their businesses and signed lease agreements for furniture, automobiles, beer stein services, and appliances that included televisions, video recorders, and stereos.

The two suspects, Anthony Saint and Robert Wayne Powell, were part of a cleaning service that worked late at night when the offices were usually empty.

One of their customers was Gulf Oil (now Chevron), whose headquarters were located on Holcombe Boulevard in the West University area of Houston. On one particular night, while working there the two "hoodlums" decided the go through Gulf Oil personnel files and make copies of most of the employee applications.

The crooks then went out and leased a couple of houses in the Alief neighborhood using the stolen identifications of a few of the Gulf employees, plus went to numerous businesses that leased furniture, appliances, and any other item that a person could lease. This was way before anyone had ever heard of the term "identity theft."

I had one of our Special Crimes ADAs to help me draft a search-and-arrest warrant for the two culprits.

I got my partner, DA Investigator Joe Vara, and two HCSO deputies, Gaston Rangel and Donnie McGeough, that are assigned to our Fugitive Apprehension Unit (Donnie's wife, Cheryl, was one of our secretaries), and together we headed out to the Alief area with eight large trucks behind us. When we got there, I made the vendors stay out of sight of the house until we had Robert Powell in custody. As we were walking up the driveway, we heard the phone ringing inside the garage. We also heard Powell answer it. So, we knew he or someone else was there.

I knocked on the door and there was no answer. I didn't really want to kick the door in because it really wasn't his house. Powell had only been arrested before for possession of a small amount of marijuana, so I didn't think that he'd be dangerous or aggressive.

I told my guys, "Let's just walk around the house and see if we can find an open window." So, we walked around and found a window that was taller than a normal window and it had a kitchen chair beneath it like he'd used it before when he or someone was locked out. The unlocked window was in the living room and it had a cathedral ceiling plus a loft.

I decided to go through the window myself because I wouldn't ask one of "my guys" to do something that I wouldn't do myself. I got on the chair and raised the window and said, "Police, we're coming in!"

I stuck my leg through the window and heard a loud boom and found myself laying on the ground, my eyeglasses broken.

"Whose gun went off?" I asked. All the guys were checking their guns when we saw that the shot came from inside, leaving tons of "bird shot" markings on the house next door. The shot missed my head by less than an inch!

I started hollering out to Powell to surrender or that he'd be shot. He said that he thought we were from one of the rental companies and that he wouldn't come out until he saw a uniform.

I was thinking: *Are you kidding me? We're in raid jackets with police markings, and he wants a uniform? He probably thought that we were going to beat the ever-living shit out of him, which I wouldn't do and have never done before or since.*

After the patrol car came and arrested him, I told the vendors to get their stuff.

A few hours later, I started thinking about what happened and realized that I was almost killed and had the top of my head blown off by a guy who stole a bunch of cheap furniture and appliances.

The following Monday I went to the house of Powell's partner, Anthony Saint, along with Investigator Wally Zeringue. Wally was a highly respected retired HPD officer and was in his late sixties or early seventies at the time. He had more energy than most twenty-year-old officers that I knew. What a great guy and investigator.

When we got to this "stolen" house, I told Wally, "So much for being nice and not kicking in the door. I'm not taking any chances. This guy's been arrested for possessing a handgun before, so we're going through the door this time."

I knocked on the door, saying, "Police, open the door!" two or three times. So, I took a few steps back and took off running and hit the door with my right foot. I bounced off like a rubber ball and landed on my backside. I came off the door so hard that I noticed that I'd ripped the crotch out of my blue jeans. Wally and I were laughing so hard that I could hardly get back on my feet.

I turned to Wally and said, "These guys are starting to be a major pain in my ass and now I'm lying on it." We laughed again and finally got the door open after several strong kicks.

Once in the house, I began sweating like an atheist in a crowded revival tent. I knew that Saint was hiding in the house and might have a gun. We had our guns and flashlights out, going door to door. While Wally searched the bedrooms, I checked the hallway closets. When I opened the second door in the entry hallway, I immediately saw four eyes when I pointed my flashlight. That scared the daylights out of me. I said, "Hands up and don't move."

It was Saint's daughter, who was probably in her mid or late twenties, and granddaughter, who looked to be six or seven years old. I don't know who was more scared, them or me. In fact, one of them pooped in their pants. I felt bad for them and was embarrassed that one of them had an accident. I asked the daughter where her dad was, and she pointed to the attic.

I asked Wally to watch them while I looked in the attic. I pulled the attic stairs down and took a few steps up and hollered, "Anthony, stand up with your hands up."

I said this several times to no avail. I went out to my "county ride" and got my sawed-off shotgun. I went back in and took several steps up the stairs and jacked a shell in the chamber. I hollered, "Anthony if you don't come out now, I'm going to the den and start shooting through the ceiling."

Right after I said that, he jumped up with his hands up. He was only wearing his designer underwear and was covered with the asbestos from the insulation in the attic.

I called for a HCSO patrol unit to transport him to the county jail. I told Wally, "Don't you think that SOB is itching his ass off right now."

"Oh, don't you know it," Wally said. "Can you imagine being covered in asbestos and itching and not being able to scratch?"

I called Terrell Newberry and told him to call his buddies to come get the rest of their property.

Powell pled to nine years of probation for Attempted Capital Murder of a Police Officer. Less than a year later it was revoked, and he was sent to the Texas Department of Corrections. After his release from prison, he was arrested on several occasions for minor offenses.

Saint was sentenced to eighty-two days in the Harris County Jail. He was never arrested or charged again.

Robert Powell

Anthony Saint

Conn's letter

Robert Wayne Powell

CHAPTER 17

ODDS AND ENDS

It's always been a safe bet to say most plainclothes law enforcement officers will have some kind of encounter with a crook. It could come while you're on duty clad in no uniform of any agency. Or it could happen when you're off-duty trying to mind your own business.

On one occasion while Joe Vara and I were on an electronic surveillance of a pyramid scam meeting when we had Barry Neff, one of our Special Crimes investigators, posing as a potential investor in the scheme, a guy came up to our surveillance van and tried to steal our battery.

Joe and I were in the parking lot of the meeting location near the Shepherd/Durham intersection of the Katy Freeway – or Interstate 10 West – when this guy unlatched the hood and began the mechanical manipulation necessary to remove the battery. Our van had a separate battery, just in case one went dead. We got out quickly and arrested him and quietly quartered him inside the vehicle, not wanting to draw any unwanted attention to our task at hand.

Once we had enough evidence and/or probable cause to effect an arrest and charges, we went in the meeting, along with our handcuffed battery thief and arrested the culprit "running the show." Then we shut down the meeting. We explained to those present what crime had been committed. We said that at some point in the near future they would not receive any more money after their original investment. We ended up transporting the battery thief and the ramrod of the pyramid scheme to jail.

The leader of the scheme went to trial in Judge Jimmy Duncan's misdemeanor court. Jimmy Duncan was the "Judge Roy Bean" of the Harris County Courthouse. He carried a Colt .45 under his judicial robe.

If you were a police officer and less than a minute late to a trial or case setting, he'd chew you out in front of everyone. This proverbial "ass-chewing" also was in effect for assistant DAs, defense attorneys and defendants. This well-established habit was the primary reason Judge Duncan almost always finished at the bottom of the annual judicial conduct poll sponsored by the Houston Bar Association.

As you might expect, he had his favorites. If he were your friend or liked you, it was a different story. I became a good friend of the judge when I was assigned to the chief investigator in the DA's office because we'd meet at his courtroom during lunch time and play 42 dominos. We started playing at noon, so if you were going to the game, you'd better pick up something to eat on your way to the courtroom. And don't be late!

The pyramid schemer was represented by Sherman Ross, later a county criminal court judge like Duncan. When Vara and I testified, Judge Duncan told the jurors, "I know Kenny and Joe very well, and you can believe everything that they say." You should have seen Sherman's face when he heard the judge say that. I almost laughed out loud. I did giggle a little bit. I have to admit that what Duncan said may have helped. The jury found the defendant guilty. He was required to pay a hefty fine.

■ ■ ■

If I weren't working late on Friday night, we made it a habit to go visit my in-laws, Frank and Emily Bugaj. We'd have dinner and play 42. If my brother-in-law, Leslie Haas, and his wife, Cynthia, didn't show up, it'd be Shoot the Moon dominos because you only needed three players instead of four. The Bugajs lived in Garden Oaks, across from St. Rose of Lima Catholic Church, where we all attended.

On one Friday night after dinner and dominos, I was headed home with my older son, Kyle, who was about six or seven years old at the time. My wife was driving her car in front of us with our daughter Kristin and other son, Keith. We lived in Hidden Valley, a small subdivision located on I-45 between Highway 249 and West Gulfbank Road. I grew up in Hidden Valley and moved back in 1974. We'd take the back roads home and pass by our alma mater, St. Pius X, on Donovan and North Shepherd.

Just past West 43rd Street on Alba Street, two guys were walking down the side of the road. One was carrying a six- or twelve-pack of beer and the other guy had a ten-pound bag of ice. When I got even with the ice man, he took the bag and hit the side of my county undercover vehicle, a 1976 Super Bee. I hit the brakes and told Kyle, "Get down on the floorboard and don't get up until I say so."

I reached down and removed my .357 from my ankle holster and held it in my hand where this idiot couldn't see it.

"Hey man, what in the hell are you doing hitting the side of my car with a bag of ice?"

He approached my window and said, "My friend and I need a ride, so we're taking your car."

Without missing a beat, I stuck my fully-loaded gun to his forehead.

"You've got a ride all right," I said. "You're going to ride to jail."

I placed them both under arrest for public intoxication (PI). I had them lay on the ground until HPD arrived. I thought about arresting the ice man for attempted robbery by an ice bag. But I knew I'd never hear the end of that, so PI was going to work. They were both pretty drunk.

I got on my HPD radio and called for a unit to stop by for a jail transport. HPD's North Shepherd Station was only two blocks away, so the officers were there in less than a minute. When they arrived, I told the turds, "Hey, guys, your ride is here."

■ ■ ■

I have to say that when Joe Vara and I worked together, we had a lot of weird things happen to us. While investigating a "credit fixer" on one occasion, I was talking to Joe on the phone about the case strategy.

We had contacted a former girlfriend of one of our suspects who was going to help us get probable cause. I was going to get her "wired up," as the old saying went. This way we could record her conversation with our target.

The woman appeared to be in her late twenties and well-built. No one would have any problem describing her as attractive. Please understand that I wasn't about to apply the Nagra recorder to her body the same way I would have wired a male. Besides the recorder there also was a wireless transmitter. I gave her these devices and some tape.

Using my body – outside my shirt, of course – I showed her where to place them on *her* body. I very professionally instructed her to go into the bathroom and "wire yourself up."

Joe was still on the phone with me. While I was talking to him, all of a sudden, the woman came out of the bathroom nude from the waist up! I remember the innocent look in her eyes.

"Is this okay?" she asked, her natural gifts rampant with the mic, the tape, and the transmitter.

I started choking and told her to go back to the bathroom, shut the door, and put her clothes back on.

Joe could understand that something was going on. In a concerned voice he asked, "Are you okay?"

"You wouldn't believe it if I told you," I said, still choking a bit. "I'll have to tell you later."

Our wired-up undercover witness met with the suspect. Her work enabled us to get enough information to take the case to the next level. We would meet with an employee of the Greater Houston Credit Bureau. For "a fee" she would remove negative information on a credit report.

We called the female employee and Joe arranged to meet her in the parking lot of the Holiday Inn on Fannin and the Southwest Freeway. I wired up Joe with the Nagra recorder and Kell transmitter. We also set up a signal in case the Kell quit working for some reason. After the woman, the target of our efforts, had incriminated herself by what she said to Joe, he was to rub his hair. I would rush in and arrest them both.

Joe paid her $50 to "fix" his credit. There was just one major hitch. She said she wouldn't complete the task until Joe kissed her. On the lips, not the cheek!

At this point I should note that this rather large woman was nowhere near as attractive as our "undercover wire." Had she been even close, Joe very likely would have complied. I was within eyesight while he started rubbing his head.

I was laughing so hard that I totally missed the "bust signal." Joe about rubbed most of his hair out for fear he would be compelled to perform a dreaded undercover duty.

After I arrested Joe and the woman, Joe said, "Jesus, Kenny you didn't see me rubbing my head? Man, my head is really sore."

"Sorry, Joe, I was laughing so hard that I missed the signal."

The credit bureau didn't want to file charges, so we had to cut her loose without a kiss.

■ ■ ■

On August 7, 1978, Detective Jerry Carpenter came to me and asked if I had any "comp days" that I could use to work an extra job for him escorting a friend of his to Madisonville, about 125 miles north of Houston on Interstate 45.

"Sure," I said. "I could use the money. Who is it and what do I need to do?"

He told me that it was Mary Jo Wood, whose name I recognized from the book, *Blood and Money*, the best seller of the 1970s written by Thomas Thompson, a well-known author who got his start as a journalist in Houston.

Jerry investigated the case and it became a lifelong pastime recounting the "what-ifs" surrounding the complexities and characters who came to life in the best seller. Jerry's assignment to Special Crimes didn't dampen his determination to see justice done. Bob Bennett, the previous chief of Special Crimes, participated in the investigation and served as lead prosecutor in the ensuing criminal cases. The vast majority of the investigation happened before my arrival.

The case centered around the mysterious death of River Oaks socialite and horsewoman Joan Robinson Hill after a determined – and some would say rigged – grand jury investigation resulted in the heretofore unused charge of Murder by Neglect filed against Joan's husband, Houston plastic surgeon Dr. John Hill.

Joan suffered from flu-like symptoms which worsened over several days before her doctor husband had her admitted to a hospital, where she died.

Grand jurors heard evidence showing Dr. Hill neglected Joan's health and may have poisoned her. They indicted the doctor, but the trial ended in a dramatic mistrial amid incriminating testimony by Hill's second wife. Then the plot thickened. Before a second trial a masked intruder entered the Hill mansion to shoot and kill John Hill.

The only motive that arose pointed to a widespread belief by police and prosecutors that Hill's estranged father-in-law, oilman Ash Robinson, hired a hitman. In doing so, he had to go through an intermediary, long-time madame, Lilla Paulus, to engage the services of Bobby Wayne Vandiver, a lifelong hoodlum. Paulus was once known around Houston and other environs as being "the fastest whore around." Jerry Carpenter later verified that the middle-aged madame from the Houston suburb of Bellaire would pimp any female who could walk and lie on her back.

When Paulus stood trial for serving as the "middleman" in the murder-for-hire plot, this latter point was made clear. Her daughter Mary Jo Wood testified that her mother pimped her out when she was only three years old. Mother and daughter were estranged, although Mary Jo was plying the family trade in Las Vegas. Ash Robinson and Lilla Paulus went back a number of years, ever since Mary Jo and Joan took horseback riding lessons in their younger years. Ironically, Paulus received a sentence of thirty-five years in prison and died there on May 16, 1986, for her role in Dr. Hill's death. Robinson was never charged, a fact that irked Jerry Carpenter for the rest of his life. Ash Robinson died of natural causes on February 16, 1985, in Pensacola, Florida.

Carpenter got to be good friends with Mary Jo during HPD's homicide investigation and had stayed in touch with her over the past few years. My Special Crimes colleague told me that Mary Jo was coming to town to visit relatives in Madisonville regarding the estate of her grandmother, Annie Paulus. The family needed to meet to discuss her estate. Mary Jo obviously hadn't been close to these family members. She feared there might be trouble at the meeting that might result in violence. She wanted what amounted to a "throw-down boyfriend."

That was my extra job, compliments of Jerry Carpenter. I asked Jerry what she was doing now, and he told me that she was still a prostitute in Las Vegas. Her husband kept the business all in the family – he was her pimp.

"You've got to be kidding me," I said to Carpenter.

"Nope, it's true," Jerry said through a sly smile, "but she makes a whole lot of money and is a pretty nice person."

I wanted to say, *I bet she is nice, she's got a job where she's on her back all day and gets paid for it.* But I didn't.

I had second thoughts but knew I needed the money. We agreed to terms and I dutifully went to her fancy hotel in the Galleria. I sensed what I was in for but remained professional. I knocked on the door of her room. I had been expecting to see a hump-shouldered hag with buck teeth.

An attractive, tall redhead answered. She was loosely clad in a red see-through blouse and dark pants. I mean you could see every ample inch of her bare breasts.

I was embarrassed.

"Are you married?" the strident thirtyish woman asked.

Not looking at her, I said, "Yes ma'am, happily."

"That goddamn Carpenter sends me a married cop. What the fuck was he thinking?" she asserted. I laugh about it now but at the time I lost my normal "smart ass" nature. I was speechless.

She calmed down and said that she was ready to go.

I had to drum up some courage to say what I was about to say. But I was getting paid to be a professional bodyguard.

"Ma'am," I said respectfully. "I can't take you dressed like that."

"And why not?"

"When we get to the lobby, we'll have to shoot our way out to exit the hotel and I don't feel like the hassle."

Thank God! She changed her see-through top.

I have to say that I was proud of myself for not succumbing to temptation. This woman was temptation personified – just as her profession required her to be. She was a very attractive woman. It was plain and easy to see why she made so much money for her services in the high-rollers' capital of the world. She was, indeed, a "high-dollar hooker." I felt a little sorry for her knowing that her crappy mother forced her into prostitution at such a young age.

I was praying that we wouldn't run into someone that I knew because I wasn't quick-thinking enough to figure out what I would say to them. As we walked through the lobby, I could sense the heads turning. And these eyes weren't focusing on me.

Once at Madisonville, I had no idea of what to expect from her brother and the other relatives. I was nervous about the possible conversations about her family history. In the designated meeting room, we encountered another fifteen people. They were fairly friendly to me after she introduced me to them as her boyfriend. I felt like they were afraid of her. They began talking about the estate and everything seemed to go well. I didn't say one word except when she'd whisper in my ear about one of her relatives. Even then I would only make a short, meaningless comment.

Finally, one of her relatives came over to me and said, "Man, you haven't said a single word. Cat got your tongue or something?"

"Well, you know how it is with Mary Jo around. You can't say much."

What I really wanted to say was, *What in the world would I say to a bunch of idiot hillbillies that are dumber than a box of rocks?*

On the way home, I felt comfortable with her (but not *that* comfortable). I asked her if I could ask her a personal question.

"Sure, fire away. Nothing will bother me or hurt my feelings." I knew that she wouldn't mind because she was tougher than a box of nails.

"It's hard for me to understand how your husband would not only allow you to be a prostitute, but he's your pimp, as well. I just don't get it."

"We live in a nice house and drive nice cars. We have a lot of money and can buy what we want to."

"I still don't get it, but money isn't everything."

"Hey, here's how it works. I get a 'date' and then meet them in a hotel room. I tell them that before sex, I have to wash their penis. I take a warm washcloth and bar of soap and start washing their penis.

"Almost every single one of them ejaculates while I'm doing this. They are so embarrassed that they pay me and tell me 'we're good' and I leave."

I didn't say anything, but I did laugh and then said, "Easy come, easy go."

I took her back to her hotel, got paid, and never heard from her or saw her again.

Mary Jo Paulus Wood

Attorney Dick Deguerin and Lilla Paulos

Joe Vara

CHAPTER 18

THE DISAPPEARANCE

On May 20, 1985, Joyce Redmond Salame Lomas failed to show up for her daughter's high school graduation. Later, her daughter, Lucretia King, called HPD and filed a missing person report. She told police that after the graduation ceremony she went to her mom's apartment and found her mother's purse and her car, which was still parked in the garage. This was strikingly odd. She also told police that she didn't trust her mom's "new" husband, Robert Lomas.

Lomas was a thirty-four-year-old ex-con, previously convicted for assault to murder and auto theft. He received a ten-year sentence to TDC for the assault. He was also a part time chauffeur for a friend of mine, Aron Frank. Aron was a "high dollar" jeweler, whose store was located on the fourteenth floor of an upscale bank building in downtown Houston. Most of his customers were police officers and a few of the others were known crooks. Aron got all of his customers through "word of mouth."

I met Aron through his business partner, Roland Harris, a narcotics officer with the Pasadena Police Department. I also recovered a diamond ring for Aron from a former college classmate and Austin police officer (Chapter 5). Another one of his "famous" customers was Markham Duff-Smith, who was convicted of having his mother murdered for an inheritance.

There were numerous others, but Aron didn't know that they were crooks. For some reason, cops and crooks liked to buy or wear a lot of jewelry. Aron was one of my best friends. I remember the time he got so angry at me when I asked him, "Man, you have a lot of customers who are crooks." He didn't speak to me for months. I later apologized and we made up.

Eventually, HPD Detectives Frank S. Dobyanski and Charles R. Williams were assigned the missing person case. They called in Lomas and asked him some questions regarding his wife's disappearance. His answers were evasive. He later failed a polygraph test. Soon after the test he was pawning some of Mrs. Lomas' jewelry. Sometime later, detectives also learned from some of his "friends" that he'd been bragging about killing his wife and getting rid of her body. The problem was that the body hadn't been found. Detectives also learned that Robert Lomas had gone to Joyce's attorney, Bruce Wolfson, and had the car title changed from her name to his. Lomas also saw to it that a new will was written that included some major changes in it. Wolfson commented to detectives that it was strange for Joyce to leave town without calling her daughter. He further stated that Joyce "thought the world" of her daughter, Lucretia, and it was very odd for her not to contact her.

Lucretia also told detectives that she'd seen Lomas assault her mother on several occasions. One time he'd actually tried to pull off her clothes during one of the assaults. Detectives received a phone call from one of Joyce's friends, Jackie Freeman, who lived fourteen miles north of Katy, the west Houston suburb. Freeman said that on the afternoon of Lucretia's graduation, which they were going to together, she drove to Joyce's home and knocked on the door several times. There was no answer. She said she got back into her car and waited to see if anyone would come out.

She later saw Robert Lomas, carrying a large black garbage bag that he placed in the back seat of his 1979 Oldsmobile Cutlass. She further stated that it had to be heavy because of the way that Lomas struggled with it. She said he then went back into the house and he came out carrying an overnight bag. He noticed Ms. Freeman and went to her car.

"Is Joyce home?" she asked him. "We're supposed to go to graduation together."

"I left her at home this morning when I went to get a sausage sandwich," he replied. "When I returned, she was gone."

Freeman thought that was very odd because Joyce would not miss her daughter's graduation under any circumstances.

Detectives spoke to many other friends of Joyce Lomas. They said

Joyce really didn't trust Robert Lomas. She told them that she would hide her jewelry from him. She also told them that he had a violent temper. Sometimes bruises were visible on Joyce's body. Most of her friends said that they knew Joyce was bisexual. They said they worried about him blackmailing her so her family would not find out. It was obvious to these friends that Joyce and Robert had an odd relationship. One witness said that Lucretia lived with her mother but moved when Robert tried to rape her. The witness said that Lucretia hated him.

Later, Detective Dobyanski received a call from the Stockton, California Police Department about the investigation. Police there said that they'd received information from a source that Moryn Kraft and her boyfriend, Robert Lomas, were in Stockton and that Kraft was calling some of the victim's friends in Houston, pretending to be Joyce Lomas. When the California authorities approached Moryn about the Houston investigation, she agreed to cooperate.

Upon Moryn Kraft's return to Houston, she met with HPD detectives and gave them a statement about what Lomas had told her. She said that Robert admitted to her that he killed Joyce and disposed of the body. They then took Kraft to the DA's office and met with ADAs Terry Wilson and Chuck Rosenthal in the Major Offenders Division. Both were formerly assigned to Special Crimes. They had the reputation for being tough prosecutors. Kraft related to them what she'd told Dobyanski and Williams. She said she thought Lomas disposed of the body near a place in Galveston where they'd go crabbing together.

Detectives and Kraft met with a deputy sheriff assigned to the Galveston County Organized Crime Unit. His name was Wayne Kessler and he was working with a Galveston police detective, Harry Millok.

Kraft directed the law officers to Pelican Island, where she thought Joyce and Robert Lomas went crabbing. This area off the north side of Galveston consisted of open fields, barren sand, and grassy marshland. The officers spent several hours searching to no avail.

Kraft was staying in the downstairs of a garage apartment behind her sister's apartment, located in Jacinto City, a suburb east of Houston. Lomas was still in California, but had been calling Kraft every day. Detectives placed a recorder on her phone to see if he'd say anything that might incriminate him in the murder. But that didn't happen.

Later, Lomas returned to Houston and wanted to meet with Kraft the next day at her garage apartment. ADAs Wilson and Rosenthal requested that I "wire" her and the apartment for the meeting. The next morning, June 7, 1985, DA Investigator Les Ramsey and I went to the garage apartment.

Les was a retired Oklahoma City police detective assigned to the Major Offender Division of the DA's office. Les was a hard-nosed investigator, very thorough and knowledgeable about investigative technics. He was distant enough that many of the ADAs were afraid of him. I figured this intimidating air was just an act. Once you got to know him, he was a very smart, good-humored fellow.

Les appeared to have somewhat of a temper. But I thought this was part of the act. In actuality, he was hard on the outside, soft on the inside. He didn't care much for some of the ADAs. When they'd ask him to do what you might think was pretty stupid, he'd give them a skeptical look that seemed to communicate, "That's the dumbest thing I've ever heard."

When I later was his supervisor in Special Crimes, he'd come to me and tell me, "You can't believe what this ADA wants me to do."

"I know it's stupid," I would tell him, "but that's what we get paid to do sometimes. Take out your ID and read it. It says District Attorney Investigator, not District Investigator. I know that we get asked to do some stupid shit sometimes by some of the ADAs. But unless we can talk them out of it, we just have to do it."

We both laughed and he'd go off and do the "stupid request."

So, on June 7, 1985, just a little more than two weeks after the disappearance of Joyce Lomas, there was no body and not quite enough evidence to charge Robert Lomas with murder in her death. Also, HPD Detectives L. S. "Larry" Ott and D. L. "Dave" Collier were working on the case with Dobyanski and Williams.

Les and I went to Kraft's apartment, where I had her put a wireless transmitter on her body and the Nagra recorder hidden behind a picture. Kraft was a good looking little petite blonde, about twenty-three years old. We hid out, poised to listen and stay on guard.

Later, Lomas showed up with nothing to say about what happened to his wife. He did remind Kraft of what he wanted her to say if the police questioned her. He did make one thing clear: he was there to have sex.

"Come on, baby," he said. "Let's fuck. I'm horny."

"I'm having my period right now," the wired-up little blonde said, thinking fast.

"I don't care."

"No way."

He continued applying the pressure, finally saying, "I just want to feel your pussy."

He began chasing her through the small apartment, causing her to panic – she knew that he'd find the transmitter if he got near her private parts. She kept running away.

"Just let me look at that pussy," Lomas pleaded, not knowing he was being recorded.

By this time, Les and I were biting our tongues to keep from laughing out loud. We rolled around on the floor, snickering so much that he heard it and asked her, "What's that noise upstairs?"

"Probably the neighbors upstairs or some rats in the ceiling," she said excitedly. "I don't know."

While this was happening, Lomas was still chasing her around trying to get her to pull her pants down. He finally gave up long enough to get her to go with him to get something to eat.

Dobyanski and Williams had an audio receiver in order to hear what was being said. When Lomas and Kraft left, they deduced that the only thing they learned from the wire was that Lomas was horny.

Kraft eventually told Lomas about the wire. She admitted to him what she told investigators. Hearing all this, Lomas told her he was going to Seattle, Washington to hide out.

After that, ADAs Wilson and Rosenthal decided to charge Kraft with credit card abuse for using Joyce's credit card to purchase airline tickets to and from California. This was done to get the attention of Lomas' once-reluctant sex partner. They wanted her to realize the seriousness of her cooperation in a probable murder case. They also were tired of her telling Lomas what the detectives and assistant district attorneys were saying about the case.

At this juncture, detectives were putting more pressure on Lomas about what really happened to his wife. They had caught him telling them so many lies it was time to rev up their tough questions. The situation got serious enough for Lomas to accuse Dobyanski of harassing him

On June 10, 1985, a Pasadena man, Rick Shannon, and a friend were wade fishing off Pelican Island when they discovered a bucket containing a human skull.

Five days later he called HPD Homicide to tell detectives all about it, saying he just dumped out the skull and kept the bucket. I'd be afraid to even use or put dead bait in that bucket.

After getting a description of where Shannon found the skull, Detectives Dobyanski, Williams, Ott, and Collier headed to Pelican Island to see if they could find any other remains. When they found the area that Shannon described, they discovered a culvert and the remnants of a fire. They dug around the ashen area, eventually finding a skull, fifteen parts of a skeleton, and many small bone fragments. They also found a blouse and a pair of pants.

They later learned that two off-duty Galveston police officers, Jason Chide and Brian Riedel, were crabbing at the Pelican Island location about a month before. They said they saw a man burning something. When they asked him about it, he used what they deemed to be a fake Mexican accent to say he was just burning some trash. They thought he was suspicious, so they wrote down his license number. When they learned that a burned body was found there, they called HPD Homicide.

Determining that the registration confirmed that the vehicle belonged to Lomas, the Pasadena officers picked him out in a photo spread. Meanwhile, an autopsy revealed that the teeth recovered at the fire scene were those of Joyce Lomas.

Later, the detectives and Kraft appeared in front of a Harris County grand jury. Their testimony led to Lomas being indicted for murder in his wife's death. When detectives went to arrest Lomas, they learned that he'd left to live with his uncle in Mexico City. He was finally arrested in January 1986 in Mexico City, but escaped the next day. He was arrested again in Mexico in February 1987 and extradited to Houston to stand trial.

On March 10, 1988, the Harris County lead prosecutor was Roberto Gutierrez, a former KPRC (Channel 2) news reporter, who later said that he had to reach a plea agreement with Lomas because there was a problem in proving the cause of death and type of weapon or means that was used to kill Joyce Lomas.

In addition to killing his wife, Lomas pleaded guilty to robbing a woman named Sandra K. Richbourg of $13,000 in jewels on January 1, 1985, beating her up, stealing her car, and setting it afire. His forty- and twenty-year sentences for robbery, auto theft, and arson ran concurrently with his murder sentence.

He was released from prison on June 9, 2000, after serving a third of his sentence. Between 2003 and 2005, he was charged with three cases of Indecency with a Child, but all were dismissed. He did receive 180 days in jail on May 15, 2006 for possession of marijuana.

Joyce Lomas

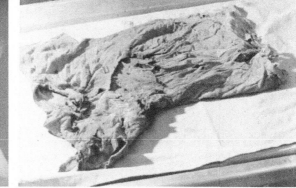
Joyce's clothing recovered

Site where Joyce Lomas' remains was found

HPD Homicide detectives who found her body and the culvert

CHAPTER 19

THE WIRETAPPING KILLER

In September of 1985, I was asked by Harris County Sheriff's Detectives Tony Rossi and J. J. Freeze to assist them with a wiretapping case in the east part of Harris County. I admit I was qualified to answer their call. In 1979, I had successfully completed a two-week class at the National Intelligence Academy in Fort Lauderdale, Florida, where you learned how to do wiretaps and pick locks. I had already learned these crafts from my former partner, the chief investigator in the DA's office, Bobby Blaylock. I also had excellent instructors in Florida; they were all former CIA agents. This was a school unlike any other, and I really enjoyed it.

In the case the detectives brought to me, the complainant, Yolanda Placker, said her phone had quit working, prompting a call to Southwestern Bell to solve the problem. Ma Bell found a tape recorder in her attic with several other attachments to her phone. These devices caused the malfunction. Ms. Placker suspected that her ex-husband, Gene Placker, had something to do with the tap. The couple had separated the past May.

The Texas Department of Public Safety was notified about the wiretap, as was the Harris County Sheriff's Office.

Gene Placker was well known in law enforcement circles, especially in Baytown, east of Houston. He was in the business of selling manufactured homes, most of which were either stolen or had major flaws. He was also known as a major "fence" in the east part of Harris County. Placker had a criminal history that would make Al Capone look like a saint.

Yolanda also mentioned that her live-in maid and nanny, Rocio Del Carmen Rueda, had mysteriously disappeared from her house in July. She'd taken all of her clothes and other items and was not at the house when Yolanda returned home from work one day.

On February 12, 1986, Placker's girlfriend, Brenda Anna Smith Brack, gave a ten-page affidavit to detectives, detailing everything she knew about Placker and his sidekick, Ricky Dean Mayhew. Brack said that in June 1985 she originally contacted Placker about selling her mobile home. She said she and her husband were splitting up because she needed to move somewhere else. He agreed to help her and even lent her some money. She later started dating Placker and eventually moved in with him. It was during that time that she met Ricky Mayhew, who also stayed at Placker's house.

She noticed that Placker would sometimes leave the house in the early morning hours, sometimes accompanied by Mayhew.

Brack also asked Mayhew about it and he told her that they'd wire-tapped Yolanda's phone by placing a recorder in the attic. He also told her that they'd periodically go over and retrieve the tapes, but that most of the time it was in Spanish because the maid was on the phone all day.

Mayhew said that Placker would throw a fit every time that this would happen and start throwing the cassette tapes against the walls, smashing them to bits. Placker eventually told Mayhew that he was going to have to do something about the Spanish-laced recordings because they were wasting his time.

During this time, Placker was in and out of jail on several different charges. On one occasion while he was in jail, Brack listened to some tapes, but they were in Spanish. In August 1985, Placker was arrested for having a pistol in his possession. Brack said, "He'd asked me if I would tell the authorities that the gun was mine." Brack agreed to the plan and met with Placker's attorney at the courthouse when the case was set.

"After his attorney told them that I would testify that the gun was mine, they reset the case to a later date," Brack said.

THE DEADLY DETAILS

On February 4, 1986, Freeze, Rossi, and I went to the Harris County Jail and met with Mayhew. He told us about the killing of the maid, Rocio Del Carmen Rueda. He said that Placker had stolen a plastic badge from

Kmart. He also revealed to us that Placker was with him at Just Boots when he bought a cowboy hat. Placker took the hat, put it on and said, "Look, I look like a Texas Ranger or police officer." Placker also flashed the plastic badge for effect.

Placker went on to tell him about his plan to "arrest" the maid and take some of Yolanda's jewelry, along with the maid's clothing, making it look like she took off back to Mexico.

Mayhew said that on or about July 3, 1985, Placker called and said that he was going to pick him up at the office; they were going to kidnap the maid. Placker also said he planned for them to change into clothes that made them look like police officers. He said Placker was wearing a suit and Mayhew was dressed in slacks and a nice shirt. Placker even borrowed a car that resembled a police vehicle. Placker took some black electrical tape and changed the numbers on the license plate.

The phony police officer had a chrome-plated semi-automatic .22-caliber pistol and a .380 caliber blue-steel semi-automatic. The two men drove to Yolanda's house. At the moment their plan was thwarted by the fact that some people were standing outside across the street. They waited for the people to leave before returning and pulling into the driveway. Placker got out of the car wearing sunglasses and the new cowboy hat.

When they got to the door, Placker pulled out his wallet with the plastic badge and knocked on the door. He said that when the maid opened the door, Placker showed her the badge and claimed to be a police officer with Immigration.

Mayhew said the maid wanted to call Yolanda, but Placker wouldn't let her. The maid tried picking up the phone a couple of times, provoking Packer to pistol-whip the helpless woman, violently striking her in the face. The maid cried. Her tormenter ordered her to sit on the couch.

"Placker told me to watch her while he searched the house looking for Yolanda's jewelry and the maid's clothes," Mayhew told investigators. Placker got angry when he couldn't find any jewelry. He grabbed the maid by the arm, pulled her into her bedroom, and ordered her to start packing her clothes. Alas, she couldn't understand what he wanted. So Placker started making motions with his hands in such a way that she understood well enough to start packing.

According to Mayhew, the three of them finally left and drove to Placker's storage lot. Along the way, Placker said that now he'll be able to listen to all of the tapes. Once at the storage lot, they drove to a double-

wide trailer that was used for storage and took the maid inside. All this
time, the terrified maid was crying her eyes out. It was far from the end of
the terror she would face.

Placker had rape in mind. He took Rocio Del Carmen Rueda into the
bedroom, while Mayhew sat on the couch in the living room area. Minutes
later Placker came out of the bedroom with Rocio – who was completely
naked. The would-be rapist had placed some cushions on the bar and laid
her on them. The terrorism continued. Rocio resisted. Placker made her
spread her legs, even though she was begging him not to attack her.

Placker slapped her violently. Then he discovered a small white string
protruding from her vagina. It was her "time of the month." The attacker
backed off and let go. He allowed her to go into the bedroom and put her
clothes back on.

Despite the temporary reprieve, poor Rocio was doomed.

As she got dressed, Placker told Mayhew that earlier in the day he'd
dug a grave. Now it was only a matter of killing the woman, whose only
mishap was talking on the phone in Spanish to her friends while her
employer was at work.

The three of them left the trailer bound for the freshly-dug gravesite.
The innocent victim's time remaining on earth was quickly ticking away.

Placker made the maid stand in front of the grave. He carefully put a
disposable diaper over the barrel of his pistol. He closely aimed the gun
behind the woman's head and pulled the trigger.

It misfired.

The panic-stricken Rocio cried and prayed in Spanish.

Remaining calm, collected and – one might say – cold-blooded, Placker
ejected the clip, slammed it back in, and promptly shot his victim in the
back of her head.

According to Mayhew, the eyewitness, Rocio fell halfway into the
hole. Placker had two shovels, which the two men used to bury the victim
deeper into what looms as a final resting place where no human being will
be able to find her or place a marker.

Mayhew said that the grave was above a drainage ditch. They placed
a cement block on top of the body to keep her under water. They took the
maid's clothes and the .22 pistol and threw them in the San Jacinto River.

The next morning Placker went to Yolanda's house to retrieve the latest
tape. The next time Mayhew saw Placker the cold-blooded killer was wearing
a big smile. He would now be able to listen to the tapes with no Spanish.

After the Mayhew interview, Rossi, Freeze, and I got some jail trustees with digging tools to follow Mayhew to the gravesite. When we got there, you could see that something had been recently buried there. Once the trustees got to the water line, we used a shovel to see if we could find anything. When the men pulled up part of a skeleton, the putrid odor was something I will always remember. It was the foulest smell I have ever taken into my nostrils.

We recovered the entire skeleton except for the skull. It was found about six months later in someone's front yard several blocks away from this grotesque death scene.

According to law, Rocio's remains were shipped to her native country. We had to match the newly-found skull with the skeletal remains that were recovered. It took months to have the remains transported from Mexico back to the United States for evidentiary purposes. We had to go through U. S. diplomatic authorities.

While Placker was in jail awaiting charges and/or indictment, he became ill and was taken to Rosewood Hospital in Houston, where he later died from pancreatic cancer.

Poor Rocio was buried in Mexico City.

Gene Placker

OFFICIAL IDENTIFICATION
OFFICE OF THE
DISTRICT ATTORNEY
HARRIS COUNTY, TEXAS

KENNETH K. RODGERS
NAME
LIEUTENANT INVESTIGATOR
TITLE
08/04/80
SIGNATURE   DATE

Kenny Rodgers, Lieutenant Investigator ID
August 1980

CHAPTER 20

ANOTHER HALLOWEEN TRAGEDY

On Halloween of 1985, ten-year-old Mary Stiles disappeared from her home at the Woodhollow Apartment complex located at 1300 Northwood in Baytown, shortly after 4:30 in the afternoon.

Baytown is located about thirty miles east of Houston, but inside Harris County. When one thinks of Baytown, one thinks of the Texas oil industry, for the small city primarily consists of people employed by one of the many oil and gas refineries, the largest of which are Exxon and Chevron Phillips. If you're in Baytown, you see oil and water mix, for the city sits at the mouth of the San Jacinto River, which empties into Trinity Bay and connects with Galveston Bay and the Gulf of Mexico.

Let me digress a bit to put the Stiles case in perspective. On Halloween night of 1973, Ronald Clark O'Bryan poisoned his nine-year-old son, Timothy, by giving him a giant Pixy Stix tube of sugar candy laced with cyanide. Timothy died in his father's arms within a few seconds. O'Bryan's motive was life insurance money. He needed these ill-gotten gains because he was going broke. It didn't take a jury of his peers very long to return a guilty verdict and assess him the death penalty.

The ADA who helped lead the investigation by Deer Park Police and also prosecute the case was Mike Hinton, a member of the Special Crimes prosecuting team at the time. Hinton took on the personality of the bulldog that he was, passionately arguing for justice. He and fellow prosecutor Vic Driscoll effectively prevailed.

O'Bryan languished on Death Row and survived State District Judge Michael McSpadden's order to execute him on a Halloween night when a last-minute appeal was granted. Finally, the so-called "Candy Man" was executed on March 31, 1984.

There were around three hundred demonstrators at the Walls Unit in Huntsville, where all executions take place. These citizens were peppered with candy by the pro-death-penalty counter demonstrators who were hollering, "Trick or Treat."

People around Harris County and beyond believe O'Bryan went down as "the man who ruined Halloween." Trick or treating was never the same: all candy given out to the costumed kiddos had to be wrapped. Then there was this other Halloween twelve years later. Little Mary was dressed as a Care Bear for Halloween. She asked her dad, Gary, if she could go to the office of the apartment complex to get some candy. "Sure," the father said, "but come right back."

That was the last time he saw his little girl alive.

After a while, Gary got concerned when Mary didn't return home. He called the Baytown police about his missing sixth grader. When Baytown Officers R. A. Clifford and J. Connaly showed up at the scene, they immediately started looking for Mary around the swimming pool, maintenance closets, and everywhere else you can think of. They eventually called for more officers and went door to door and set up a road block at the entrance and exit of the complex.

Over the next few days the majority of the police force was searching for Mary and seeking anybody with any information about her where-abouts. They drew a total blank. Gary called the media for help, a move resulting in more than one hundred phone calls to the police with no positive results.

Posters with the little girl's photo were placed in all the stores in town – a tactic that also failed to produce results. Mary didn't have any enemies and was well liked by everyone. Her dad and police were perplexed by the situation until nine days later when the police got a letter in the mail.

The letter gave details of how Mary was killed and the location of her body. Authorities were certain that the letter was from the person who caused her disappearance. The letter also said, "Please give her a proper burial." The letter was signed by "The Madman who wishes he never was."

When officers followed the instructions on an enclosed map, they found Mary's body covered with debris. She was still in her Care Bear costume with her panties pulled down to her ankles. She'd been stabbed in the neck about four times and had many defensive wounds.

After the recovery of her body, P. J. Kuehn and Max Gore – the lead detectives in the case – brought the letter, map, and detailed offense report to ADA Ted Wilson in Special Crimes. Baytown police were frequent visitors to our floor and always seemed to consist of experienced detectives who were easy to work with.

These detectives also sent the same evidence or copies of it to Special Agent John Douglas of the FBI Behavior Research Department in Quantico, Virginia. Douglas has authored many books on profile analysis in crimes like this one. Profiling was his internationally recognized specialty. Within days, Douglas advised the Baytown detectives that the subject who wrote the letter was probably a teenager who lived nearby, knew the area and the victim, had family and emotional problems, plus more information that ended up being "right on."

The letter also said that the self-proclaimed "Madman" would continue to kill if the police didn't answer his riddles that he was going to send in another letter. For each correct answer this deadly perpetrator promised to send police a letter of his name. The police would have to answer the question by placing the answer in the *Baytown Sun*.

"This killer is an evil monster," veteran prosecutor Wilson said upon reading the letter. The individual's first riddle and question dealt with Egyptian mythology. Wilson took the letter to ADA Ray Speece, recognized in the DA's office as being "an expert on everything." Speece was a walking/talking *Encyclopedia Britannica*. It was well known that you could ask him a question about anything, and he'd know the answer. He could probably be a millionaire just being on game shows. Speece was assigned to the appellate section of the DA's office, where most of the brainy attorneys didn't relish courtrooms and trials but they definitely knew the law and had the brilliance to use it for the good guys.

Speece gave Wilson the answer and the police had it posted in the *Baytown Sun*. However, it turned out that Speece's answer was connected to Greek mythology, not Egyptian. The Madman let the police know the difference in his next letter.

By then the U. S. Postal Inspector had learned that the original letter was mailed from a postal box located in the apartment complex where

Mary had resided. Police set up a video camera on the postal box and had a surveillance team, that included a postal inspector. Every time someone dropped a letter in the box, the postal inspector would retrieve it and see if it was addressed to the Baytown Police Department.

Days later a teenaged kid rode up on a bicycle and dropped an envelope in the box. It was a letter to Baytown PD! Officers were following anyone mailing a letter at this box location. They followed this individual, who was identified as Joseph Lee Fordham, a Baytown Sterling High School student.

Detectives asked for our help with a twenty-four-hour surveillance on "the kid." I'm happy to say that we hit paydirt when we retrieved some trash that he put in the garbage dumpster located in the apartment complex. Inside the trash bag were copies of the detailed map and drafts of his letters to police. It was enough for us to get an arrest and search warrant for Fordham.

So the next day when he was stepping off his school bus at the apartments, we and the Baytown police officers arrested him. I videotaped the arrest and the search of his room in his apartment, where we found the murder weapon, mythology books, notes regarding the murder, and other pertinent evidence which later led to his conviction as an adult. We also went to Sterling High to search his locker, where we found even more evidence. We spoke to the principal and teachers regarding his behavior and his other activities as a student.

Meanwhile, as Detective Kuehn interrogated Fordham at the police station the teenager confessed to the murder. He showed no remorse or emotion. He said that on Halloween he was depressed because of his current family life. In short, he was just an angry person. He further stated to Kuehn that his stepsister was one of Mary Stiles' best friends. Mary visited often, always so happy and cheerful, and that it made him jealous and angry.

Ted Wilson had the teenaged madman certified to be tried as an adult. The court appointed Roger Bridgewater as Fordham's attorney. (Bridgewater later became a criminal district judge).

Fordham was found guilty in May 1987, but it was apparent that the jury felt sorry for the defendant because they only gave him twenty-five years in prison. Even Wilson said he felt "bad" for the kid because no one from his family ever bothered to show up for moral support during the trial.

The state released Fordham on parole in 1994. He went to visit his grandmother in Georgia in 1998 and was returned to prison for a parole violation. He was given six more years. Fordham tried to commit suicide in 2014. He survived and, at last account, was living in Georgia.

In 2017, Wilson, Bridgewater, Kuehn, and I appeared in the TV show, *On the Case with Paula Zahn, The Mary Stiles Case.*

In the business of crime fighting, some times your success stories make television. We were on TV, but we couldn't bring little Mary back.

Mary Stiles　　　　*Joseph Fordham*　　　　*Ted Wilson, ADA*

CHAPTER 21

GUNSMOKE FRIDAY

It was Friday, January 3, 1986, a routine Special Crimes Friday because you knew that something was always going to happen that would make changes to your weekend. I got a call from Detective Art Woolery of the Harris County Sheriff's Office regarding a kidnapping case. Art told me he needed my help.

He came to the office along with Freddy Bradshaw, whose friend had been kidnapped by a group of guys that he and the kidnap victim "had done a drug deal with." Apparently, Bradshaw and his partner, Cecil Tyner, had purchased $500 worth of marijuana from a group and failed to pay them in timely fashion. So the drug dealers kidnapped Tyner and wanted $50,000 in cash in order to release him.

I must explain that at this point in time, ten years after the Garth Bates case, our forfeiture fund – proceeds from drug and gambling cases – had grown substantially. We weren't sweating $50,000.

I met with Don Stricklin, chief of Special Crimes, and we decided to make arrangements to pay the ransom and arrest the suspects for aggravated kidnapping. According to plan, I took a $50,000 check co-signed by Stricklin and District Attorney Johnny Holmes to the Bank of America, where we had about $5 million in our forfeiture fund account.

I instructed Investigator Mike Feary to drive me to the bank, which was near our downtown Houston office, and told him, "Don't leave this spot. I'm going to be coming out of this bank with $50,000 in cash and I don't want to be standing around waiting for you while you're circling the block."

I got into details: "I guarantee you that Officer Albrecht is going to come by and tell you to move. So, tell him that your supervisor is coming out with a large amount of cash and that you were instructed to stay put, no matter what."

I already knew what was going to happen. Albrecht was a well-known downtown HPD traffic enforcement officer who loved to write tickets to other officers, including his fellow Houston police officers. He had a reputation at 61 Reisner (HPD Headquarters) that had extended over many years. He'd write a ticket to his mother even if she was driving to the emergency room with his grandmother. This guy was ruthless, and that's putting it mildly. I can't tell you how many run-ins there had been between us – even when I was dutifully trying to serve a grand jury subpoena on Albrecht's downtown beat.

I used to work a lot of cases with HPD Burglary and Theft Detectives J. C. Davis and Billy Sims. On one occasion, Sims and I were driving through downtown in Sims' HPD vehicle and Albrecht stopped us for speeding. He got out his ticket book to write Sims a citation. "Fuck you and your ticket," Sims said with more than just a little bit of conviction. "Meet me at HQ and write it to me there, if you think your balls are that big, asshole." Sims then sped off. I laughed my ass off.

So, I came out of the bank, and guess what? Feary was not in his assigned spot. I was pissed, but really couldn't be angry at Mike. I said to him, "I told you that asshole would come by. And I knew that you would move because no one likes to get into it with him, so I understand."

I did eventually get even with Albrecht years later when I was chief investigator under Holmes when he was district attorney. I had to pick up Holmes after he gave a speech at the Houston Club downtown one day. While I was parked in front of the club, I knew that Albrecht would stop by and order me to move. Sure enough, he showed up and told me to move my vehicle. "No way," I told him. "I'm picking up the district attorney and he expects me to be sitting here when he's finished." We started arguing when Holmes came out. You should have seen the look on Officer Albrecht's face. Thereafter I never had any problem with him.

Art Woolery and I decided to have Bradshaw call the crooks, who wanted to meet in the El Dorado Restaurant off North Main, near the Interstate 45 intersection. They specified 7 p.m. I called HPD and arranged to have patrol cars assist us in the arrest of the kidnappers. I wired Bradshaw so we could monitor the transaction.

About an hour before the meeting, Investigators Mark Argo and Gary Johnson parked behind the restaurant. Woolery and I were parked in the north side of the parking lot in our surveillance van. Investigator Dann Fisher was parked on the east side of the lot. Freddy Bradshaw was parked in his truck near the middle of the lot with the $50,000 in cash in his possession. We had HPD patrol cars in radio communications so we could tell them when to move in.

The suspects, Sergio Botello, Sergio Borgos, and Raul Garcia Jimenez showed up in their "weed van" and parked near Bradshaw's truck. Bradshaw shows the trio $10,000 of the $50,000 that he had in his truck. Before we could call in the patrol officers, Botello pointed a gun at Bradshaw's head.

Argo and Johnson were inside the closest vehicle and could see what was happening. They swiftly moved to tell the suspects they were under arrest. Botello fired his gun at them and Johnson was wounded in the foot by one of the shots. Fisher got out of his vehicle and opened fire. Woolery and I drove closer and jumped out, our guns blazing. We were in a cross fire with our fellow good guys. They were shooting from the south and east sides and we were shooting from the north side.

Woolery and I felt bullets whizzing by our heads. There was a total of fourteen rounds fired by the five of us. I was carrying my two-and-a-half-inch stainless steel Smith and Wesson .357 revolver, while Woolery had a Colt .45 semi-automatic pistol. My guess was that in those days most officers carried revolvers, which were either .38- or .357-caliber. Most of the semi-automatic pistols carried were .45 caliber. It happened so fast that neither one of us had time to think about what was happening. After the gun smoke settled, we just looked at each other and didn't say a word. We both had looks of, "Wow, what just happened?"

Botello was wounded with a gunshot to the head, Borgos was trying to hide underneath the van with a pistol and Jimenez was hiding inside the weed van. Borgos was lucky to be alive because he refused to give up his weapon. I assumed that he thought we were drug dealers, even though we had on our raid jackets and by then there were ten of us surrounding him. We had to drag Borgos from beneath the van after he finally gave up his weapon.

Gunsmoke hung in the air once the shooting stopped.

Besides me being blown out of a window (another chapter) and this shooting, I don't think we've ever had any other shootings outside of a couple of accidents in all my years as a DA investigator. Investigator Milton Ojeman, who worked in the Fugitive Apprehension Unit, almost had his leg blown off when his partner accidently discharged his shotgun while attempting to arrest a suspect. The other shooting happened while two Special Crimes investigators were attempting to arrest a suspect and an accidental discharge hit investigator Nelson Cox in the arm.

Botello died from the wound to his head en route to Ben Taub General Hospital. Borgos was charged with four counts of aggravated robbery and one count of kidnapping. Jimenez was charged with one count of kidnapping and one count of unlawful carrying of a weapon.

Our Civil Rights Division investigated the shooting. As a result, a Harris County grand jury no-billed Argo, Johnson, Fisher, Woolery, and me. The charge would have been murder. Jimenez was sentenced to twenty years and no records could be found on Borgos.

All in all, it was just another Friday at the office. Gunsmoke Friday.

Raul Garcia Jimenez   *Sergio Botello*

Sergio Borgos   *Me with $50,000*

CHAPTER 22

HUMP NIGHT

Every Wednesday night there was what became known as "Hump Night," which meant three drinks for the price of one at the Steak and Ale Restaurants throughout the Houston area.

Working in Special Crimes was very stressful for many reasons. Most of our cases were "high profile," like a political corruption case of an elected official, solicitation to commit capital murder, complicated murder cases, and organized crime investigations. The latter inevitably involved gambling, narcotics, and aggravated promotion of prostitution. We worked on very sensitive cases that we could only share or talk about amongst ourselves.

So, on Wednesday nights you'd find some of our staff at one of our local hangouts, the Steak and Ale on Memorial Drive, just west of downtown. There also would be a lot of other folks who worked at the courthouse present for the rounds of drinks. But you'd find the Special Crimes group at one table.

One of the very few "outsiders" allowed at the table was himself a former insider. Or was Ron Woods really outside his former realm of Special Crimes. To say he couldn't be trusted was flat wrong. Woods was a former FBI agent and the U. S. Attorney for the Southern District of Texas from 1990 to 1993.

When you became a member of the Special Crimes staff, you became part of a family – once you became trustworthy, of course. We worked and played together. If someone in Special Crimes was having a party on a weekend, you'd usually see mostly people from – you guessed it – Special Crimes. Some of the DA's staff didn't look kindly on us. They thought we got special treatment because of our job description. The ADAs there had county cars and carried guns. Many of the other prosecutors didn't like that. They'd call our prosecutors "police wannabes."

Anita Myers, a secretary in the misdemeanor division called us "Special Effects," which I thought was too funny. I picked up on and used the term. Anita wasn't being mean, she was just poking fun at us. She liked teasing everyone. She was a great secretary and knew as much law as some of the ADAs. The knowledgeable secretary had a great personality and was a good person to know. She later married Ken Magidson, a former ADA who, like Woods, later became the U. S. Attorney for the Southern District of Texas (2011 to 2017). He also was appointed the Harris County District Attorney during 2008. His real forté? He was the centerfielder on our softball team. His "softball nickname" was "Maggot." Anita died at an early age from cancer in 2012. They had one daughter and now have four granddaughters that all currently live with Maggot.

Another hang-out was Otto's, which was across the street from the Steak and Ale. These great eateries served a multitude of purposes. Otto's was the favorite go-to place for the Indictments, our softball team, after our games in the Houston Law Enforcement League. A lot of our team members consisted of Special Crimes staff members.

We were a pretty damn good team. We won the league champion-ship on several occasions. One of my best memories was the game in which Gary Dibello pitched a no hitter in a slow pitch game. Gary worked in Special Crimes and had gone to Hump Night prior to that night's game. He was so intoxicated that he could hardly stand up straight on the pitcher's mound. Yet he pitched a no hitter in a slow pitch game. That's unheard of. Gary was a John Belushi lookalike. You would've thought he was the famous comedian – until he started pitching to you. He was very funny, smart, and just a very nice guy. He and his wife, Barbara, an Adult Probation officer, were killed by a drunk driver in an automobile accident in east Texas while on vacation. It was very sad that two great people died so young.

I can't believe no one was ever killed on a "Hump Night." Actually, it almost did happen at the Steak and Ale one late evening when one of the busboys was smoking behind the dumpster outside the restaurant. One of my buddies was talking about selling one of his handguns to another guy. The prospective buyer wanted to test fire it before he bought it. So, we all went to the back side of the fine establishment to fire a few shots.

After firing one round into the dumpster, we heard a loud scream and saw a kid dressed in a white uniform – who we later learned was the busboy – take off running in a flash to scale a ten-foot chain link fence at lightning speed. I'd never seen anyone move that fast in my entire life on either the football or baseball field. He was never seen again at the Steak and Ale.

On another Hump Night, a former ADA cleverly pilfered the penny loafers of a current ADA, who was known to take off his shoes and put them under the table. The shoe thief threw the loafers into the flower bed that was proudly maintained by Steak and Ale.

You'd never see this "theft victim" wearing anything but penny loafers. He probably didn't want to take the time to tie his shoes because he couldn't hold still for that long, with his antsy movements inside and outside the courtroom. When he went looking for his shoes sometime later, he was told where he could find them. Somewhat sotted, he proceeded to pull up all the shrubs until he found his pennies in the shrub stack.

We later went out in put the uprooted plants in the back seat of the ADA's "county ride." The next morning, he woke up and found all the shrubs in his back seat. Later in the day, he got a call from the manager of the Steak and Ale, who told this loyal customer, "We'd appreciate it if you took your business elsewhere."

Sometimes after work, we'd stop by Otto's for a beer or two. Even Johnny Holmes would tip a few. He's the only person that I've seen to be able to pick up a full beer bottle and just pour it down his throat. So, he'd usually only stay a few minutes.

Another stress release practice was playing of practical jokes. It was a common thing because sometimes there was a time to just take a break from the "high stress assignments." Most occurred on Thursday nights because two of the Special Crimes personnel would have to stay late while the offices were cleaned. We'd sometimes include the cleaning lady in on the prank.

On one occasion, we had her hold some inflated balloons in both of her hands, with arms extended while we'd try to pop them with a "blow gun." Good thing we weren't using poison darts. We never forced her to do it. She was having as much fun as we were, and she got to take a break from her cleaning duties.

There was usually alcohol involved as well. Sometimes you'd come in the next morning and might find your office furniture in the restroom, which I attributed to either Dan McAnulty and/or Mike Feary. I volunteered a lot for cleaning duty, so it wouldn't happen to me to be a victim.

Part of our work duties included accompanying vice officers on raids of "sex stores," and we'd store some of the important evidence in Special Crimes for trials. I actually thought it was a waste of time and manpower.

One piece of "crucial" evidence was a huge purple dildo. One "cleaning" night I conveniently placed the sex toy in the hanging plant, located in the corner of the ceiling of Special Crimes prosecutor Judy Police Mingledorff's office. Judy was a former schoolteacher and could spew some "words" if needed. Otherwise, she appeared to be the most "prim and proper lady." Not only was she a great prosecutor, she was very pretty and could take anything that could be dished out. Nothing would faze her. She was just a calm professional and beautiful lady. Just don't piss her off. Her husband, Ken Mingledorff, was also a former Special Crimes prosecutor.

She never even noticed the huge purple penis, which was so large it could probably be used as a deadly weapon. Sometime later, a news crew from KPRC came to her office to do a story regarding a major fraud case that she was handling. When the news segment of her interview aired, you could see the sex toy dangling from the plant in the background.

The purple toy later became a "weekly award" in Special Crimes. If you'd find it in your office, you'd have to "hang" onto it for a week before you could pass it on to the next award winner.

During one of our famous Special Crimes Christmas parties, it ended up in the middle of a huge bowl of potato salad. No one would even touch these eats – except for one prosecutor, nicknamed "Safeway." He just "spooned" around the purple giant sea cucumber and ate away.

"Man, this is really good potato salad," he raved. I stuck it in the purse of one of our inebriated secretaries. Her name was Melinda. When she left to go home, the huge purple banana was dangling out of the top of her purse and she didn't even notice. I wonder who has the award today?

Sometime in the eighties, Harris County went to automated elevators which left the elevator operators with nothing to do. The county decided to place them in the entrance of each county building at an "information desk" to answer questions and provide directions. We were assigned

Dorothy, who absolutely knew nothing about our office. She spent her whole day just sitting there with nothing to do. She had a phone on her desk which never rang, and no one to ask her any questions. If someone asked her something, she had to fumble around looking for an answer.

So, Joe Vara and I decided to put some excitement in her life by super-gluing her phone receiver to her phone. When it finally rang, she picked up the receiver and the entire phone was attached as one piece, so she couldn't answer. That took a while because her phone never rang. Once discovered, she was supplied with a new phone. We then removed the earpiece, so when she'd answer the phone, she couldn't hear anything. We later removed her mouthpiece, as well. She proved to be a good sport about all these sticky predicaments.

Our security guard, Dick Rutledge, a retired deputy sheriff, was stationed next to Dorothy's desk and would get a good laugh. Dick later became one of our investigators.

Nowadays, you'd end up in prison pulling some of the pranks that we pulled on people.

Gary Dibello

CHAPTER 23

THE LATER YEARS

In the late 1980s, Don Stricklin, the chief of Special Crimes, was promoted as the first assistant Harris County District Attorney upon the departure of Henry Oncken, who became a state district judge hearing criminal cases. Bobby Blaylock had already left to become the chief investigator under District Attorney Johnny Holmes.

The new chief of Special Crimes was Bill Taylor, aka "the Colonel," a veteran prosecutor who leaned more toward major fraud (financial crime) investigations. He was a colonel in the U. S. Army Reserves assigned to the Adjutant General's Office. After he graduated from Texas A&M, where he was in the Corps of Cadets, he was assigned to serve in the U. S. Army as a second lieutenant.

I really didn't fit in, even though I was still assisting other law enforcement agencies with electronic surveillance investigations. Over the years we had developed the best electronic equipment of any law enforcement agency in Texas. This is not braggadocio but the plain facts. I'm not sure that Taylor realized this well-known fact because I was usually out of the office helping another agency.

My office requirements had grown so much that I'd moved to the floor below Special Crimes to the former quarters of a county criminal court judge. The office was huge and even had a bathroom. I had so much equipment and taped evidence that I actually needed the space.

The other plain fact was I was out of sight and out of mind. I think that the new boss thought I was "screwing off" somewhere. I was ready for the transfer in many ways. All the late-night assignments and stressful cases were beginning to wear on me. I moved to Division D of the DA's Trial Bureau as a lieutenant over the investigators. It was a huge change for me.

I went from being a primary hands-on investigator working the big cases to a desk-bound supervisor. This wasn't my cup of tea. I knew in my gut that my calling was in the action, albeit sometimes fruitless and boring. Supervising investigators was not my favorite thing to do. I sorely missed working on actual cases, but took solace by often assisting other investigators. A major discomfort, however, was giving up my blue jeans for the less functional coat and tie every day.

I have to say that the Trial Bureau was the "bread and butter" of the DA's office. The prosecutors there handled ninety-nine percent of the county's criminal docket – from capital murder on down. What Joe Six-Pack doesn't understand or realize is that in order to prosecute a criminal case you need witnesses. Otherwise, you don't go to trial. Many witnesses for the prosecution move out of town or hide somewhere to avoid being subpoenaed to testify in public. They have all sorts of reasons that investigators must deal with on a regular basis.

The other investigators and I realized that this trial factor made our jobs extremely critical. The prosecutors had to rely on us to "beat the bushes" looking for these reluctant folks. Most of the time they weren't easy to find. They would purposely disappear from the face of Houston, Harris County, and often from the State of Texas.

These missing and reluctant witnesses didn't usually live in the "high-dollar" Houston neighborhoods. Our investigators usually had to venture alone into a low-income apartment complex in a high-crime area, walking around wearing a coat and tie, which was a red flag for *cop*. I told my guys that they could go without wearing the "dress wardrobe" as long as they had their badge displayed.

The *residents* in these areas would suspect that you were either a bill collector, repo man, or a cop. Chances were good that they wouldn't mess with a cop. Some of the "higher ups" didn't like my policy, but they weren't usually the ones walking around in sweltering heat in "the hood." I knew that Johnny Holmes would agree with me.

Without a prime witness, you had no case and couldn't go to trial. We had a thankless job that some prosecutors sometimes didn't appreciate. They usually concentrated on the bottom line: *Did you find him or not?*

A GOOD BIRDDOGGING

I spent the year 1973 assigned to the 184th District Court and really liked it because the judge, Pete Moore, a former Army pilot during World War II, and my prosecutors really appreciated my efforts. Most of the ADAs would write a memo to the personnel file of their investigator in some of the difficult cases when they would find the missing or hiding witness and then get them to court. This show of appreciation made you work harder for them. I have to say that some of the female clerks thought Judge Moore was a hero. One of them even suggested that Robert Redford play the judge in a movie about his life.

The first murder case that I investigated for the prosecutors in his court was the robbery and shooting death of Carlos Rubi, a freshman at the University of Houston. This victim worked nights at the old Foley's Department Store in downtown Houston. He was valedictorian of his graduating class at nearby Stephen F. Austin High School, from where coincidentally both my parents had graduated in the late 1940s.

On April 4, 1973, near the front door of China Garden Restaurant in the 1700 block of Dallas Street on the east side of downtown, Rubi was gunned down and robbed. The violent perpetrators were Leonard Page and Revert Weston, a duo who'd just fled from New Orleans after shooting and robbing two victims as innocent as Rubi was. Rubi was taking his dinner break that night while working and was executed just outside China Garden's front door.

China Garden was then – and still is now – owned by the Jue family, who immigrated from China to Houston in the 1960s. The family started a Chinese food import store in 1968. A year later, David and Marian Jue opened the restaurant, a lunchtime stop-off for innumerable noon crowds from the courthouse to practically every other high-rise office building in downtown. Marian still manages the place. The family has strong ties to the community.

The husband of daughter Carol is Richard Churchill, at this writing a retired Houston police officer. The Jue's son, Richard, who also played a role in managing the restaurant and was a young man at the time of this violent act, discovered Rubi's body at the front door. Richard called HPD. He knew how to act – years later he became a reserve deputy constable. He killed a man who tried to rob him in the late 1990s, while operating a parking lot adjoining Toyota Center during Houston Rockets games.

When HPD officers arrived, they learned that the only eyewitness was William Robert Gillespie. This individual was far from a solid citizen whose credibility likely wouldn't produce a high winning percentage in the courtroom. Gillespie was a drifter and a day laborer in a labor pool. Formerly a worker in Los Angeles and San Francisco, he had broken his leg and resided in a room in a rundown building with a "Rooms for Rent" sign on the front. The room was located atop the Hello Bar and Grill, across from the murder scene. After the first shot, Gillespie rose from his bed and observed the next few shots closely aimed at the young victim's body.

Later, the police arrested the two killers while they attempted another robbery. Gillespie picked them out of a police line-up.

Assistant District Attorney Stu Stewart, an outstanding prosecutor and the chief in our court, had a problem. He needed the mercurial day laborer, Gillespie. Without this star witness, the State had no case and would have to free Leonard Page and Revert Weston. We would have to send them back to New Orleans to stand trial for their pending cases there.

We didn't think Gillespie was purposely hiding from us. He was just off doing what he was in the habit of doing from the West Coast to our middle coast. He checked out of his room, telling anyone who cared that he was "movin' on."

My search was on. I called the homicide divisions of both the Los Angeles and San Francisco police departments to ask for their help. Just like HPD's highly respected Homicide Division, the investigators from the two widely-acclaimed counterparts in California didn't relish seeing murder cases dismissed because of a missing eyewitness.

Like the clock at a football game, time started ticking away as the trial date neared – with no star witness. I had played quarterback for St. Pius X High School and well knew time factors like this one.

I contacted the FBI for help. Agents sent me everything they had on Gillespie, including intel on his sister, a resident of Brandon, Florida. Wasting none of the precious time left on the clock, I contacted her. She said the last time she saw him he was living under a bridge in Brandon. Yep, he had completed the circuit – from the West Coast to the Middle Coast to the East Coast. I sincerely appealed to this woman. I told her he was the eyewitness in a Houston murder trial. I asked for her to please go by the bridge to see if he was still there. A couple of hours later, I got a collect call from Gillespie.

I explained the situation.

"I don't have any money to come to Houston," he said.

"No worries," I told him. "We're paying for everything."

There was still time left on the clock! I made all the arrangements to fly him to Houston. When I picked him up at the airport, his body odor overwhelmed me. Pity the poor fellow passengers on the plane – especially if he were in the middle seat. I got him in a downtown hotel but didn't leave until I made him take a shower. I laughed. The things we do for taxpayers!

His clothes also smelled, so I sent them to the hotel's valet service. I gave the hotel manager my business card and home phone number and asked him to please keep an eye on this distinguished hotel guest as a special favor to me and the taxpayers who regularly demand justice in their court system.

The manager called me a short time later and told me that Gillespie was walking around the lobby "acting very oddly." I reiterated that this odd wad would only be there for one night and would be leaving the next morning.

"Thanks," the manager said, "but we don't need someone like him wandering around the lobby area. It's not good for business."

I got lucky. Gillespie settled down and stayed the night. The next day he testified against both defendants. Thanks mainly to him – and my birddogging him – a jury found both men guilty of murder in the death of Rubi and sentenced each of them to at least fifty years in prison. Fortunately for those Texas taxpayers I've mentioned herewith, Louisiana law enforcement authorities claimed them, took them for trial in New Orleans and never returned them to Texas.

THE BULLDOGS

I have recalled in great detail in some other chapters the noteworthy case of Texas Supreme Court Justice Donald B. Yarbrough. I got a phone call in 1977 – when the case was broken wide open in *The Houston Post*. Tom Kennedy was the *Post* reporter who broke the story and succeeded in getting Yarbrough to surrender his law license and resign from the state's highest civil appeals court. In one of his prize-winning stories, Tom outlined the details of how I located the star witness against Yarbrough. After his resignation Yarbrough faced criminal charges of aggravated perjury and forgery of an automobile title.

The phone call was from one of our investigators, R. O. "Robert" Biggs, a retired Houston homicide detective assigned to the Grand Jury Division in the DA's office. Robert was usually a "grumpy old fart" who seemed to complain about everything, especially the prosecutors with whom he worked. Yet once I got to know him better, I learned that he really was a very likable, funny, and "a nice guy." I also found him to be an intelligent investigator. But he held Special Crimes in contempt because he thought we got special treatment. Given this background and Robert's known feelings, I was puzzled when I got his call.

"Kenny," he said, "R. O. Biggs here. How are you doing?"

"Okay, sir, how are you?"

"I just want to thank you on your article in the paper this morning. No one has ever given the investigators in our office any recognition about our work. You did it. Thank you so much. I really appreciate it and I know most of the other investigators do as well."

It was the longest "conversation" he'd ever carried on with me. I felt good. I let him talk! I was totally astounded by his call and remember it to this day. Don't let anybody – especially law enforcement investigators – have you believe they don't bust with pride when they get compliments.

In Carol Vance's book, *Boomtown DA,* he wrote, "Ken was an affable little bulldog of an investigator, most resourceful and tenacious."

At this former Harris County district attorney's book-signing party, I thanked him for his kind words about me in two of his chapters. I took the opportunity to let him know just about all of the DA investigators were tenacious bulldogs. It was my belief that Carol just never realized it because some of his prosecutors didn't give their investigators the proper credit that they duly deserved – but most of them did, I am happy to say.

THE IMPORTANCE OF LEEWAY

In the late eighties I supervised the Division D investigators. I didn't regard this as a big deal because these guys already knew what they were doing. They didn't need me or anybody else telling them what to do. They knew how to find the bad guys. They knew how to corral important witnesses.

Because there were only four district courts in Division D, the powers-that-be added the Fugitive Apprehension Unit, Civil Rights Division, and Family Violence Division investigators to my supervision.

Investigator Tom Wilson, assigned to FAU, was already pretty much "running the show" there. I did Tom's initial interview when he first applied as a DA Investigator, while I was in Special Crimes. He came to my house, which happened to be in the same Hidden Valley neighborhood where I grew up.

I began with what I thought was one of those typical "discussion questions."

"So, you want to leave your job as a detective with the sheriff's office where you're investigating murders, robberies, and other hideous crimes to become a DA investigator," I said, "where you'll start out in the Misdemeanor Division investigating someone who stole a dozen eggs?"

"Yep, I do," Tom replied.

"Have you lost your mind? You're going to be so bored working on chickenshit little misdemeanors after working on the cases that you're used to working."

"I know what I'm getting into."

"Good luck, buddy. If you get the job, you're going to come to me one day and say, 'I should've listened to you Kenny.' "

The only time that I really got involved as a "supervisor" was on the occasions when an investigator had a problem with an ADA, or vice versa. It only happened in Family Violence, where division chief Cindy Merrill was a micro-manager. She would call me almost every day about the most mundane things, such as when her investigators, Larry Boucher and Pat Daly, wouldn't answer their radio or pager right away. I finally asked her to come to my office one day after a meeting of the DA's upper echelon staff.

I explained to her that her two investigators were professionals. They knew what they were doing. I told her she would probably get better results if she gave them some leeway. She must have taken what I said to heart, for I never heard much from her again. We later became good friends and are to this day.

HUMOR AND LACK THEREOF

Milton Ojeman, Don O'Dell, Jim Jackson, and Leo Michna were the four district court investigators in Division D. Milton was a former Harris County deputy sheriff who almost lost his leg when working in the Fugitive Apprehension Unit. While attempting to arrest a perpetrator, his partner accidently discharged his riot shotgun when exiting their vehicle.

Don O'Dell was a retired HPD detective who got a case dismissed when he was interviewing a witness and learned we were prosecuting the wrong person. I had never seen that happen before. He got a nice "atta-boy" memo in his personnel file for that one.

Leo Michna, was a retired HPD lieutenant, very seasoned and reliable. Jim Jackson, assigned as an investigator in a district court in Division D, had an excellent reputation as a Harris County Deputy Sheriff. Again, experience paid off in those days at the courthouse. Also adding experience to the roster was Bill Bryan, another retired HPD street cop. Bill worked in the Civil Rights Division.

What I'm saying here is that I worked with some highly capable, motivated law enforcement officers who hated to see the bad guys get away. They didn't have to prove themselves as investigators. They were already very capable.

The four of us liked to play practical jokes on prosecutors who had a sense of humor. Michna's chief, Jan Krocker, wasn't much of a fan of our jokes. Krocker had some of the dumbest requests that she didn't really need on a case or for a trial. It would drive Michna crazy, so he eventually retired early. He didn't tell anybody why he took this early retirement. But I knew. Krocker later became a criminal district court judge.

A GOOD JOE

Joe Roach was a prosecutor in Division D who could take a prank or two. Joe later became a Houston City Council member and served his three-term limit before becoming a defense attorney. Joe was a little person, as was his wife Becky. Both were good people. They couldn't have children, so they adopted three little persons.

Every day after Joe left for court, we'd either put phone books in his chair, lower or raise his chair and/or desk. Each time when he returned from court, you'd hear, "Goddammit, Kenny."

His office was right across from mine. I can't tell you how many times I heard him say that. On one occasion, my youngest son, Keith, was visiting my office when he was only twelve or thirteen years old. I had recently caught him smoking one day. We were on the elevator during his visit as Joe Roach got on in front of us.

I didn't miss a beat.

"See what happens when you smoke," I said to my son.

Joe turned around and said, "Goddammit, Kenny."

I returned to the DA's office in 2009 and in 2011 I ran into Joe in the lobby of the Criminal Justice Center.

"Hey, Joe," I said to him, "you still mad at me about the jokes?"

"Hell, no, it was fun, and I liked the attention."

"You know, Joe, I wouldn't have played any jokes on you if I didn't like and love you,"

"I know that. I love you, too. Those were the good ole days, weren't they?"

A month later, Joe died from a disease that's common amongst little people. He wasn't always the tallest guy in the room, but it didn't seem to matter. I sensed there were other of his colleagues at City Hall who felt the same way about him.

FROM PROSECUTOR TO JUDGE

ADA Leslie Brock, now Leslie Yates, was always a good target for our pranks. I gave her the same message that I gave to Andy Tobias: "Please call L. E. Fant at this number," which was the Houston Zoo. She brought the message in laughing after calling the zoo and said, "That's a really good one."

Leslie was from Ormond Beach, Florida, very smart and athletic. She played on our women's office softball team that I coached along with another investigator, Pat Smith. Leslie was one of our best players and always hustled on the field, trying to take the extra base. In one game she tripped while running to first base and fell. I never let her live that down.

She later married one of my friends, Terry Yates, a former Special Crimes prosecutor. They have two sons that are great baseball players. *I wonder where they got that from?* Their oldest son received a baseball scholarship to Centenary in Louisiana. Leslie became a district court judge. I know in this volume of memories and memorable people and cases that I have let it be known that many of the prosecutors in Harris County became criminal district judges. To tell you the truth, I have lost count of the number.

A GOOD JO

As the chief investigator in the DA's office, I had to drive Johnny to various places but sometimes he would drive himself and I'd ride with him. He sure didn't need me for protection because he carried a Colt .45. Johnny, Jo Tinkle, and I would usually go to lunch together. That was a great benefit for Jo and me because the district attorney always picked up the tab.

Jo was Johnny's secretary and I'd drive her to many places. It was usually for shopping or some other reason, so I nicknamed her "Miss Daisy" after the movie, *Driving Miss Daisy*. Jo was a good-hearted soul, the essence of kindness. I loved the woman like she was my mother. Every time that she'd get a jury summons, she'd bring it to me because she thought that I could "take care of it." I would just throw it in the trash.

About five years later after we both retired, she called me about getting another jury summons. I told her, "Just throw it in the trash like I always did."

"You mean to tell me you didn't have somebody in the clerk's office take care of it?"

"Hell, no. They don't send those by certified mail. They can't prove if you got it or not."

"Well, I'm surprised that I haven't been to jail."

I just laughed and told her that she was a worry wart. A few hours later, she had a stroke and never recovered. I went to see her in ICU before she moved on. I told her daughter, Diane Tinkle Corbett, "I'm going to miss driving Miss Daisy. I loved that woman."

THE BOSS' MONIKER

Johnny was funny about some things, especially when eating out. If the waitress was too slow or rude, he'd get up before walking out and say, "I'll never come here again."

I heard him say this so many times that I wound up saying to him one day, "Johnny, we're running out of places to eat. We're going to have to start driving through Jack in the Box and you with a bag over your head."

I must have heard him say, "I'm an asshole," on so many occasions that I lost count years ago. I'd always say, "No, you're not," and usually leave it at that. He would usually say that when he thought that he did or said something wrong, which really wasn't too often.

Our office mailbox was located on the second floor of 201 Fannin, where the administrative staff was located. As I was walking in the office one day, I heard Cheryl Lewandowski, our administrative assistant, say, "Mr. Holmes, you're not an asshole."

I happened to be nearby and took Cheryl's remark as a cue.

"Hey, Asshole," I said, "what's going on?"

I wish I had a picture of Cheryl's face when I said that. You'd have thought that she was having a baby or that someone was touching her inappropriately. I knew he wouldn't get pissed at me because he had verified his asshole status so many times before.

One morning he was dropping off his daughter's car to be repaired at Jack Roach Ford on the Southwest Freeway and Buffalo Speedway. I was supposed to pick him up around 8 a.m. and drive him to work. An hour later I realized I had forgotten to pick him up!

I picked up our radio and said, "Unit 10 to Unit 1."

A second later he said, "Go ahead."

He was standing in my office doorway.

"Oh, shit. Johnny, I forgot. How'd you get to the office?"

"I walked. I needed the exercise."

I apologized again and he said that while on the walk he got an offer for a lift from an HPD patrol car but told them that his mother always said, "Never ride with strangers."

So, he just walked more than ten miles to get to work.

CANDY GIRL

My secretary then was Candy Roch, with whom I worked while in Special Crimes. Candy was very able, intelligent, and pretty as well. The fact that she could put up with some of my antics was somewhat of a miracle in itself.

At my retirement party in 2001, I forgot to mention her for some unknown reason. Most likely it was because I had so much to say about my thirty years on this special job. I felt so bad about it and have never forgotten her because I'm not sure I could have done anything without her. Candy was awesome in dealing with the other investigators and other personnel in the office. Her work and social skills were admirable, and I appreciated her very much. I'll never forget her – ever again.

HELPING PEOPLE

One thing that I didn't like hearing from a prosecutor was, "Well, he might not have done this case, but he's probably done something else."

"Are you kidding me," I would usually respond. "We're the good guys and play by the rules. That's the difference between us and the bad guys."

Good guys follow the rules and bad guys don't. You can bet your ass that you'd never hear Bob Bennett, Johnny Holmes, Henry Oncken, Don Stricklin, Ted Wilson, and many others ever say that. They had too much integrity and honesty. I followed those same rules.

I used to hear through the "grapevine" about officers planting evidence on suspects so they'd have a "good case." Now, that makes the good guy a bad guy, and they've crossed the line.

I had my suspicions about some of the good guys that might've crossed that line, so I wouldn't work with them. Several times I was told to work with a certain officer on a case and I refused. I believed I had integrity and certain ethics that I follow. Please note that I'm not naming any names here.

I might have done a lot of goofy things in my career but setting up someone by planting evidence and lying weren't part of my character. Stealing things while on a search warrant weren't anything that I'd ever done or ever thought about doing. I think that 99.9 percent of law enforcement officers are like me. That's why we became law enforcement officers – to enforce the law, not break it.

I used to teach at several community colleges that had a police academy. On my first day in the class, I would ask them, "How many of you are here because you like helping people?" About ninety-five percent would raise their hands.

I then asked, "How many are here because you like beating the ever-living shit out of someone?"

They'd raise their hands and I'd say, "You guys need to find another profession because you're probably not going to make it."

Another thing that I didn't particularly like was the use of stats to evaluate the ADAs. I had the JIMS (Justice Information Management System) programmers create a database that would keep track of the dismissals of the ADAs' cases, which were later used at the end of an election cycle to determine an ADA's performance. It could be used as a factor in determining if they would retain their job for the next four years. I told Johnny that I didn't think that was fair, because, "What if you just happened to get some cases in your court where they were actually innocent?"

"Yes, I guess that could happen," he said.

WATCH OUT FOR SNAKES

In 1975 a small group of recently hired young investigators, including Larry Dehnert, Bernard Ash, Mark Argo, and I were hanging out at Bernard's house located off Highway 6 and Interstate 10 on the far west side of Houston. It was one Sunday afternoon. We were talking about our age difference with the older investigators. We weren't complaining about them, but just discussing the differences of our work product, ideas, etc.

We also talked about creating an investigators association like other police and law enforcement agencies, but not a police union that would dictate pay, insurance, rank (which we didn't have), or anything else regarding an organized union. It was just about creating a social group where we could all get together once a month, and that's all.

At this time, I had recently returned from Washington, D. C., where I'd attended a three-month training session with the U. S. Alcohol Tobacco and Firearms agency. It dealt with explosives, firearms, and gun tracing.

When I returned, I was assigned to the Chief Investigator's Office, dealing with some of his daily tasks, which mainly included serving out-of-state and county subpoenas and assisting ADA Don Lambright, who was helping Carol Vance in the prosecution of Dean Arnold Corll, David Owen Brooks, and Elmer Wayne Henley. They'd abducted, raped, tortured, and murdered at least twenty-eight teenaged boys and young men in a series of killings between 1970 and 1973.

When I got to work the next morning, after the get-together at Ash's house, Johnny Fox, the chief investigator, called me into his office. He was upset. "I hear you are the 'ringleader' of the effort trying to start a police union here."

I replied by chuckling and said, "No, that didn't happen." I explained to him exactly what we talked about the previous day. "I'm not that stupid to try to start a union. Are you kidding me?"

He finally calmed down and we never spoke about it again. I had a good idea where the erroneous report came from and correctly assumed that it was taken out of context by the time it got back to Fox. I really didn't care because I had three other witnesses that could back up what I said.

A funny thing is that when Fox retired in the early eighties, we had become really good friends. He sold me his "new" 1980 International Harvester Scout, which was in mint condition. When I picked up the vehicle, he gave me his 12-gauge riot shotgun and a huge flashlight as well.

This background leads to my story of the creation of the DA's Criminal Investigators Association. It happened in the late 1980s. Investigator Wayne Bashara was our first president. We had shirts, caps, coffee cups, briefcases, and other items that we sold to the entire staff. Johnny Holmes was our best customer.

We had an annual Christmas party, which included the entire staff of the DA's office. All of our proceeds went into a fund used for various charities, flowers for ill staff members, or their families, etc. We later created a cooking team that would participate in the Harris County Annual Law Enforcement Cook-Off, a huge event.

One funny thing that we'd have at the cook-off was an Igloo cooler marked with a sign that said, "Free Beer." When you opened the lid a huge realistic-looking rattlesnake would come at you because we'd have a monofilament fishing line connected to the lid and the head of the "snake." It would scare the hell out of people who thought that they were getting a "free" alcoholic beverage. It looked so realistic that I thought it might cause someone to have a heart attack.

On one occasion, an old man approached and said, "Do you really have free beer?"

"No, it's a rubber snake inside," I said, not wanting him to have a heart attack.

"Really?" he said.

"Yes, sir, there's a rubber snake in there."

Not heeding what I said, he opened the lid, screamed, and ran off faster than I thought a man of his age could ever do.

About thirty minutes later, he returned panting, while our team members Sonny Dollar, Cliff Moseley, Bill Bryan, Larry Dehnert, and I were still laughing our asses off.

"That scared the shit out of me," he said.

"I told you there was a snake in there," I said.

"I guess I should've listened to you," he said. We gave him some beer.

Even after most of us retired, we continued with the cook-off team for several years.

GOOD GUYS RETIRE

I have to say that I didn't much like being a supervisor as much as I did investigating cases. Shortly after Johnny Holmes' retirement as – in my opinion – the best Harris County DA in history, I retired, as well.

There will never be another Carol Vance or Johnny Holmes. Politics never played a part of the way they conducted their offices. Now, it's all politics. That's sad, especially for those taxpayers I've talked about.

In the thirty-three years that I worked as a DA's investigator, I have to say that I loved the adventure every day. I admit that law enforcement was not always exciting. But when it was, I felt it to be larger than life, it was the life that I loved and lived.

Tom Wilson, Larry Dehnert, Me, Bobby Blaylock

Me, Les Ramsay, and Tom Wilson

Keno Henderson, Me, Jo Tinkle, John Holmes, and Bert Graham

Law Enforcement Torch Run for Special Olympics, Me, Rueben Diaz, Lynn Robideau, Joe Vara, Carlos Ramirez

Division D Investigators, left to right: Don O'Dell, Me, Leo Michna, Jim Jackson, Pat Daly, Larry Boucher, Milton Ojeman, Bill Bryan

Candy Roch, Jo Tinkle, John Holmes,
and Cheryl Lewandowski

Milton Ojeman

Candy Roch and Gary Zallar

Dick Rutledge and Elevator Lady

Me and Pat Daley when he was
promoted to Lieutenant

CHAPTER 24

DIM WIT

In 1989, soon after I returned from the three-month FBI National Academy, I was promoted to captain and assigned back to Special Crimes. I was back home! I also served as the project analyst for our office, a volunteer position without extra pay, but plenty of additional responsibility.

The "job" entailed my interaction between the DA computer users and the computer programmers. I tried to make it easier for our employees to utilize all of the justice data computer systems.

There were plenty of technical challenges. In 1990 the Texas Department of Public Safety came to my office with a four-part form regarding a law newly passed – Chapter 60 of the Texas Code of Criminal Procedure – regarding the tracking of criminal histories. This was very important to our office. In the old days, investigators would spend a countless number of hours trying to match arrest records with court records. I used to see DPS personnel trying to do the same thing. It was a tedious task for both.

This data was critically important to law enforcement people. If a defendant had multiple convictions, he or she would get a higher bond, and, if convicted again, a higher sentence. When you'd look at a DPS criminal history, you could see all of an individual's arrests based on fingerprints, but no final information on the adjudication of the arrest.

After DPS handed me the four-part Criminal Justice Information System, or CJIS form, I started laughing. They asked me, "What's so funny?"

"You have to be kidding me," I contended. "We have over 125 law enforcement agencies in Harris County and you expect them to fill out the arrest portion of this form, that includes the fingerprint card, and then bring us the DA's portion of the form? Some of these agencies are over thirty miles away. This isn't going to work here or in any other large Texas city."

"Well, it's the new law," the DPS representative said, doing his duty.

"It might be the new law," I countered, "but this just won't work here. The concept is great, but a four-part form isn't viable here. I have an idea, so let me get back to you on this."

I'd been talking to Johnny Holmes, the Harris County DA, about the need for an AFIS (Automated Fingerprint Identification System) for a few months.

As the project analyst, I was spending countless "volunteer hours" consolidating records of persons using aliases, which were sometimes that of a suspect's relative who'd never been arrested, or just a completely new name. Our general counsel, Scott "Scooter" Durfee, would get a letter from the "innocent person," voicing words to the effect, "I think my brother used my name when he was arrested."

The problem got so bad that I contacted my long-time friend and *Houston Post* reporter Tom Kennedy and told him the situation. By this time Tom was writing a twice-a-week column on the *Post*'s editorial page about city politics and criminal justice issues. He interviewed the always-accessible Holmes and outlined the problem in a column. A short time later, Holmes agreed to finance the AFIS using funds from the DA's drug and gambling forfeiture fund. The U. S. Marshal's Office agreed to kick in a large amount of seized funds as well.

At the same time, I was in the process of designing a new database for the process of filing cases called DIMS (District Attorney Intake Management System). DA Intake was then working via fax machines, "walk-ins," phone calls, etc. Nothing was automated.

So, I spent the next two years working on this project. I had help from our computer guru, Gary Zallar, and ADA Bill Taylor, who was in charge of Intake at the time, and Debbie Mills, our day shift dispatcher.

In 2020, Zallar was still in charge of the DA's office computers and, in my opinion, ranked as one of the top-notch law enforcement computer experts in the United States. He taught me about computers, and I taught him about the legal process.

Two years later, Gary and I talked about how much money we

could've made by creating DIMS software and selling it to other agencies across Texas.

Also, I can't say enough good things about Debbie. She was as adept as any good investigator we had. After retirement she came to work for my company, Gulf Coast AccuSearch, which is primarily a pre-employment research company, as well as being equipped to perform some private investigative work.

During this time period, Jimmy Ray, the director of JIMS (Justice Information Management System), had already created a highly efficient computerized system for tracking criminal and civil cases. There was no other system like this one in the United States. I was a big user of JIMS when it was created in the mid 1970s and primarily used it as a tracking and investigative tool. The county had recently bought a new software program and DIMS was going to be the first major project. I know: JIMS and DIMS. It has a ring to it.

I spent countless hours working with JIMS Assistant Director Mike Shannon and programmers Jason and Robbie Miley, Paul and Lisa Clements, Shirley Knight, and many others in JIMS working on DIMS. I also had to work with the other project analysts from the sheriff's office, Pat Diaz, Hank Husky, and Kermit Kurtz, and Steve Stuchlik, with the civil district courts, and Debbie Rankin of the Harris County District Clerk's Office.

After two years of hard work by many dedicated individuals, both DIMS and AFIS kicked off on January 1, 1992. One significant issue was the training of the officers from 125 law enforcement agencies. Shirley Knight, head of the training at JIMS, had a major task. So did I. When I trained the other investigators, they said, "It's impossible; it won't work."

"It will," I insisted. "Hide and watch."

The investigators could volunteer to work Intake, where they made some pretty good extra pay. With DIMS, it was the investigators' job to print out the initial DIMS report and attach the criminal history. That began the process. It took many months to get it started. What a nightmare it was for our daytime dispatcher, Debbie Mills, and the other investigators. Not a night went by that I didn't get a phone call from Intake.

One of the greatest things about DIMS was that it was a great investigative tool. It allowed officers of different agencies to see the summaries of the cases filed by other agencies and officers which had never been available before. You could track a criminal's modus operandi in each case filed against a defendant, which could be a valuable tool in investigating cases and easy accessibility.

In mid-2020, DIMS was still being used! After thirty years!

Sure, there have been some changes in the technicalities but, basically, it's still the same. Prosecutors used to call me the "Father of DIMS." I still consider that title a sincere compliment for which I'm very grateful. Most of the newer ADAs knew that I was the chief investigator and the JIMS security guy but had no idea about my past or my role in "the old Special Crimes."

To this day I take great satisfaction in knowing this hard work by so many people still makes it easier for the good guys to identify and catch the bad guys.

Gary Zallar *Debbie Mills*

Kenny Rodgers, Captain of Investigators ID
November 1989

CHAPTER 25

HERE COMES ANOTHER JUDGE

"Here it is Friday the thirteenth and we're soliciting capital murder."
— Texas Supreme Court Justice Donald B. Yarbrough

This is one of the most famous recorded quotes in the history of the Harris County Special Crimes Bureau. Justice Yarbrough clearly uttered this wonderment in the presence of former business partner and coin dealer John William "Bill" Rothkopf. The two men were sitting in Yarbrough's car on the parking lot of the Sage Department Store at one of Houston's major intersections – the Katy Freeway and West Belt.

The story didn't begin here at this location. At this time Yarbrough had served the first few months of a six-year term. In November 1976, Texans duly elected Yarbrough to be one of nine justices on the Texas Supreme Court. They did so, thinking he was Don Yarborough, who'd been a candidate for governor and lieutenant governor in the 1960s. This person, whom we grew to call "the real Yarborough," narrowly lost in a runoff for governor against John B. Connally, Jr. as a Democrat in 1962. Yarborough – with the extra "o" in his name – was still a revered liberal among Texas Democrats.

Donald B. Yarbrough had only paid the filing fees and spent little or no money campaigning, but easily won the election with more than 1.2 million votes. Yarbrough had more than thirty grievances filed against him with the State Bar of Texas resulting from his faulty representation of various clients. He was hardly qualified to sit on such a prestigious civil appellate bench. During 1976 there were numerous lawsuits filed against Yarbrough, most of which were fallouts from his various business interests and dealings with clients.

Yarbrough was also the subject of an investigation by the U. S. Attorney's Office regarding a forged letter of credit that he used to purchase the Commercial State Bank of Victoria. Also allegedly involved in the scheme was former Commercial Bank president Bill Kemp.

The State Bar's investigation was growing more complex. In the spring of 1977, District Attorney Carol Vance sent Sam Robertson, his first assistant, along with Special Crimes Bureau Chief Johnny Holmes, to Austin to meet with State Bar General Counsel Steve Peterson. Their question: Were any of the allegations against the justice criminal in nature?

Robertson and Holmes learned that the State Bar was very interested in locating John William Rothkopf, a former Yarbrough associate and business partner in a company called Gold and Silver Ltd. They needed Rothkopf in their disbarment lawsuit against Yarbrough but had no luck in locating him. They felt that he might be dead because he seemed to have just disappeared from the face of the earth.

Holmes ran Rothkopf's criminal history and learned that he had an open warrant in Harris County regarding a theft of some gold coins. Holmes also learned that the FBI, Texas Rangers, the Houston Police Department Burglary and Theft Division, and the Harris County Sheriff's Office Warrant Division had been looking for him for more than two years.

Upon Holmes' return to Houston, he tossed a file on my desk.

"See if you can find this guy when you get a chance," he said. "He's got an open warrant for felony theft."

He also told me a few of the details about the State Bar's investigation, but not much more than that, just that the guy was a very important witness.

Two weeks later, on a Friday afternoon, I decided to go by his last known address in some apartments located near the corner of Westview and Silber Road in the Spring Branch area. I was on my way home and this would be easy. I met with the apartment manager, a little old gray-haired lady who only stood about 4-foot-9 and must've been in her mid-seventies. She told me that she hadn't seen Rothkopf for at least two years. She further stated that he lived with his daughter, Carole Rothkopf. She had no idea where they moved. I left her my business card and told her to call me if she ever ran into them again.

The next day while mowing my grass, I got a call from Teresa Landry at DA Intake, which is open twenty-four hours a day because they process all of the criminal charges in the county. Teresa said, "Some little old lady called wanting to speak to you about your visit with her yesterday." She gave me the woman's phone number and I immediately gave her a call.

"You're not going to believe this," she said, "but I ran into Carole Rothkopf at the grocery store yesterday and she gave me her address."

I quickly wrote down the address, with a plan in mind. I would stop by there first thing Monday morning. I had no idea that my trip there would change my life forever.

■ ■ ■

On Monday, May 2, 1977, I drove into the complex and parked near the apartment number that the lady had given me. I radioed Special Crimes Investigator Don Baker to advise him I needed to execute an arrest warrant. I asked him to check in with me on his way to work.

"No problem," he said, "I'm on my way."

While parking my 1973 Army green Dodge "Police Package" Fury – which was out of alignment because of being wrecked by the previous driver – I saw through a window a frail little man smoking a cigarette and reading a newspaper. From this quick assessment, I felt this gentleman would pose no physical challenge if he took exception to his arrest.

The man fit Rothkopf's description but I still wasn't sure it was him. I was thinking: *How could I be so lucky?*

I decided to arrest him without Baker's help. I had him in view. I didn't think I would encounter resistance. I didn't even bother checking out with our dispatcher on my police radio as I got out of my "green machine." I knocked on the door. The man with the cigarette and newspaper answered almost immediately.

"John William Rothkopf?" I inquired.

"Yes, I am," he responded.

"I hate to be the bearer of bad news, but you're under arrest."

"Thank God, what a relief. I'm glad it's over. I'm tired of running and hiding."

Ironically, this was going to be the beginning of a lasting friendship.

Rothkopf initially asked me if he could call his friend, Don Yarbrough. I told him, "Sorry, you can't make a call until you get downtown."

As I put him in my car, I didn't even bother placing any handcuffs on him. I knew he wasn't going anywhere because he looked tired and worn out. He was only fifty-eight years old but looked much older. He surely didn't look like someone who'd been easily evading the FBI and Texas Rangers for such a long time.

I read Rothkopf his "blue card" legal warnings before heading downtown to Special Crimes. I used the radio channel to call Holmes. I asked him to meet me in the office because I had a surprise for him. Holmes was always near a police radio. I think he slept with one because any time you'd call him, he'd answer promptly. I knew that he had Bearcat police scanners in his home and office. He monitored HPD, the Harris County Sheriff's Office, and the Texas Department of Public Safety day and night.

Only Special Crimes employees had access to our radio channel except for the DA himself and his first assistant. I always thought we were a little paranoid, but at the same time, it was better to be safer than sorrier. We had no need of letting just anybody "out there" know what we were doing.

Rothkopf told me he was confused as to what to do. He kept saying how relieved he was. He had been running scared for two years because so many angry people wanted him for legal proceedings against Yarbrough.

On the way to the office he began telling me that Yarbrough wanted to kill a Victoria banker by the name of Bill Kemp because he knew too much about Yarbrough's complicated business affairs that were under investigation by the state bar, state and federal grand juries, and state governmental agencies. Kemp was a key witness against him. Rothkopf said Kemp owned a small airplane and Yarbrough wanted to put sugar in the gas tank so he'd crash and die.

Rothkopf said he'd met Yarbrough around Easter when Yarbrough pulled $2,000 out of his pocket and said he was serious about Rothkopf getting a Mexican national to kill Kemp. Rothkopf had told Yarbrough earlier that he knew a "hit man" from Mexico named Pete. He then admitted to me that Pete was a fictitious character made up in order to placate Yarbrough.

"I will pay $2,000 down," Yarbrough told Rothkopf, "and the other half when Kemp is gone."

My guess was that Bill Rothkopf knew as much about Yarbrough's criminal activities as Kemp did, so he was thinking that he could be

HERE COMES ANOTHER JUDGE | 219

Yarbrough's next assassination target as well. However, Bill said that he was relying on Yarbrough to pay his living expenses and stated, "I'm under Yarbrough's thumb." There was dread in his tone. Then he went on to say that Yarbrough was so adamant that he even talked about killing Kemp himself.

Bill – we got on a first-name basis really quick – told me that Yarbrough was a big-time crook, the virtual mastermind behind this gold coin business where they'd sell coins to people, then hire burglars to steal back the coins to resell. They sold the same coins over and over.

I sensed an opportunity here I thought would be as good as a gold coin. Would he be willing "to wear a wire" to get evidence against Justice Yarbrough? He quickly agreed. I have no doubt that he figured the state would go easy against him relative to the charges against him were he to cooperate in this manner. I told him that there were some authorities who wanted to talk to him about Yarbrough in other cases. His recorded cooperation also might also help in these cases.

I read the HPD offense report of the pending case against Rothkopf. I applied an oft-used law enforcement description: "a chicken-shit case." I figured it was probably a ploy to get him to cooperate. Well, I guess it was going to work.

I took Rothkopf straight to the Special Crimes offices where Holmes gave him his legal warning again, advised him of the charges against him, and read a summary of the police offense report.

Rothkopf had an attitude about him. He didn't appear to be too worried. It was like he felt he was the one in charge, not Johnny Holmes or Kenny Rodgers. From this "driver's seat," he asked to call his attorney, Don Yarbrough. Now wait a minute, I thought, why would he want to do that after our previous conversation about wiring him up to get evidence against the man he now wanted to call for legal advice?

Once Holmes explained the nature of the charges against him, Rothkopf came to his senses. He didn't want to call Yarbrough after all. He told us he was broke, prompting Holmes to remind him that he could get a court-appointed attorney for representation.

Holmes also told Rothkopf that we weren't really interested in Yarbrough's activities; it was the State Bar of Texas legal counsel who was extremely interested in meeting with him. Yarbrough wasn't just an attorney; he was a justice on the state's highest civil appeals court.

Holmes and I took Rothkopf to the 174th District Court where a visiting judge appointed attorney Jim Beauchamp to represent this star defendant.

Once we got back to Special Crimes, Holmes called Beauchamp to ask him to meet with us regarding the Rothkopf case. In the subsequent meeting in our conference room we told Beauchamp – pronounced BEE-chum – that we weren't really interested in Rothkopf's information, that the State Bar was. When Beauchamp pledged his new client's cooperation, Holmes called State Bar legal counsel Steve Peterson in Beauchamp's presence.

I was present and I soon realized I was experiencing a glitch. I never had a chance to tell Homes about the details of my conversation with Rothkopf. We hadn't settled down from the excitement related to finding him and undertaking the legal proceedings that followed. Quite frankly, I wasn't really sure if I were dealing with a fine-tuned bullshit artist or a man ready to go straight by helping the good guys.

I knew I had to get more information after Peterson and the State Bar had what was needed to proceed with their grievances. I later advised Holmes of my conversation with Rothkopf when driving him to Special Crimes after I arrested him. Holmes raised his eyebrows into the partly cloudy Houston skies.

I would be meeting Steve Peterson for the first time. When he showed up in my office, I thought the son of a bitch was going to have an orgasm when he realized that Rothkopf had finally been captured. The FBI and Texas Rangers had failed but a young DA investigator with due diligence in his routine had succeeded.

There was a meeting of the minds. Present were Rothkopf, Beauchamp, and Peterson, along with a court reporter. They met in our conference room. I returned the executed warrant to the sheriff's office and Holmes arranged for a personal bond for Rothkopf. At the time we probably should've left the warrant unexecuted so the records would show him to be a fugitive. This would become a significant problem later into the investigation.

The next morning, we learned that the interview lasted until 4 a.m. the next day. We also learned that Yarbrough had been hiding Rothkopf because his information and testimony could absolutely ruin his career and possibly send him to federal prison.

Holmes pulled me aside and told me not to tell anyone where Rothkopf was living, not even him. He said that I would be solely responsible for his safety and well-being because he also could become a target of Yarbrough and his cronies.

Upon leaving the office that night, I gave Rothkopf an old double-barrel shotgun that I had, along with one of our walkie-talkie police radios. My radio unit number (call sign) was 307, so I told him that he was 307B if he ever called anyone on the radio.

For the next several days and months, I would pick up Rothkopf at his apartment in the morning and bring him to the office, where he was still meeting with bar officials; I would drop him off after work.

During this time between May 2 and May 12, I got to know Bill Rothkopf pretty well. I couldn't help but like the chain-smoking, self-styled peddler, a red-faced elfish man who spoke with a Northern accent.

You have to understand what was taking place here. Rothkopf was becoming a star "CI" – a confidential informant – whose trust in me was equally as important as the trust that I, and others, had in him. This strong trustworthiness quickly becomes "a must" when you and the CI might be placed in dangerous situations. My feeling was then – and remains so to this day – that our bond became stronger than ever because we both loved to laugh.

When a reporter later asked him about his life's work, he used one term. "I'm a peddler," he said. He said he could sell anything. He hailed from South Bend, Indiana, and came to Houston because his wife Margaret had cancer and needed treatment at M. D. Anderson Hospital. Sad to say Margaret died shortly after the move to Houston.

Rothkopf set up a coin business in the River Oaks Bank and Trust building located on the corner of San Felipe and Kirby, near the ritzy River Oaks subdivision. Yarbrough's law office was in the same building. It was only natural that the two would meet. Rothkopf dealt in gold coins, Yarbrough had a love of gold. He believed that paper money would eventually become extinct. Everyone in the United States and the rest of the world would resort to using gold coins. Rothkopf and Yarbrough got into the business of buying, selling, trading, and – as we learned – stealing gold coins.

Rothkopf told me that whenever they sold more than a few gold coins, that Yarbrough would send some burglar buddies of his to their house in a few days and steal the coins back for resale. It was the same story he told me the day I found him in Spring Branch. He told me that Yarbrough was "crookeder than a cow's hind leg." He must've used this expression to me and many others at least twenty times over the next few months in the spring of 1977. Each time he used it to describe Yarbrough, the crook he was describing was wearing the robe of a supposedly highly respected appellate judge.

At first nobody except me believed what Rothkopf said about Yarbrough wanting this ex-banker named Kemp killed. I was only in my mid-twenties – still "the new kid on the block" in Special Crimes. I had earned respect at this early point in my career as an investigator – but *not that much respect.*

Once Rothkopf and I returned from a taped meeting between him and Yarbrough on the Sage parking lot on May 12, 1977, my stock rose. The majority of opinions changed around the office. Prior to this tape-recorded meeting I was having problems getting any of the other DA investigators interested in helping me. I had to "draft" HPD Detective Jerry Carpenter to go in his city ride to help me observe the Sage parking lot meeting. Jerry really didn't want to go, but I made him feel guilty, so he finally agreed.

On that day Rothkopf called Yarbrough from Special Crimes. They agreed to meet early in the afternoon "at the office," which was this Sage parking lot. This was their go-to place to meet during the months Rothkopf was "missing." Ironically, Yarbrough was paranoid about the government listening in on his phone calls. Little did he know we were listening to every word he spoke into Rothkopf's recording device that we had hidden on his body.

I had fixed up Rothkopf with a wireless transmitter and micro-cassette tape recorder. We were able to monitor their conversation, while also seeing to Rothkopf's safety. I had placed the transmitter in his waistband, securing it with athletic tape. I hid the recorder in his shirt pocket behind some folded notes. The microphone for the transmitter ran up over his stomach and was taped to his chest. Sometimes the noise created from the clothes rubbing against the microphone was annoying. The resulting static made it difficult for Jerry and me to hear.

I took pictures while Carpenter observed the meeting. We were the only two investigators on the scene.

Things got a little nerve-racking when they left the location and went to a Church's Fried Chicken on nearby Memorial Drive. We weren't sure where they were headed but once we heard, "give us two number threes," we were relieved to know they were just getting lunch. With all the talk about murder, we weren't sure of Yarbrough's intentions. Was he capable of killing Rothkopf?

The meeting between the two began with a discussion of the recent publicity of Yarbrough and the general condition of the various pending lawsuits against him. In this context Yarbrough said he still wanted Bill Kemp killed. He went into a detailed discussion of how this would be accomplished, asking Rothkopf if his "Mexican friends" were still available to do the job.

Rothkopf said he would try to connect with this Mexican hitman named Pete to see if he would still do the job for $2,000. Pete was a totally fictitious character. Rothkopf created him in his imagination in order to appease Yarbrough. Rothkopf told me that he had actually heard about a hitman named "Pete," but never met him. He took care to make it clear to me that he never had any intentions of assisting Yarbrough to knock off Kemp.

At the end of the meeting, they agreed to meet again at "the office" the next day.

Once we returned to Special Crimes and listened to the micro-cassette, everyone was pretty much satisfied that Rothkopf had been telling the truth. This was "the real deal." One problem was that the sound quality of the tape wasn't that good.

Low tape quality or not, the real deal meant the cast of good guys increased. FBI Special Agent John McGauley, assigned to assist the U. S. Attorney's Office in its investigation of Yarbrough's banking scheme, showed up in our office to offer his assistance. Actually, it was pretty rare for an FBI agent to help or share any information with local agencies, but I felt McGauley was sincere and could be trusted. I asked him if the FBI had any kind of equipment that we could "borrow" for this investigation. He left us for about an hour and returned with a Nagra reel-to-reel recorder that was thin and a little larger than a pack of cigarettes.

Coincidently, McGauley got the small recorder that would do the job for more than three and a half hours from their FBI tech agent, Dick Suter, a good friend of mine. I'd attended St. Pius X High School in north Houston with three of his sons. During my senior year, I met Dick and talked to him about working for the FBI as a clerk while I attended college. Such a clerkship was the first step in the route toward becoming a special agent after graduation. I had wanted to be an FBI agent since I was ten years old after watching James Stewart in *The FBI Story.* I also had visited the FBI headquarters with my parents in 1959. I read every book available about the FBI. I knew at a very young age that I was going to be involved in law enforcement.

In this ongoing FBI-involved investigation, I was excited about the fact that Rothkopf was telling the truth about Yarbrough wanting to kill someone. I believed him when the other investigators didn't.

Now, I had no problems getting any assistance from the other investigators, plus Holmes had officially put me in charge of the investigation. My credibility was on the rise. The fact that this was such a "high profile" case, everyone wanted to help, including a few of the lower level DAs in the Special Crimes Bureau.

Since this was such a sensitive investigation, I decided to use code names for Yarbrough and Rothkopf. There was always a lot of "courthouse talk." I worried that someone would make mention of the Rothkopf arrest and blow the case. Plus, for the purposes of radio communications while on surveillance, we didn't want anyone to know what we were working on and the individuals involved.

I decided that Yarbrough would be known as *Yankee* and Rothkopf as *Dog*. I don't know why or how I came up with those names, but Holmes and others involved in the case liked them. Many law enforcement people from the South often used references to Yankee or "a Yankee" as derogatory terms to describe a bad dude of any sort. They also appreciated any efforts to "dog" these bad dudes. A Yankee was bad, a Dog was good.

Holmes and Rodgers reviewing
the Yarbrough case

CHAPTER 26

YANKEE AND THE DOG

References to Yankee and the Dog took hold. Steve Peterson, the State Bar general counsel and investigator, made mention of "Dog's arrest" to Bill Kemp's attorney, Tommy Thomas. This really put a new wrinkle in the present picture. Attorney Thomas seized upon the opportunity to seek federal immunity for Kemp.

Not only did Peterson mention "Dog's" arrest to Thomas, but he also told him about "Yankee's" plan to kill Kemp.

Oh shit!

Just a week after Dog's arrest, Thomas fired off a letter to Jack O'Donnell, the assistant United States attorney representing the government in the Yarbrough-Kemp Commercial Bank investigation. In the letter, Thomas said that Peterson told him that Rothkopf had been found and that there was a threat against his client's life. He also demanded federal protection for Kemp.

Worse yet, he sent a copy of this letter to Judge Bert Tunks, an appellate judge who was set to hear the State Bar's disbarment lawsuit against Justice Yarbrough, aka "Yankee."

The possibility that Tunks would advise Yarbrough's attorney, Waggoner Carr – the former Democratic Speaker of the Texas House and Texas State Attorney General – of the fact that a DA investigator had found Rothkopf and that Rothkopf contended Yarbrough wanted Kemp killed was information that could very likely ruin our ongoing investigation.

Upon learning this, Holmes contacted Thomas and leveled with him about where we were going with the investigation. Thomas agreed to keep quiet only if we would agree to give Kemp protection. Holmes reluctantly agreed because Thomas had us over a barrel. We put Kemp and his family in the Rice Hotel, several blocks from the courthouse, during this time period. This meant neither Kemp nor his attorney would go public on this matter. Our investigation was safe!

Meanwhile, Thomas and Peterson spoke to Judge Tunks so that he'd keep the contents of the letter confidential. Judge Tunks agreed to do this for "a reasonable time" in order for us to proceed with our investigation. Ironically, the decisions of Tunks and his two fellow appellate panel members could be appealed to the court on which Yankee held a duly elected seat.

Kemp was given state's immunity. A grand jury heard his testimony about the facts surrounding the Commercial Bank deal. During his appearances he was wearing a bullet-proof vest because he knew Yarbrough and felt that what Rothkopf was saying was true. Kemp's testimony verified that the acquisition of the Commercial Bank was a criminal matter and that he in fact was involved along with Yarbrough.

■ ■ ■

Now, let's get back to the Friday, May 13, 1977 meeting that Dog had set up with Yankee at "the office." Dog was wired with our Westinghouse one-watt transmitter, which allowed us to monitor live conversations, along with the Nagra mini reel-to-reel recorder borrowed from the FBI.

This time all of the Special Crimes investigators became a part of a surveillance team that covered "the office" like a human blanket. A surveillance van parked across the street at the Sheraton Inn, a van at the IHOP just to the south, one at a nearby convenience store, an investigator inside the Sage nursery that fronted to the parking lot, and an FBI motor home inconspicuously established over a small acreage of parking spaces.

Yankee and the Dog were sitting in Dog's blue 1974 Chevrolet Monte Carlo – which was supposedly registered to a fictitious Billy Ray Waller – parked on the east side of the Sage store, next to a cedar fence. Blaylock and I were parked in a county ride on the other side of the cedar slats, some of which were missing, thus enabling us to actually see the Dog's car as we monitored the conversation.

My adrenaline was pumping like I was at bat with the bases loaded and had a 3-2 count. I just couldn't believe that we were so close. I didn't want to blow the case and I was worried about Rothkopf's safety. All we needed for Solicitation for Capital Murder was for money to change hands. Had Yankee handed the Dog a hundred bucks we had a go.

They were so close to us that I had to turn down the volume on my receiver so it didn't squeal with feedback. If it did, Yankee surely would hear it. We would be outed and over. It would become a "he said, he said case." Who would believe what Rothkopf had to say over a Texas Supreme Court justice?

I could hear Yarbrough refer to "Pete" and say, "The best thing would be to do it myself if I had a gun with a silencer. We don't know for sure that they don't fuck it up. Then where would we be?"

He continued to say that Kemp could really hurt him during his scheduled deposition on May 27 regarding the Commercial Bank of Victoria dealings in 1974-75. Yarbrough said that something needed to happen before the deposition to make sure Kemp couldn't talk.

"He'll take the Fifth Amendment and that's going to hurt me," Yankee ventured to say. "It makes me look bad. He's not going to be loyal to me and as far as I'm concerned Kemp deserves to die."

"How do you want it done?" Rothkopf asked.

Yarbrough explained that he wanted Kemp killed, his body taken to Mexico, and his car left at the airport so "it appears like he just went away somewhere."

Blaylock and I were going crazy listening. I couldn't believe what we were hearing. This made Judge Bates look like an angel compared to Justice Yarbrough.

Yarbrough proposed to Rothkopf that they both go get a $2,000 loan at an Austin bank on May 16 in order to make a down payment for "the hit." The justice would provide Rothkopf with a fake financial statement so he could sign the loan.

Yankee stayed on the subject at hand. "Kemp is a motherfucking, a motherfucking toad," he stated.

He had plenty of animosity to go around, too. He talked about Doug Ford, who was involved with him in an oil well deal near Graham, Texas; it entailed Ford's $35,000 investment.

"I want Kemp wiped away and Doug Ford wiped away," he said, showing a mean streak. "After that I don't give a shit."

It was at this recording session that we dutifully heard and preserved perhaps the most famous tape-recorded quotations in Special Crimes history.

After discussing the proposed murder of Bill Kemp, Yankee turned to the Dog and said, "Here it is Friday the thirteenth and we're soliciting capital murder."

Spoken like a true doctor of laws.

There was plenty in this conversation to prove that Yankee trusted the Dog inherently. He went on to say that if authorities found out about him and investigated their activities, "they could send us both to the pen for over twenty years."

About this time, he pulled Rothkopf's oversized, brightly colored ball-point pen from his shirt's breast pocket and said, "This looks like it could be a microphone."

I heard that and thought: *Holy shit, if he only knew we were less than twenty feet from him. If he searches the Dog, we're busted!*

Rothkopf just laughed it off. He conjured up enough cool to make a smart-ass comment that caused them both to laugh. We breathed a sigh of relief.

At the end of this meeting it was clear that Rothkopf was to travel to Austin and meet Yarbrough at the Austin Motel prior to going to the bank to apply for the loan.

Johnny Holmes and I immediately began arrangements to handle surveillance in Travis County during this meeting. A list of persons, vehicles, associated recording, surveillance, and camera equipment had to be prepared and readied for the Austin adventure. Because of the sensitive nature of the investigation, we felt that no other jurisdiction should be notified of our presence.

At this juncture, I have to admit that every serious DA's investigation involves human beings caught in the act of being human. Sometimes laughs are involved.

That night, Holmes and I went to the offices to prepare for the trip to Austin on Monday. When we arrived, we saw one of our staff cars parked in front of the door located on Caroline.

That's weird.

Once we got on the floor, we noticed all lights were off. Total darkness. We thought no one was in the office. After we started making noise, an office door opened and out came a red-faced staff member along with an exotic dancer. A CI perhaps? He claimed he was interviewing the "witness" regarding a case. As he spoke nervously she nonchalantly brushed her long brown hair.

Holmes and I put on our game faces. Once out of sight, we couldn't stop laughing.

■ ■ ■

Holmes and investigators from Special Crimes traveled to Austin on Sunday to get ready for the meeting the next day. We had eight investigators and ADAs, including Holmes, and all the necessary equipment.

We stayed Sunday night at Holmes' parents' house on Lake Travis after spending the day drawing detailed area maps of the meeting location. Each agent was given a specific assignment so there would be no slip-ups. We went over the route carefully, staking out each surveillance location.

Early Monday morning, Rothkopf arrived at Holmes' house on the lake with Jim Beauchamp. I wired the Dog and Holmes and I briefed him about what he should do. We were very cautious about entrapment, and we did not want him to participate in a federal bank fraud in any form or fashion unless it was totally and completely under the direction and insistence of Yarbrough.

The Austin Motel is located on South Congress, literally downhill from the State Capitol. We learned from earlier conversations that Yarbrough was using that as his home-away-from-home during the work week. He still lived with his family in Houston.

Surveillance was established well in advance of the meeting time. Our surveillance van with its cameras was inconspicuously parked in an abandoned beauty shop parking lot across the street from the restaurant where the meeting was to take place.

Rothkopf, having been previously wired, arrived on time. Yarbrough did not. He was several minutes late. During the ensuing conversation Yarbrough advised Rothkopf that the bank deal was off.

The bank officer couldn't lend him the money without messing up some financial statements of the borrower and that just wasn't possible using the identification that Yarbrough had furnished Rothkopf. They would have to figure some other way to get the money for the hit.

Additionally, Yarbrough felt that they would have to delay "hitting"

Kemp. Since it was getting so close to the disbarment suit being heard, people might suspect him of having it done.

Yarbrough and Rothkopf began talking about the automobile that Rothkopf was driving. We would later learn that this sleek, late-model sports coupe was originally owned by one of Yarbrough's companies. The company had transferred the title to Yarbrough personally. Yarbrough in turn transferred the car to Rothkopf.

Earlier, during the Commercial Bank dealings, Yarbrough had instructed Rothkopf to take the car to Bill Kemp, then president of the Yarbrough-owned bank in Victoria, ninety miles south of Houston. His instructions were to borrow money against the car. This money was later to be used to pay the expenses incurred to hide Rothkopf. Rothkopf did as he was instructed, and the car was used to borrow the money, as planned. The bank took a lien on it.

Later the car ended up with an Alabama registration showing it to be owned by one Billy Ray Waller. We surmised this. After Rothkopf got the loan from the bank and pledged the automobile as security, Yarbrough fictitiously registered the car in Alabama using a bill of sale on the car to Billy Ray Waller. At that time Alabama was a non-title state and this could be easily done.

The state's position on this matter was that Yarbrough used this tactic to defeat the Commercial Bank's lien on the car. This Billy Ray Waller had made application for license plates from Alabama by letter; however, the address where the plates were to be mailed turned out to be Don Yarbrough's office address.

Yarbrough brought up the car during the tape-recorded Austin conversation. Rothkopf made it clear he didn't like driving around Houston and Huntsville – where Yarbrough thought he resided – with the Alabama plates. He also was using a phony Texas Driver License. Yarbrough got the point and agreed. He indicated to Rothkopf that he did not have the Alabama "title" with him and that he had to go to his office to get it. They agreed to meet back at the motel at 12:30 p.m.

Yarbrough left, circled the motel, and fell in behind Rothkopf's automobile. He turned around after following Rothkopf for a minute or two and headed north toward the Capitol. Investigators met Rothkopf away from the location, removed the tape, and listened to what had transpired. This was done behind a commercial shopping center, inside the surveillance van.

Rothkopf returned to the motel at the appointed time. So did Justice Yarbrough. The two talked briefly and went into the room behind the motel's restaurant. Investigators grew extremely apprehensive about this turn of events since it would now be impossible to see Rothkopf and ensure the integrity of our surveillance as well as Rothkopf's safety. We were very glad to see them both reappear after thirty minutes. They got in their respective cars and left the scene.

Again, we met Rothkopf, removed the tape recorder, and listened to the conversation. Quite to the surprise of all of us Yarbrough went into the motel room with Rothkopf and began putting on gloves to remove the Alabama title. Next, Yarbrough instructed Rothkopf how to forge Billy Ray Waller's name to show conveyance of the vehicle to Rothkopf, who was known on this document as "Roger Conway."

I don't think a story can be effectively written without having listened to this thrilling audiotape. It was something to hear, and still is today more than four decades later.

Obviously, all of us were really surprised about what we heard. A Texas Supreme Court justice instructing John William Rothkopf how to effectively forge an automobile title, clearly with the intent to defraud.

At this point Holmes thought it would be most appropriate to discuss the way Rothkopf assumed the name of Roger Conway. During the period that Yarbrough started getting into State Bar troubles and civil suits filed against him, it became obvious to him that his former associate should get lost. In an effort to assist him in this endeavor, Yarbrough obtained the birth certificate of a Beaumont lawyer by the name of Roger Joel Conway. He selected this name because of the close age and description to John William Rothkopf.

Yarbrough instructed Rothkopf how to present himself at the Department of Public Safety and fill out an affidavit of lost driver license using the Roger Joel Conway birth certificate as his identification. The plan worked. Rothkopf got a Texas Driver License showing his photograph with Conway's name on it. Rothkopf used one of his former addresses. Yarbrough orchestrated this entire name change scheme. According to Rothkopf, Yarbrough actually accompanied him to the DPS office to fill out the false affidavit of lost license and got the new phony identification issued.

The duo now known to us as Yankee and the Dog were scheduled to meet again three days later. They were to return to "the office." Naturally, we "wired" the Dog and set up adequate surveillance. We would watch every move. This meeting lasted only twenty to thirty minutes. Yankee discussed the Alabama car title. He said Rothkopf should wait until his Alabama plates expired before taking the steps to get a Texas title and plates.

They briefly talked about the Kemp deal. But nothing definite was arranged. Yankee still wanted Kemp eliminated. The next meeting was arranged to be a week later, June 3, 1977 at the office at 8:30 p.m. Wire in place, as usual. Surveillance set up. The Dog waited more than an hour. He called Yankee at home to learn that the justice was having trouble getting away. His wife was out of the house and he was babysitting.

Almost two hours after the originally scheduled time, Yankee showed up. He said he couldn't afford the down payment and went so far as to ask the Dog if he could cough up the money and go forward with Kemp's murder with his blessings. Yankee said to contact him again in a week.

They met a week later at the office. Again, the conversation was about Kemp and how he might testify against him. Yankee wanted to see Kemp dead but cautioned against the murder taking place before the State Bar's lawsuit went to court.

Although Yankee and the Dog set up another meeting before the end of the week, Johnny Holmes instructed the Dog to call it off. Holmes, always thinking ahead of the game, believed there were too many people in too many agencies who knew the DA's men had found John William Rothkopf and had him "wired" to get evidence against Justice Yarbrough.

Let me discuss the identities of these people and how they learned these details. Obviously, Steve Peterson knew what was going on because of his relationship with the State Bar and the detailed information Rothkopf had provided. Had Rothkopf initially told me what he ended up telling Peterson, we wouldn't have called Peterson, we would have worked Rothkopf in secret. Peterson told everything to the State Bar officials. Unquestionably, he made a very bad error in judgment by telling Kemp's lawyer, Tommy Thomas. He also told Frank Bean, the lawyer the State Bar appointed to try the disbarment suit against Yarbrough.

Of course, the Kemp letter to Jack O'Donnell and Judge Tunks was problematic. Those individuals who knew included each and every one of the DA investigators in Special Crimes. With such a high-profile investigation taking place, the courthouse press corps was bound to pick up some clues and go running to their microphones, cameras, and printing presses.

Interestingly, only one criminal and civil courts reporter knew what was happening. Tom Kennedy of *The Houston Post* was documenting the growing number of civil lawsuits against Justice Yarbrough. He had covered one civil damage trial in which Yarbrough prevailed against two angry plaintiffs, one of whom was Doug Ford, a man he told the Dog he wanted killed.

Kennedy proved to have the characteristics needed to be an effective newspaper reporter – sharp eyes, open ears, and the ability to be "off the record" when appropriate. He was in the process of developing the trust needed between a reporter and his sources that led to his later becoming a columnist specializing in criminal and civil justice issues.

Kennedy hadn't printed one word about the discovery of Rothkopf. Holmes wanted to know why this newspaper reporter knew so many facts – possibly even something the ongoing investigation hadn't yet turned up.

In early May 1977, Bob Bennett, former chief of Special Crimes, called Holmes about Tom Kennedy snooping around the federal courthouse, asking questions about Rothkopf and Yarbrough. Bob knew what we were doing because Holmes originally called him to advise him of Rothkopf's capture. Bennett represented a plaintiff in one of the numerous civil cases against Yarbrough, and Holmes wanted him to know what was happening. Rothkopf was automatically a person who would become a "star witness" in most of these cases.

The purpose of Bob's call to Holmes was to warn him of the possibility that Kennedy might find the return of the warrant on Rothkopf when snooping around in the files. Also, he would find out that Rothkopf was on a personal bond recommended by Holmes.

This would be a significant story for Kennedy, who was already on Yarbrough's enemy list, having been banned from a news conference Yarbrough held in his law office before being sworn in as a justice. Bennett knew Kennedy from his courthouse reporting assignment. So did Holmes.

Holmes decided that we could not run the risk of Kennedy discovering who was holding the bag. Therefore, Holmes took a calculated risk. He summoned Kennedy to his office. To this day, Kennedy likes to quote "the other Kenny Rogers" when we discuss his approach to *The Post*'s Yarbrough coverage. "You've got to know when to hold 'em and when to fold 'em. I was holding 'em." Kennedy smelled a scoop and agreed to stay quiet and "off the record" about Rothkopf and the Yarbrough investigation.

Meanwhile, he researched and found more than twenty lawsuits against the justice, many involving deception and failure to keep his end of legal representation and business agreements.

Kennedy also detailed Frank Bean's disbarment lawsuit, which was frequently amended as the number of "counts" against the justice increased rapidly. They eventually grew to become the first-ever one-hundred-count disbarment lawsuit in Texas history. He knew it was just a matter of time before he would be writing an exclusive story for page one of *The Houston Post*.

The days ticked on. Some of them saw patience overwhelm anxiety. Many people knew and they were keeping their mouths shut – an exceptionally strong indicator that Yarbrough had no trusted friends in high places. By June 10 there were many people "wired in" to what was happening and who the major players were. Many of them even knew the players by their code names, Yankee and the Dog.

CHAPTER 27

THE POST SCRIPT

Johnny Holmes was the quarterback calling the plays. He had approached Jack O'Donnell, assistant United States attorney, in late May to discuss the possibility of going forward with the federal grand jury investigation of the Commercial Bank deal involving Texas Supreme Court Justice Donald B. Yarbrough.

Holmes' suggestion to O'Donnell was to subpoena or invite Justice Yarbrough to appear before the grand jurors. Questions would be posed about the bank purchase. Furthermore, Holmes suggested that the prosecutor make inquiries about whether or not Yarbrough knew the whereabouts of John William Rothkopf, a material witness in their investigation.

Knowing Yarbrough as Holmes did, and knowing the public stance about Rothkopf that he had previously taken on television, Holmes felt sure that Yarbrough would appear and perjure himself. Yankee would keep secret the Dog's whereabouts, in other words.

Prosecutor O'Donnell rejected Holmes' suggestions at this time because these tactics weren't part of his timetable. The grand jury would not be going into the bank matter again until August.

Holmes told him that he didn't know how much longer we could keep the Yarbrough ordeal quiet. Ever the chess board tactician, the Special Crimes chief suggested that O'Donnell move forward now and not wait until August. O'Donnell rejected the advice.

The signal caller felt time was growing more crucial by the minute. The clock was tick, tick, ticking down. So many people knew of the ongoing crime saga that there was a very substantial risk that Yarbrough might get word of the fact Rothkopf had been arrested and was obviously in our camp. The last thing we needed was for Yankee to confront the physically weaker Dog and discover a concealed tape recorder or transmitter.

Even worse, Yankee might take a future meeting as an opportunity to fill the recorder with all sorts of self-serving bullshit about the previous efforts to kill Kemp. For all of these reasons, Holmes called a halt to any future meetings between Yankee and the Dog at the very instant we were wiring up the Dog to get him in the ready. I was the lead investigator. The other investigators – as well as the Dog himself – voiced our disagreement.

Each of us felt that Yarbrough would go forward with the Kemp hit deal. We would close in on him with a Solicitation of Capital Murder charge against the judge. We knew we would dutifully follow the orders of our well-respected quarterback. And so we did.

Tom Kennedy and *The Houston Post* were poised and well prepared to publish "the story" whenever Holmes declared the ongoing investigation to be at a major milestone or termination point. Holmes used logic as a prosecutor just like Kennedy did as a reporter. The next step in the process: Kennedy should interview John William Rothkopf, aka "the Dog."

Holmes told Kennedy that he figured Rothkopf would be agreeable to meeting with him. But any interview would have to be arranged through Jim Beauchamp, Rothkopf's court-appointed attorney. Initially, Kennedy felt Rothkopf would "lawyer up" and, therefore, clam up. He knew the lawyerly routine in such interview scenarios: "No, you can't print that – it's off the record." Holmes said that shouldn't be the case here. And he was right.

Holmes and Kennedy were like the lawyers who know the answers to questions before they asked them. Rothkopf would claim that he became disenchanted with Yarbrough and decided to go the Special Crimes Bureau to tell the story of the justice wanting to engineer the death of an adverse grand jury witness, Bill Kemp. Rothkopf would then tell Kennedy that we didn't believe him and that even if we did there was no way to substantiate what he was claiming.

It was only natural for Kennedy to establish the facts, just the facts. The facts as he knew them were that Rothkopf had been wired in conversations with Yarbrough. The tapes would back up any charges against the judge. This key fact of the case represented the absolutely necessary backup any reporter needed for a story.

The reporter, who had been patiently secretive up to this point, wanted to use details of the taping and surveillance plan, and, for certain, the conversations that were on the tapes.

Johnny Holmes, as open and sincere as ever, told Kennedy this would be impossible. He knew that for Kennedy to use the tape-recorded details, he would have to play them for the reporter. Then Holmes played his hole card – unless he agreed not to write about the tapes at this time, he would not be allowed to talk to Rothkopf.

Journalists rely on sources, the more sources, the better the story. Kennedy knew Rothkopf was a primary source. He knew Yarbrough would give birth to a black cat when he learned Rothkopf was spilling the beans to *The Houston Post*. And, too, it was not as if top-notch sources like Holmes and me were not source aces in the hole.

Kennedy agreed to the terms. He did so after what he called "a prayer meeting" with Carol Vance. He knew – like any reporter worth his/her salt – that a "no" today might turn into a "yes" on the next day. The newspaper business in Houston at this time was highly competitive. Kennedy liked nothing better than to beat the prime competition, the *Houston Chronicle*. He already had his story written. All he needed was enlightening quotations from Rothkopf. Reporters call this "collaboration." It's a magic word in journalism.

Ever keeping cool, Kennedy nonchalantly answered the phone in the Civil Courthouse press room, taking great care to make sure none of his competitors knew what he was up to. It was Rothkopf, who introduced himself and said, "Why not bop on over and we'll talk." Kennedy bopped over the two blocks to the Special Crimes headquarters.

By this time, Kennedy and I had developed a mutual trust. He told me Yarbrough delighted in filing lawsuits against people. He would relish with delight a suit against *The Post* corporately and Kennedy personally. We both sensed a unique cooperative attitude between *The Post* and the DA. Machinations moved quietly in the background above our pay grades.

Vance and Holmes trusted Kennedy and *The Post* to keep their vow. This set the stage for Vance and/or Holmes to meet with *Post* legal counsel Jim Crowther for a prayer meeting about the tapes. Legally, if *The Post* knew there were in fact tapes to back up every word printed on page one, it was a go-ahead. It didn't hurt matters that Vance and Crowther went back many years.

Even better, Vance and Holmes arranged to play the tapes for Kennedy the next day. Kennedy, Crowther, *Post* Managing Editor Kuyk Logan, and City Editor John Boudreaux knew they had bigger bait on the fish line than Yarbrough could imagine. Without detailing the existence of the tapes in the initial story, *The Post* would see Yarbrough cry foul – until it published a follow-up story with the direct quotes and other details from tape recordings made by Rothkopf.

On Saturday, June 25, 1977, *The Houston Post* ran Kennedy's page one story "at the top of the fold" with the headline: **Yarbrough Wanted Witness Killed.** Talk about impact. It went into detail about Yarbrough's legal problems, the Rothkopf revelations without mentioning tape recordings, and the Austin, Travis County, car title forgery. The die was cast. The justice would soon be turning in his robe – and his bar card.

On the following Monday, Vance and Homes traveled to Austin to discuss the matter with Travis County District Attorney Ronnie Earle. Naturally there was lots of publicity surrounding this trip. They discussed the matter in private with Earle suggesting that a joint press conference be held advising the media that John William Rothkopf had made certain admissions about a Texas Supreme Court justice's conduct in Travis County. A grand jury in Austin would soon hear from Mr. Rothkopf.

The impression we wanted to leave with the media – and we achieved this – was that this was just the testimony of a disgruntled former associate. We would present Rothkopf's testimony before a Travis County grand jury for whatever it was worth. It was suggested in that press conference that surely Mr. Justice Yarbrough would be invited to attend and tell his side of the Rothkopf "story."

Yarbrough took the bait. Apparently without even counseling with his lawyers Yarbrough advised District Attorney Earle that he wished to appear and negate "this preposterous story."

Yarbrough made some very foolish press releases and interviews about the absurdity of Rothkopf's story. He said publicly it was just a continuing attempt by the State Bar of Texas to discredit him, and that this too would pass, that there was not a shred of truth to Rothkopf's allegations.

■ ■ ■

On June 28, 1977, Johnny Holmes went before the Travis County Grand

Jury and told them the Rothkopf story about the car title forgery.

Holmes purposely did not tell them the *whole story* about the arrest, tape recordings, and related details. He just told them about what Rothkopf had said about the forgery in Austin and intended to leave it at that. The grand jury was to think that they were just hearing the allegations of a former associate about the Austin event.

Holmes was not going to tell them anything further for the time being. He stuck to his guns: it was a forgery investigation. Ronnie Earle was present in the grand jury room and, much to Holmes' dismay, interrupted the Harris County Special Crimes chief and told them the whole story. This would be significant later.

Holmes was against spilling all the prosecutorial beans at this time. He thought he made this clear to Ronnie Earle. Yet, for some reason known only to Earle, he related the whole matter to the grand jurors.

Prosecutors called Rothkopf to testify about the meetings and the car title forgery. I was called to testify about the surveillance and the various tapes.

This set an important stage. Here came the judge – not Garth Bates; this time it was Donald B. Yarbrough. They treated the justice with respect. He was told about the nature of the investigation, that the grand jury was looking into an alleged forgery about which Rothkopf testified. It allegedly happened at the Austin Motel on May 16, 1977.

Yarbrough, the witness, was allowed to proceed in a narrative presentation, only interrupted by Holmes to ask specific questions. Holmes knew that in a perjury matter that care must be exercised not to allow the witness an out. When he lies, move on to another subject. Don't allow the witness a chance to reconsider, and say, "I don't recall" or "It is my best recollection" or equivocating words of this nature.

Accordingly, Holmes had previously advised the grand jury not to ask him any questions. He told them any questions that they wanted answered must be in writing and submitted to him. He then would ask them if he felt they were appropriate.

Just as everyone suspected would happen, Yarbrough did a classic job of lying. He maintained true to form and true to the public image that he had allowed the news media to formulate. He said that he did not meet with Rothkopf, did not know where he had been, and that Rothkopf's reappearance was a complete surprise. He said that Rothkopf's story was completely false, totally absurd. Holmes asked the carefully prepared specific question: "Did you meet with John William Rothkopf in Travis County, Texas, on May 16, 1977?"

When leaving the Travis County Courthouse after our testimony, the Dog had picked up a paper bag that had contained the lunch of a Travis County ADA, who was eating in the waiting room for the grand jury witnesses. The Dog placed the bag over his head to conceal his identity from newspaper photographers without any suggestion from me, Blaylock, or his attorney. The video of his leaving was the opening for KPRC news for a number of years. Every major newspaper in Texas had the photo on their front page the next day.

The answer was as expected. The grand jury did not return indictments for Forgery and Perjury that day. The reason was that they had not been prepared since we did not know the exact wording that the perjury indictment would take. Also, the Travis County district attorney's first assistant, Phil Nelson, was very meticulous about how the indictment was to be worded and wanted to do some research.

Holmes became concerned that Yarbrough might hear of the tapes and ask to reappear before the grand jury to recant his story.

Vance had returned to Houston that same Monday and had not stayed for the grand jury presentation. He left Holmes to handle it. Johnny ended up staying all week. The two communicated by telephone daily, sometimes talking several times a day.

The evening after the grand jury witnesses were heard, Holmes decided to call Vance and suggest that he have a press conference and reveal that there were tapes of the Rothkopf/Yarbrough meetings. The reason for this was to advise publicly that there existed corroboration of Rothkopf's allegations and thereby cut off Yarbrough from recanting his previous perjured testimony. Under state law, if he had recanted prior to these circumstances, changing it would be a defense to perjury.

Publicizing the tapes would obviously show a change of circumstance and even if he came back before the grand jury and told the truth he would be nevertheless a criminal perjurer.

Remember, Kennedy had already listened to each of the tapes and heard the now-infamous "Friday the 13th" capital murder quote from the justice. The tapes were not only publicized, but Vance played portions of them the next morning. The press went wild. That evening of the day the tapes were released to the media, Yarbrough called Holmes at his sister's house where he was staying in Austin. It was about two o'clock in the morning. Don Shelby, a Channel 2 (KPRC) newsman, had gone over to Yarbrough's house and talked to him into the night. Yarbrough told Shelby that he wanted to talk to Holmes and sought Shelby's help.

Shelby contacted DA Intake, who in turn, called Holmes' Houston residence. His wife, Diane, told them that Johnny was staying at his sister's house in Austin. Intake called Holmes to ascertain if he would take a call from Yarbrough.

Yes, was the answer.

Yarbrough talked to Holmes for a few minutes, admitting that he had lied, and said that he wanted to go back before the grand jury and tell the truth. Holmes advised him that he would communicate that to the foreman of the grand jury, also named Kemp, but was not related to the target of Yarbrough's hit-man intentions. Holmes told him that it would be up to foreman Kemp as to whether or not they would hear from him again.

Yarbrough said that he was traveling to Austin later and provided Holmes a number where he could be reached. This later became unnecessary because Yarbrough talked to his lawyers and took their advice not to go back in front of them.

As it developed, our decision to release the tapes was a wise one.

On July 2, 1977, Tom Kennedy wrote a front-page story in *The Post* about me titled, "Investigator found, then hid the 'Dog.' " As I said, he also had timely published a detailed story about the tapes – the one he had carefully crafted after hearing them exclusively, according to his agreement with Vance and Holmes. This story effectively eliminated any hopes Yarbrough ever had of suing *The Post* for libel.

There always seems to be extra drama in cases like this one. The next day my four-year-old son Kyle was missing. We all assumed that Yarbrough might have had something to do with it. Holmes called HPD and DPS and got their helicopters up within minutes. They flew over my neighborhood looking for Kyle. I was worried to death. About an hour later, my stepdad, Jim Haymon, called me, and said he found Kyle walking under Interstate 45 and West Gulfbank Road.

I was relieved but wondered how in the world did he get that far by walking.

After the forgery and aggravated perjury indictments were returned, the State Legislature began in earnest to oust Yarbrough. They were in a special session at the time, the Governor having called them back to Austin to consider special matters of interest and concern. Legislators introduced a resolution of address in both the House and Senate. They set the matter for presentation before a joint Senate-House committee. We were happy to cooperate fully with their presentation. Vance and Holmes traveled to Austin to provide assistance.

On the first meeting scheduled for Austin, I'd overslept because of working an extra job late into the night. The office kept calling me on my police radio asking me where I was. I was driving the old green county clunker, which had a bent frame and would shimmy when you got over seventy-five miles per hour. I did learn that once I went faster that the car would smooth out. I drove one hundred MPH for a long way along the route to Austin.

Once there, I found it to be a circus atmosphere. Vance introduced me to a couple of state senators and promptly left in order to go play tennis with his son, who was a student at the University of Texas. It really didn't bother me because Johnny and I knew more about the case than anyone else, including the Harris County DA.

The senators began asking me questions about the case. I answered all of them but could tell that none of these legislators knew much about the case or the facts. One of them even asked me if I kept the evidence in the case in the trunk of my car. *I'm thinking: Are you nuts?* He said that he used to be a Texas highway patrolman and that he kept any evidence in the trunk of his state patrol car. I advised him that we had a large safe where we kept our evidence and only a few of us had the combination. I was one of them.

The committee met several times. I had to set up their sound system in order to play the audio tapes.

A week before going to Austin, Rothkopf and I were supposed to go fishing in Galveston with Galveston County Criminal District Attorney Mike Guarino, and his chief investigator, Felix Mares. I'd taken Bill fishing on several occasions in Matagorda. We'd become pretty good friends since I'd usually see him every day. I'd pick him up every morning and take him to the office and then back home after work. If I didn't see him, we'd talk on the phone.

Rothkopf decided that he didn't want to go to Galveston, so I went fishing without him. Mike, Felix, and I went out in a boat and I lost the largest flounder that I've ever seen because I didn't wait for someone to net the fish.

After fishing we went to the home of a Galveston County assistant DA for dinner. While there, I decided to call Rothkopf and tell him about the big fish that got away. While talking to him on the phone, I heard him gasp and fall to the ground. The sad thing was that I didn't remember his address. I called Johnny Holmes at home and told him what happened and that we needed to get an ambulance to his house *now*.

I did tell him that I could direct someone there. He called my partner, Bobby Blaylock, on his other phone and advised him of what was happening and for him to get in his county car. Johnny told him over the police radio to go to the intersection of Silber Road and Interstate 10 (the Katy Freeway) to meet the ambulance. Once the ambulance got there, I directed Johnny on how to get to his apartment located near the intersection of Silber and Westview Drive. Once they arrived, they found him lying on the kitchen floor barely alive. They learned that he had a collapsed lung. They got him to a hospital, and he survived.

A few days later, the sergeant at arms of the Texas House served me a subpoena to appear at the Joint Special Session of the Texas Senate and House on July 15, 1977. Johnny told me later that I was the first and only peace officer in the State of Texas to ever be subpoenaed in a joint session.

Later, the sergeant at arms asked me for Rothkopf's address. He needed it in order to subpoena him to appear before the joint committee. I started laughing.

"What's so funny?" the man asked.

"Besides his daughter," I told him, "I'm the only person in the world that knows where he is located."

He told me in a threatening manner that the Texas Rangers could find him.

"Good luck with that."

"We'll see."

I laughed again and he got pissed off.

Several days later, he approached me in a very friendly manner and asked if I could serve Rothkopf for him. I said sure and they flew me to Houston Hobby Airport on the DPS helicopter.

One of my buddies from the DA's office met me at the airport, while the helicopter waited, and took me to the hospital. I spent some time telling Rothkopf about the circus that he was missing, and we just laughed.

Returning to Austin, they flew me over the nudist camp located in Boling, which was a waste of time because no one was there.

A few days later, Yarbrough's attorney, Waggoner Carr, filed a motion for continuance, which was overruled, and Yarbrough sent a letter of resignation to the Governor of Texas. The House and Senate remained in session until Governor Dolph Briscoe received the resignation and acted upon it, making Justice Yarbrough a private citizen again. The joint resolution was no longer necessary.

Next it was the State Bar's turn. Armed with the newly available evidence, they set about with a renewed vengeance to get the case set for trial. Again, at the eleventh hour, Yarbrough surrendered his law license, making the historic disbarment lawsuit totally moot.

There was much disagreement about this and there were many members of the bar who wanted to move forward with the suit even though Yarbrough resigned his license. Their concern was that at some time in the future the former justice might be able to get his license back. The State Bar contended that unless it actually proceeded to litigate the issue and succeeded in getting a disbarment by the Texas Supreme Court, that he could get his license back.

The issue was never litigated. Judge Bert Tunks dismissed the cause on the grounds it was now moot.

Thus, the only item remaining was the criminal suit which was pending in Travis County for forgery and aggravated perjury.

Our office began preparations to assist the Travis County district attorney in the preparation of the case. It was decided that Vance would participate in the trial, although Holmes personally preferred that our office, with Ronnie Earle's consent, would actually tackle the monster. There was still lots to do and many loose ends to tie down. We still wanted to know how Yarbrough got the Alabama plates and just who this Billy Ray Waller was.

Throughout the fall of 1977, during two resets of the case in Austin, we were picking up these loose ends. It appeared that the case would actually be tried in January 1978.

Shortly before trial I was successful in locating the Billy Ray Waller in question. We interviewed him about the automobile transaction and how Yarbrough could have gotten his driver's license to make the title transfer on the car Rothkopf was driving. Waller claimed to know nothing about it, telling us he did not know, nor had he ever met, Don Yarbrough.

Frankly, we believed him. That is one of the unanswered questions in the case: How did Yarbrough get Waller's driver's license to make this transfer? It is still an unanswered question. DA investigators don't like unanswered questions.

Waller was used as a witness in the trial and his testimony was devastating. So much so, coupled with all of the other overwhelming evidence, that after the close of the presentation of the evidence Waggoner Carr did not even argue the case before the jury.

The defense was: yes, he perjured himself; however, he did not perjure himself on a material matter in that what he perjured himself on would not have affected the course or outcome of the grand jury's decision.

This is the point that Holmes had believed was very nearly a fatal mistake. If the defense's argument was valid, Yarbrough was only guilty of misdemeanor perjury, not aggravated perjury, a felony.

Ronnie Earle should not have told the grand jury the whole story until after Yarbrough testified. That way there would have been no question that his lies would have affected the "course and outcome of the grand jury's deliberations."

The defense's position was that since the grand jury knew about the tapes before Yarbrough testified, the fact that he lied about what occurred could have in no way affected the outcome of their decision. A very clever argument. This was overruled at the trial court level but would be a contention on appeal.

On January 26, 1978, a jury found Yarbrough guilty of forgery and aggravated perjury and sentenced him to five years in the Texas Department of Corrections.

When Tom Kennedy and I were leaving the courthouse after the trial, we stopped by to tell Phil Nelson and Ronnie Earle goodbye and good luck. Earle, the district attorney looked at us sheepishly, smiled and asked, "Wonder whatever happened to ol' Pete?"

Kennedy and I just looked at each other in awe because they didn't remember that Pete was a fictitious person. When we got outside, we had a big-assed laugh. We still laugh about it, if you want to know the truth.

The moral of the Yarbrough (Yankee) story is that the system works. There are devices, checks and balances, and the good ole common sense of investigative techniques that work to ensure the continuation of our system of justice – in this case *for* a Supreme Court justice.

No person is above the law. Not the President of the United States, not a judge, and certainly not a Justice on the Texas Supreme Court. As long as there are dedicated public officials willing to work faithfully to ensure that the rule of law prevails, we will always enjoy our free, democratic way of life.

Yarbrough, out on bond while his case was being appealed, met with Houston doctor, Howard Siegler, about attending medical school in Grenada. Yarbrough later jumped bond and took his family to Grenada, so he could attend medical school there. We later learned that he failed his biology course. So went "Dr. Yarbrough."

U. S. marshals arrested him while he and his family were on a cruise out of Grenada to the island of St. Vincent on St. Patrick's Day in 1983. He served nineteen uneventful months in the Texas Department of Corrections. Has Yankee bit the dust?

Nagra recorder

Don Yarbrough

Yankee subpoena

*Jim Beauchamp, me,
Bill Rothkopf (incognito),
and Bobby Blaylock
exiting the Travis County
courthouse*

Me and Billy Ray Waller

Carol Vance memo of appreciation

CHAPTER 28

YANKEE RETURNS

"Yeah, I'd like to kill the people
who were responsible for putting me behind bars."

— Former Texas Supreme Court Justice Donald B. Yarbrough
to a DPS Undercover Agent

On February 6, 1985, ex-prison inmate Donald B. Yarbrough was planning his Valentine presents. He told undercover DPS Narcotics Agent David Hammons, aka "Paul Herman Burer," at the Denny's on Crosstimbers and the North Freeway his list of priorities.

Any criminal intent involving Yarbrough, aka "Yankee," was surely to entail the intervention of the Special Crimes Bureau in Yankee's hometown. In November 1984, our office received a copy of a letter from the Travis County District Attorney's Office. The author of the letter was Yarbrough's former cellmate and co-worker in the prison laundry room at the Walls Unit. His name: Bola Allen.

Many of the law enforcement officials, witnesses against him, and even several reporters joked about Yarbrough being after them with a violent vengeance. Until this letter, these were only jokes.

Allen's hand-written letter stated that Yarbrough had "plans and strong determination to do away with certain individuals connected with his downfall."

Allen urged against retaliation; he wrote that Yarbrough had made up his mind. "That speculation was further affirmed by the first letter he wrote to me which I received yesterday," Allen said in his letter to the DA in Austin. He promised to provide "details" in any subsequent investigation, writing, "I feel an urgent need to write you to exonerate myself, and most importantly, save the lives of innocent people."

The question became: *Who would Yarbrough come after first?*

Johnny Holmes, now the Harris County district attorney, informed all possible targets. Johnny called me when he got a copy of the letter and asked me to come to his office to discuss the matter. I knew that I was on the list, since I'm the man whose arrest of Bill Rothkopf was the turning point in Yarbrough's political career and his entire life for that matter. I also testified during his trial about all the recordings that I made and all the meetings that I witnessed.

Among those were KPRC (Channel 2) reporter Don Shelby – who later became an investigative reporter and television news anchor in Minnesota.

Also, on the "supposed list" were Henry Oncken – who graduated from being Holmes' first assistant to a brief service as a state district court judge – and former Victoria banker Bill Kemp, the man whose damaging state grand jury testimony in the mid-1970s incurred Yarbrough's wrath. Yarbrough wanted Kemp assassinated but never "made the down payment" necessary to charge him with solicitation of capital murder.

Tom Kennedy was also on that list because of all the stories that he'd written in *The Houston Post* during the summer of 1977. His stories provided the exclusive initial details of Yarbrough's plot to have Kemp killed. *The Post* nominated Kennedy for the Pulitzer Prize for these stories. Post Managing Editor Kuyk Logan, concerned for Kennedy's safety and that of his wife, Glenda, offered to quarter the reporter and his wife in a Galleria area hotel. Yarbrough's penchant for use of violence was well known. Kennedy found a threatening note on yellow legal paper tacked to the front door of his home. The reporter, however, subscribed to Holmes' theory about Yarbrough and he and Glenda stayed at home. The theory: "I know a coward when I see one. Judge Yarbrough is a coward." Not only that, Kennedy hadn't yet made any other enemies from his courthouse reporting.

Bill Rothkopf, aka "the Dog," was the logical choice to be at the top of Yarbrough's new hit list. No person's testimony was more damaging in the criminal case against the former Texas Supreme Court justice. But Rothkopf died in April 1984.

The conclusion was that Holmes might be Number 1. A licensed airplane pilot, he was never one to take undue risk. He began to wear a bullet-proof vest. He only wore it for a short period of time because it was too hot and heavy. He took it off while in his office, hanging it on a nearby hall tree, even though Kennedy, joking, asked to borrow it.

Bola Allen then held, and probably still holds today, the record for most money stolen by writing hot checks in Harris County. He stole more than $1 million in this manner.

Holmes told me to come up with a plan and keep him posted. I knew that Yarbrough was very vindictive but told Holmes that I didn't think he had the "cojones" to actually follow through with such a plot. Yes, I also subscribed to the coward theory, and I had "evidence." After all, after listening to him in all his conversations I came to the conclusion that he was nothing more than just a big "bullshitter," but I knew at the same time that you can't just take any chances. I told Holmes, "the first thing I need to do is meet with Bola Allen and hear what he has to say and we'll go from there."

I'd learned that Yarbrough was paroled on November 2, 1984. Days later I went to the Walls Unit of the Texas Department of Corrections and met with Warden Joe Lewis and Captain John Gilbert to advise them of my investigation. We were extremely concerned for the safety of those of us who were involved in the disbarment and criminal conviction of ex-Justice Yarbrough. Even a coward gets lucky.

These prison officials agreed to help us by doing whatever was needed to thwart these alleged assassination efforts. I told them that I would need access in person and by phone with Bola Allen. They agreed and gave me their phone numbers and said to call whenever I needed to speak with Bola.

I met him on this same occasion. They brought Bola down to an empty office that I could use and interviewed him about the details of his letter. When I finally met him, I was surprised to see how short he was. Even though he was from Nigeria, he spoke very good English. Bola told me that he and Yarbrough had been cell mates for quite a while and they also worked in the prison laundry together.

He further stated that Yarbrough spent a lot of time talking about getting even with some people that he felt were responsible for his demise.

Bola said that he had Yarbrough's new address. He was instructed to continue communicating with Yarbrough about helping him find "a hit man."

Over the next few months, via meetings and phone calls, we came up with a plan to introduce a hit man to Yarbrough. Bola was very helpful and a pretty nice guy. Just don't take a check from him.

On February 6, 1985, Yarbrough met with a prospective hit man. In reality he was meeting with a DPS undercover narcotics agent, David Hammonds. Hammonds used an alias, Paul Herman Burer. The two met at the Denny's on the North Freeway, aka Interstate 45. Yarbrough told him that he wanted him to kill some people from the DA's office – Holmes, Oncken, and Rodgers.

"That's gonna be pretty expensive," Hammonds/Burer said in a professional tone.

"It might take me a few years to raise the money," the murder solicitor said.

"That won't work for me."

Neither gave up on a possible plan. They met a few more times at Denny's, but – like the Bill Kemp murder plot – nothing materialized. It was for the same reason both times – lack of capital.

The next substantial meeting was held at the Airport Hilton on April 13, 1985, where Yarbrough met with one of our investigators who was posing as a hit man.

Yarbrough told him that at that time he's more interested in laundering money because if someone got killed, authorities would know that he'd be held responsible. I was in the adjoining room and had placed a video camera and mic in the AC vent so I could tape every word of the meeting.

We had so many meetings there that when we quit using the room as a de facto recording studio, I forgot and left the wires right there in the air conditioning vent. I had made it a practice to leave them there so I'd only have to take a camera and mic for any future meetings. I bet they're still there today.

After the last meeting, I met with the Criminal Division of the Houston Internal Revenue Service. I advised agents there of my investigation. I was later sworn in as a special deputy U. S. marshal in order to be a member of the new DEA/IRS money-laundering task force. Yarbrough was their first target.

At one meeting between Yarbrough and a "banker" – actually a "wired" IRS agent – Yarbrough commented on my surveillance van parked at the front door of the bank. He told the agent that he didn't like the "looks" of the vehicle since such undercover tactics were what got him in trouble the first time. He went so far as to look in the van where I was stationed. I could hear him because the agent was wired. I realized that my briefcase was laying on the passenger front seat with my laminated business card attached.

Yarbrough looked through the front windows to see if he could spot any evidence of undercover operations, all the while talking to the agent/banker. I thought to myself: *I'm a real dumb ass – I just blew the case because of doing something so stupid as to leave my damn business card in plain sight.*

For some unknown reason, Yarbrough missed seeing it. We were still in business!

After a series of complex meetings with undercover IRS agents and other undercover law enforcement officers – which endured almost over a year – Assistant U. S. Attorney, John Lenoir, who was part of our task force involving Yarbrough, decided that we had enough evidence to charge him with money laundering.

On April Fool's Day, our last staged meeting took place at the Hyatt Regency Downtown, where Yarbrough thought – in his own mind, at least – that the laundering plan involving $1 million was supposed to take place. But we had no cash – only a pair of handcuffs!

The agents gave me the honor of making the arrest since I brought them the case. After this meeting Yarbrough went into the men's room, which was located near one of the entry doors of the hotel. He parked himself at a urinal. I followed him in and stood next to him. We were both doing our business when I spoke up.

"Hey Don, how's it going?"

The look on his face when he saw that it was – perhaps – his major nemesis – he was surprised and dismayed. I was just glad he didn't turn toward my new Dockers while he was peeing, but I guess I could've done the same to him.

"Bad news, Don. You're under arrest – again." We then took him to our Fugitive Apprehension Unit, where we fingerprinted and photographed him. Then it was off to the Harris County Jail, where federal arrestees were taken at that time.

At Yarbrough's bond hearing the next day in U. S. Magistrate Karen Brown's court, the judge denied bond to the defendant. Assistant U. S. Attorney Lenoir told Judge Brown that Yarbrough "is an extreme flight risk and a danger to the community." Lenoir pointed out that the ex-justice had the means to alter his identity and had access to foreign bank accounts.

Evidence seized at his home included two birth certificates in different names and information about obtaining a passport in these names. Agents also seized records showing that he had bank accounts in the Cayman Islands, as well as Grenada, where he lived as a fugitive for five years before his 1983 arrest.

I then testified that Yarbrough willingly offered to launder money for undercover agents posing as large-scale cocaine dealers. I said Yarbrough told investigators that he wanted to get even with the people who were responsible for his 1978 conviction for forgery and perjury.

I added that Yarbrough talked to undercover agents about finding a hit man but decided to wait until his parole had ended before pursuing the matter. It was then that he decided to get into the money-laundering scheme.

Yarbrough pled guilty to money laundering and was sentenced to the remainder of his parole years that he owed Texas in the Federal Correctional Institution in Texarkana, Texas. He was released on March 8, 1990.

Yarbrough ended up running a medical billing collection company in Orlando, Florida. He died on August 12, 2017 at age seventy-six. The lead of his published obituary said he was the youngest man to ever be elected to the Texas Supreme Court. It made no mention of his prison record as well as his consistent inclination toward criminal activities. And there certainly was no mention of his old Special Crimes nickname – Yankee.

Bola Allen was discharged from TDC on October 16, 1996 and deported – without a checkbook – back to his native country of Nigeria.

Don Yarbrough 1986 arrest

Phony TDL of DPS Officer

Tom Kennedy, Pulitzer Prize nominated investigative reporter and columnist for The Houston Post

Kenny Rodgers, Chief Investigator ID
March 1996

CHAPTER 29

MY RETIREMENT

After thirty years of service in law enforcement I decided that I'd had enough. On my first day of retirement – July 31, 2001 – right after the noon hour, my dog Clarence and my wife's dog Shadow got into one hell of a fight. I thought Shadow was going to kill Clarence. He had him in his jaws and would not let go. I was "dead asleep" when this happened. So, me being the "peace maker" that I am and due to the fact that I just spent about $625 on Clarence's vet bill, I tried to break up the dogfight.

Clarence, named in memory of my bookmaking grandpa, was a small black and gray Australian cattle dog I found wandering the beach in Matagorda. Shadow was a very large black lab that my wife, Debbie, picked up trying to cross a busy intersection in west Houston.

Both dogs, having been lost and abandoned, really appreciated the fact that we'd found them. They loved us and we loved them. We had bonded with the dogs. Both were "alpha" dogs so there was always tension between the two of them.

Trying to break up their fight was one big mistake. After about ten bites on both my arms and hands, and even my chest and neck, I finally got them apart. It looked like a murder scene. The only blood was mine. I was the injured party. The dogs were injury-free. I was bleeding like a stuck pig. There was blood all over the townhouse.

The next day I went to my doctor. Yep, doctors are always out of town when you really need them. I had to see the "other doctor." She looked fourteen years old and still had teenage acne on her face. She told me that she did not know what to do. Great! She only knew that I needed a tetanus shot. *No shit, Sherlock!*

I became more pissed at myself because Harris County was giving free shots to county employees. I hadn't taken advantage of the free pre-retirement shot. I really didn't relish the idea of Karl the maintenance man sticking a needle in my arm.

Well, guess what? There was a back order for tetanus shots.

Dr. Acne-face just didn't know what to do. She actually went to her how-to book. When she found out that I was allergic to penicillin, she was really in a quandary. I had to tell Ms. Clearasil what to prescribe me. Hell, she should have paid *me* the co-pay. I asked the nurse assistant to find out from this doctor what medicine to put on the wounds when I was paying the bill. And guess what? "I really don't know," she said. I asked the nurse when she had to start junior high again and she just laughed.

I went to the pharmacy where my buddy Dan Pursley worked the over-night as a security guard to get my prescription filled. Surely my first day of retirement would pick up. This buddy said they were pretty sharp at this place. In hindsight, I was stupid for listening to him. I asked the pharmacist what medication I should use to treat the wounds. While I was standing under the window that said CONSULTING, she hemmed and hawed and said, "Uhm, uhm, I really don't know."

I suggested Neosporin and this consultant on the Overnight Shift replied, "Yes, that would be good," but that I needed to see a doctor and get a tetanus shot. *No shit, Sherlock!*

I wanted to say that but restrained myself for the second time that night.

I wanted to tell her that for $5, I'd bring her a small rat, and have it chew off the nasty little wart she had on her left cheek. Incidents like this one make you mean. You have to restrain yourself. I thought I was doing a good job.

At that moment I'm thinking to myself that here it is on my first day of retirement and I'm going to die in an all-night Walgreens in Montrose. People are going to think that I died from AIDS when my death came, only because I didn't get the free shot.

I returned to my blood-spattered townhouse to try and find someone in this great Bayou City who had tetanus shots available. I finally got in touch with the City of Houston Health Clinic and learned that they had it but were closed for the day. I asked the woman on duty to find out if I could wait until the morning for the shot. She referred me to Animal Control. At least she didn't say she didn't know. I decided that who would know more about dog bites than a vet?

So I up and called the vet, the same individual who had my $650 check to pay Clarence's bill. He told me he was off that day – probably cashing my check and spending the money. I asked to speak to the other vet and told the receptionist what the problem was. She had me hold the line. Finally she returned to our connection and said the vet on duty suggested I call a medical doctor. I told her that I had spent a great deal of money in her clinic and just wanted to know if I could wait another day to get the shot.

The young woman put me on terminal hold again. She finally came back and advised me that if both dogs had their shots then they should be okay. I told her that I was the one with the bites – *not* the dogs.

By now I'm feeling like the guy who called 911 after he ran over the deer and put it in his car. The deer wakes up and bites him in the neck. The guy stops the car and a dog tries to take the deer away from him.

I think you know how the rest of the story goes. Anyway, by now I'm very frustrated and told her thanks anyway.

I called my private investigator buddy, P. M. Clinton, who knows a lot of doctors. He had his son, Posey, call Dr. Sam Seigler for me. Posey then called me back and said, "Go see him right now; he's waiting for you." I called to find out where his office was and learned that he doesn't have any tetanus shots anyway.

There I sat on my first day of retirement, still bloody, and trying to get a tetanus shot that nobody had.

So instead, I took the only "shot" I knew was available – a shot of vodka. I didn't become rabid and, yes, lived to tell you this story.

Early the next day I drove to the closest City of Houston Health Clinic in order to get a tetanus shot and saw that there were no cars in the parking lot. I was thinking: *All right! I'll be outa here in minutes.*

I walked into the lobby and saw more than one hundred illegal immigrants with their kids waiting to get their shots. I got out of there about five and a half hours later.

■ ■ ■

A few months later the Criminal Investigators Association had a retirement party for me at a meeting hall on Seamist near West 11th Street at the edge of the Heights.

It was an awesome party. People came up to me and told me that it was the best retirement party that they'd ever been to.

Another buddy, investigator Sonny Dollar, put on a skit about me when I ran for constable in Harris County Precinct 4 earlier that year. He'd dressed up in a constable's uniform and looked like my opponent, who resembled Adolf Hitler. Everybody laughed their asses off.

The food was great and almost all of my family and friends were there. It left me with some very good memories.

Investigator Pat Smith, whom my kids called Uncle Buck because he used to babysit them when they were younger, did most of the work putting the party together, along with another fellow investigator, Joe Vara.

Chuck Rosenthal, the newly elected district attorney, succeeding Johnny Holmes, read my first "attaboy" memo from my personnel file. It was about me being called "a little Bill Hubbell," which was an honor to me, but probably not to others. Hubbell was an early mentor and himself a great investigator. I later mentioned the memo at Hubbell's funeral when I gave one of the eulogies. I told his family that it was an honor to be compared to such a man. I had many "attaboy" memos and letters, but Hubbell's meant the most to me.

When I spoke, I said, "As I look around this room, I have a *story* about every one of you guys."

I saw Jack Frels, then a federal prosecutor, and Don "Choo Choo" Stricklin, a state district court judge, run for cover in the back of the room. I don't remember much about what I said at that time, except that I loved my job and would miss it terribly.

One of the most important things that I forgot to mention was my administrative assistant, Candy Roch, while I was the chief investigator. I realized after my speech that I'd hurt her feelings, which really made me feel bad. I really got pissed at myself. As my administrative assistant, Candy always "had my back" and did such a great job. I know I mentioned her in a previous chapter, but she deserves to be mentioned again – as I'm sitting here.

I was a terrible speaker. Some people respond from the heart at times like this. I didn't. I learned a few years later that I could really give a great speech or tell a story if I was sitting down – just like I was when I wrote this memoir. For some unknown reason, while standing, I'd become nervous. I lost my cool and froze up on this special occasion.

While sitting I could rattle off some good bullshit. Too bad I couldn't give speeches sitting down when I was running for district clerk and constable. I might have had the bad luck to win. But, then, I might have many other dog day stories to tell.

Janie Vara, Amy Smith, and Darlene Brown.

Sonny Dollar as Hon Rickman

Clarence, Me, Debbie, and Shadow

DA Investigator
Cassandra Leach Woods

KENNY RODGERS

Kenny Rodgers...let me see
What has Kenny meant to me?
He'll call you out...he has no shame
He'll laugh at you...and call you names
Ten seconds after he's chewed you out
He'll wonder what your attitude's about
When he's done his job
which may include chewing your ass
There's no grudge, no animosity...
"That shit's in the past"
He's right back to where he's always been
Knowledgeable, Obnoxious, and being a Friend

Poem written by Cassandra Leach-Woods and presented to me
at my retirement party.

CHAPTER 30

THE BLACK WIDOW RETURNS!

"Do you know who I am? Google me!"
— Catherine Mehaffey Shelton to one of her adversaries

To the surprise of no one in Houston law enforcement and prosecution, Catherine Mehaffey, aka the Black Widow, became implicated in another shooting, this one in the Dallas metropolitan area. It was a deadly one.

Almost a decade after the shooting of Gary Taylor and the mysterious death of Dr. George Tedesco, Mehaffey married a gun dealer, Clint Shelton, and became known as Catherine Shelton. Mr. Shelton was at least ten years younger than the missus. Later, informed sources would tell reporter Howard Swindell of the *Dallas Morning News* that Mrs. Shelton treated Clint more like a son than a husband. Heck, she even took his car away as punishment on at least one occasion, according to Swindle's sources.

But in the latest shooting episode, the targets were a former employee of the law firm, Marisa Hierro, and her husband, Michael. The attacker's weapon of choice was a sawed-off 12-gauge shotgun. Part of Marisa's right arm was shot off, but she survived and implicated Mr. and Mrs. Shelton as the respective shooter and antagonist at the scene. She identified her former boss by the blonde hair sticking out from under a mask, as well as her well-manicured fingernails. She also heard her order her husband to finish the job by shooting Marisa one more time. He said he had already shot her and never pulled the trigger again. Michael later died at Baylor Medical Center in Dallas. Mr. Shelton was charged with and convicted of the crime.

As of this writing, he is serving life in the Texas Department of Criminal Justice. Despite efforts by investigators from Rowlett, a Dallas suburb where the Hierros resided, Shelton has refused to implicate his wife. Of course, the law says your spouse can't be compelled to testify against you, especially in a murder case, although he could willingly testify. He could but he won't – as I write this. I never ascertained if he knew of the loyalty of Mrs. Shelton, now in her early seventies, who at one point at a 2015 memorial service of a retired Houston police sergeant claimed to be his grieving fiancée.

I've tried to hit the high points of a low life whom many believe has gotten away with more than one or two murders. The details have been doggedly documented on *48 Hours* as well as a cable television production, *Your Worst Nightmare – The Black Widow Episode.* Howard Swindell's excellent three-part series in the *Dallas Morning News* in 2002 and an in-depth *Houston Press* report by Rose Farley and George Flynn two years earlier both shed light on this intriguing subject. Flynn, by the way, was Taylor's best friend right up until the day he died in 2013. He was a well-respected *Houston Post* reporter and editor who covered the courthouse back in what we now call the golden years of the seventies and eighties newspaper journalism. And as for the other Google listings of Catherine Mehaffey Shelton, don't forget Taylor's memoir, *Luggage by Kroger.*

Despite the vast details each of these reporters uncovered and published, the Black Widow is still out there! There's no stopping her. I discovered she had returned to her old web-weaving stomping ground known as the Bayou City. The producers of the aforementioned "Black Widow" cable episode told me to let them know when I learned Mehaffey/Shelton's latest address.

I was alarmed and concerned when I tracked her down residing in a townhouse development in Spring Branch, a west Houston suburb. This doesn't mean that I knocked on her front door and asked her, "Hey, what's happening?" Nobody likes being around Mehaffey. Marisa Hierro relocated from the Metroplex and refuses to provide her address to anyone but trusted police investigators. Yeah, the old timers who have known the Black Widow for more than forty years still call her "Mehaffey" instead of the more recent reference of "Shelton." I found that many residents of her heavily occupied townhouse development are flat afraid of her or, as one of them put it, "everybody's scared shitless." They got her number: fiery-tempered, threatening, and often scary and physically violent. In one confrontation with a woman and her mother, Mehaffey stared them down and asked the pointed question, "Do you know who I am? Google me!"

To Google Catherine Mehaffey Shelton results in a rather long read and viewing session. As if that wasn't enough, my updated investigation showed she's up to her old tricks. I also learned that she has modified her modus operandi. Now legally known as Catherine Shelton, "a retired attorney" as opposed to a disbarred lawyer/convicted felon named Mehaffey, whose real age would be seventy-two in 2020, modified her web-weaving to entrap vulnerable men in their advanced years. Her goals remained the same – money and property. And they became more advanced – money laundering and rewriting wills in order to accumulate cash and property.

The Black Widow had become "the Queen of Deception" and/or "the Predator of the Weak."

One target was a fellow townhouse resident. Gerhard Neils was the perfect man in the crosshairs. In his mid-eighties in the summer of 2018, this aging gentleman was a retired machinist very open about the fact he trusted God and His Word as guidance in every aspect of his life. On the wall in his modest abode hangs a picture of Jesus Christ, the son of God, the solidified bedrock of Christianity. In fact, he was a refugee from Nazi Germany with only four years of formal education. In Germany, he did an apprenticeship as a blacksmith.

In his later years he experienced a debilitating stroke and suffered from arthritis. Neils later expressed his thoughts that Mehaffey tried to take advantage of these medical conditions to yell at him, putting pressure on his weak heart, perhaps causing a fatal heart attack or stroke.

Mehaffey learned Gerhard's weaknesses and took advantage of them, primarily that his beliefs required him to help those in greatest need, as Jesus did. Oh, goodness, his neighbor Catherine was a poor retired lawyer who needed more security in her senior years. She also needed a permanent home that she owned because she knew, with her criminal and credit record, she couldn't rent an apartment or house.

The "poor woman in need" persuaded this kind gentleman to take out a mortgage on a three-bedroom townhouse unit Mehaffey would then occupy as his tenant. She would furnish a down payment and make monthly mortgage payments in addition to the civic association's maintenance fees and the annual property taxes. She admitted that her credit wasn't any good and that the Internal Revenue Service "had made some mistakes," putting her in tax troubles that would take a few months to settle. Were she to show that she owned property, the government would soon confiscate it in lieu of back taxes.

I keep calling her "Mehaffey" instead of "Shelton." Sorry, it's a habit developed way back when. Although Mehaffey made the down payment and continued providing monthly payments for the mortgage and fees, Mr. Neils was the one actually responsible on the mortgage paperwork.

Soon, Mehaffey picked up her victim, took him to the tax office, and persuaded him to seek a homestead exemption for the property, thereby lessening the tax burden. But wait! Neils didn't live in the townhouse and wasn't eligible for the exemption. Also, it was a rental property, another reason for the denial. A friend reminded Neils that if he went along with Mehaffey's plan, he would be subject to being charged with conspiracy to commit tax fraud.

In this same scheme, Mehaffey claimed to be his common-law wife. We had heard that claim before with Dr. Tedesco and we will hear it again when she becomes "a fiancée" later in this chapter. There was yet another problem. Throughout her law career Mehaffey preferred dealing on a cash-only basis. During his affair with her, Gary Taylor took note of the fact that when she needed money she would go through the books and desk drawers in her apartment. "There would be three or four hundred-dollar bills pressed between the pages of a book," he recalled. "She liked to deal in cash."

Perhaps a year passed, and the friendly tenant turned the tables on the aging Christian. She quit paying rent and maintenance fees, causing the owner to accumulate hundreds of dollars in penalties. She proceeded to "juggle" her funds, using her maintenance dues to pay the mortgage company in order to avoid foreclosure. The aging pensioner couldn't afford the costs, let alone the worries caused by harassment from the management and the mortgage holder.

Two friends confronted him with facts about his tenant. You must realize that the people who have had confrontations with Mehaffey don't want to be quoted for any record that might be used against the Black Widow. We will call one of these close friends Marilyn Moon, which is not her real name. The other friend involved ran NASA's super computer for more than twenty years besides also serving as a math professor at the University of Houston and Rice University. His name is Donald Hackler, a devoted churchman who apparently isn't afraid of Mehaffey or – I would bet – anything else.

Hackler has been fervent in speaking out against her and has worked together with Moon to help Gerhart Neils battle against the "retired lawyer" who still practiced law in her uniquely deceitful manner.

Hackler and Moon learned that Mehaffey had resorted to her old methods of seduction with this divorced man in his eighties. During a visit with him she sat in a provocative manner, revealing that after all these years she still didn't wear any undergarments. Neils wasn't interested.

When Mehaffey was pressed to pay her share of their deal, she refused to move out or agree to sell the property. Thus, the only alternative was to evict the stubborn tenant. She was violating the lease agreement by avoiding her fiduciary responsibilities. Plus, Moon and other residents noted, she was renting rooms to outsiders.

To stop the eviction and put added stress on Neils, Mehaffey got a legal aid attorney and filed a lawsuit in state district court. If she won the case, she would gain ownership of the townhouse while sticking Neils with the full cost of the mortgage.

She cited deceptive trade laws and accused this rather harmless kind soul of cheating her. Mehaffey must have reasoned that Neils couldn't afford a lawyer and she would be in control. She pulled the next legal maneuver – placing the case before a mediator. And get this: Mehaffey claimed poverty and got a lawyer under the auspices of a free legal service.

Neils designated Moon, a non-lawyer, as having his power of attorney solely in all matters relating to the townhouse. It was a wise move. Moon had no fear of the Black Widow.

The case bounced around through the year 2019 until two of us – myself and Tom Kennedy, the one-time *Houston Post* columnist and my book editor – succeeded in hitting up old courthouse sources and getting another free attorney, this one on the side of Moon and Neils.

Mehaffey's attorney dropped out of the case and Mehaffey the plaintiff failed to show for scheduled mediation hearings. Was the Black Widow on the run?

I'm making the point here that once an investigator, *always* an investigator. I may be retired in 2020 but I still believe in arresting, jailing, and convicting the bad guys, and Mehaffey had been getting away with

268 | SPECIAL CRIMES | KENNY RODGERS

murder (murders?) for the better part of four decades.

My further investigation found that she was trying to work her magic on at least two other aging men – a retired Houston police sergeant and a one-hundred-percent disabled Vietnam veteran.

As I write this, her recent record for success may be considered a mixed bag. But what pisses me off is that the Black Widow is still made of Teflon. Law enforcement authorities might get close but they never get the cigar.

The woman has never done any hard time in her life, much to the frustration of many of us who are either retired or currently commissioned law officers. We realize that the Texas criminal justice system isn't likely to put a seventy-two-year-old woman and ex-lawyer in prison.

So, let me tell you what she was getting away with by the middle of 2020. I also will provide you details of her failures.

Besides Gerhard Neils, Mehaffey targeted two older men for their money and property. The first was a retired Houston police sergeant, J.W. "Joe" Lorentz. Retired Houston police officers from Lorentz' era could arrange two different retirement funds: a pension that could be inherited by a spouse and a Deferred Retirement Option Program (DROP), a potentially lucrative amount that could be inherited by a designated individual that is not necessarily a spouse.

Mehaffey first dated Lorentz in 1979 before she started her short but volatile relationship with Gary Taylor. Before shooting him in the back of the head and in the back near his heart, Mehaffey revealed to Taylor that "Officer Joe" had taught her how to use a revolver. To this day the ten-year probated sentence for trying to kill the newspaper reporter/lover is the only violent crime conviction on the Mehaffey record. Hey, you can Google it!

She rekindled the relationship with J.W. in 2014. We can assume that Mehaffey was smart enough to have knowledge of her sweetheart's DROP funding, which amounted to at least $1.3 million.

A retired police captain and one of Lorentz's best friends got to know Mehaffey at one lunch get-together during this period. He was named the temporary administrator of Lorentz's estate and was called into serve when the retired sergeant died of natural causes in 2015.

Mehaffey craftily learned when the retired captain planned to open the door of Lorentz's apartment for the first time in order to start an inventory of the estate. Mehaffey met him at the door. "We have to go in there," she said, urgently. "We don't have much time."

Wait a minute! The best friend wasn't too familiar with the girlfriend's previous record with Tedesco and Taylor, much less the Dallas area shooting antics. But he had a cop's instincts and later told me he suspected she intended to throw down some papers she could later claim to be her "fiancé's will." Fortunately, he refused to allow her inside the apartment. The DROP benefit went to another friend of J.W. Lorentz.

Yet Mehaffey played every angle. She spoke at a memorial service, describing herself as the woman J. W. intended to marry. She failed to tell those gathered, which included J. W.'s colleagues from the Houston Police Department, that oh, by the way, she was still married to a Texas prison inmate serving life for murder. What's a little bigamy when an estate was involved?

Townhouse neighbors told me a framed picture of Lorentz in uniform was on prominent display at Mehaffey's residence. She also told one neighbor that she carried a picture of him next to her driver's license to show any officer if she were stopped for speeding or some other traffic offense. She could plead her case by contending that she was the grieving fiancée of a deceased retired HPD sergeant.

Yet the bottom line was she struck out in her effort to access the estate of her one-time gun tutor.

She fared better with another older male in dire need of a caregiver. Coincidentally, he had the same last name as the Black Widow – Shelton. Sam Shelton earned a Purple Heart in the Vietnam War, suffering disabling wounds that required him to be on oxygen for the rest of his life.

Mehaffey learned his family had money and that he owned a home inside Loop 610 in Houston. Mehaffey took to him and soon gained his confidence. When she learned that the local adult protective services had intentions of putting him in an assisted living facility, she quickly volunteered to open her townhouse to his every need. This happened in late 2016 or early 2017.

Any highly qualified investigator quickly learns that timing becomes Job One when a person wants to commit a crime. At this point Mehaffey faces only one charge – identity theft – in connection with her relationship with Sam Shelton.

Take a look at these circumstances: VA doctors concluded that Shelton "was doing better" by the summer of 2017. His condition was improving – he was breathing easier. Yet Mehaffey told the VA that he didn't need as much of an oxygen supply as before.

The rest of the circumstances show that prior to August 2017 Shelton changed his will, leaving at least twenty-five percent of his total estate to Mehaffey the caregiver. Seventeen days later – in the middle of Houston's dramatic recovery from the floods and fury of devastating Hurricane Harvey – Sam Shelton died.

No one investigated the death as being anything but natural. Besides, there was too much to do in the Harvey aftermath to attract the attention of law enforcement.

Normally, my investigator's instincts tell me, that a woman previously under investigation for two murders and two attempted murders – as well as a suicide and another highly suspicious deadly shooting committed by two former clients working for her – would at least be having to answer some serious questions. It didn't happen, especially in the midst of the "Houston Strong" Harvey recovery.

Funny thing but suddenly Catherine Mehaffey Shelton became a relative of the decedent, Sam Shelton. Two months after his death she actually used his credit rating as part of her effort to lease a house on Houston's westside in a high-demand, single-family neighborhood near the townhouse development. Mehaffey said she was Sam's cousin. The realtor involved was either in on the scheme or didn't mess with detailed questions. But when it became apparent that Mr. Shelton was dead and his credit non-existent, Mehaffey didn't see the lease agreement finalized.

I learned that that was not the only good or bad news for the Black Widow. Shelton's family controlled the deed to his house, meaning Mehaffey could never get her foot in that door. And, even better, HPD investigated the Shelton credit case.

I contacted Melissa McCracken, a fellow Sam Houston State criminal justice graduate who now is a Houston police officer investigating identity theft. On July 22, 2019 charges of Fraudulent Use of Identifying Information, a felony, were filed against Catherine Mehaffey Shelton. The allegations were that she used Sam Shelton's name, date of birth, and bank account number "without complainant's permission." No doubt about that. Sam Shelton was dead!

Police arrested Shelton at her townhouse and escorted her away as the neighbors watched. Among them was a civic association official in her eighties whom Mehaffey had beaten up and sent to the hospital in one of her habitual physical confrontations. Moon told me the attacker punched the slightly built woman "like a man would in a fight with another man." The victim never filed any assault charges since it was a "she-said-she-said." There was no other witness.

Too bad civic associations don't turn down residents based on their violent past. Mehaffey's began early. She earned the reputation on the grade school playground for "coming out and fighting like a man."

She proved it by bullying and beating up this frail little woman who lived down the row from her. The Black Widow punched her like they do in cowboy movies until the poor little woman was taken by ambulance to a hospital. In addition to there being no other witnesses, this victim had another key reason not to make waves – she was afraid of what the "Widow" would do when she wasn't looking. Among her various tactics was stalking.

But, remember, she's made of Teflon. Mehaffey bonded out on the identity theft charge but failed to show up for several plea hearings, always seeming to cite ill health as the reason. Meanwhile, at least one VA official discussed the "timely death of Sam Shelton" with the prosecutor involved, strongly suggesting a more serious sentence than what might have been on the table, not to mention a possible homicide investigation. This official, a retired Marine colonel, deeply regretted his role in Shelton's ordeal. He had been friends of Shelton's parents and was involved in arranging military funerals for veterans throughout the Houston area. He planned Shelton's and was sorry he had not snapped to the caregiver's background.

My investigation found yet another nickname could be added to the list under "the Black Widow." You also could call her "the Townhouse Terrorist." She has continued her decades-old habit of making friends, milking them for what money and property she could get, and then spoiling the friendship when confronted with evidence of her real motives.

At one time Marilyn Moon and Mehaffey were friends – or at least spoke with each other in friendly conversations on the commons in the townhouse complex.

Then Mehaffey "borrowed" Moon's well-used second car, failing to take responsibility for the EZ Tag bill. These townhouses are within sight of the Sam Houston Tollway. You only had to drive a fraction of a mile to access it. Mehaffey took this route very often.

A year passed and toll road authorities sent Moon a huge bill for unpaid usage fees. She appealed to the toll road authority. The possible solutions: either get Mehaffey to pay the tab or file a police report about an auto theft.

When Mehaffey declined to do the right thing, Moon filed the charges. It was yet another example of Mehaffey's bullying. Moon's resumé has robust examples of public service, including serving as a rape counselor as well as an officer in the Texas State Guard. She has the reputation as a can-do person who doesn't take bullshit lightly. She knew Mehaffey was full of it. After filing the police report, Moon no longer had to worry about the EZ Tag bill.

Mehaffey's fellow townhouse residents were either wise enough to her tactics to avoid her or were flat scared of her and walked the other way when they saw her coming.

She is routinely seen walking the complex carrying a bottle of Scotch and swigging from it. Pranks or the more legalistic "malicious mischief" complaints seem to lead to her, although nothing has been proven, possibly because people are afraid to make an issue of it. There are notable examples. The lug nuts on the wheel of a car owned by the daughter of one anti-Mehaffey resident were found loosened. Had the woman been on the freeway traveling at even an average speed she could have been involved in a serious accident.

Moon has been on Mehaffey's shit list – or "hit list" – for about a year now. One day Moon and Hackler found a tie rod wedged in the undercarriage of her Mazda 3, dangerously close to the brake line, placing Moon in danger if the brakes went out. "There's no way that was an accident," she said. "Those things just don't happen."

The term "stalker" could be applied to the woman seen peeping into Moon's window, and those of Gerhard Neils. The woman was identified as Catherine Mehaffey Shelton.

There are many reasons why Mehaffey would have it in for Moon, who filed a police report regarding alleged forgery against her when Mehaffey signed Gerhard Neils's name to an eviction notice.

Provided with the ID theft information from other sources, and the accounts of the alleged forgery, and the tie rod incident from Moon, police chose to pursue the ID theft. By May 2020, the latest hearing on that charge was postponed at least six weeks due to the Coronavirus pandemic.

Pandemic or not, things weren't going Mehaffey's way in the spring of 2020. The mediation hearing on her deceptive trade lawsuit against Neils was languishing in the LaLa Land of the legal system. Her free attorney dropped out and Mehaffey was not stepping forward pro se despite her legal training. She was headed downhill. Settlement offers were clear-cut. She could either drop the lawsuit, sell the townhouse and divide the equity, or she could pay Neils a share of the equity and get her own mortgage. Neils is not a greedy man and likely would be satisfied with paperwork legally removing him from any financial obligations.

Either one would be fair. Moon has made it clear that she has no interest in any equity; all she wants is peace for her friend Gerhard.

According to their agreement, Mehaffey would inherit the property upon Neils's death. However, that changed when he made Moon his heir to the townhouse property. As his power of attorney, Moon has stayed up to speed on the facts. She said Mehaffey had failed to pay property taxes for two years, thus provoking the mortgage company to talk about foreclosure. "She's always thought she's the smartest person in the room," Moon said. "She's not."

And those accusations just keep on a-coming. Over the past two or three years Mehaffey recruited an unknown number of friends to be part of what amounts to a money laundering scheme.

To avoid any type of serious IRS intervention, Mehaffey continued her practice of dealing in cash only. This routine went back to 1979 when Gary Taylor said she would keep one-hundred-dollar bills as bookmarks or stow them away in desk drawers.

In a recent year Mehaffey told Moon and others she was involved in an automobile accident that resulted in a lawsuit settlement in which she recovered damages believed to be in the six figures. She used some of the cash to make the down payment on the townhouse now "owned" by Neils. She used another portion to buy a used car. She still had some cash. She provided Neils some of it, requesting him to provide her $250 a month from her "savings account."

The Black Widow predator always picked on vulnerable males in more than one category. Another ceaseless custom was the use of her clients, often criminal defendants, to do her dirty work. Given the fatality record of these henchmen, it's no small wonder that she could find a willing individual to vandalize cars of her detractors at the complex or even start a fire somewhere.

Records show only three minor fires in eight years happened at the townhouse development where she has resided. However, several years ago one townhouse unit was gutted by flames, causing undue problems for neighbors who shared a common wall.

Funny thing but the couple in the smoked-out unit had gotten on the Black Widow's shit list. Coincidence? Well, don't forget the fire that destroyed a former lover's law books and papers. Then there was the theft of Gary Taylor's property during the breakup with Mehaffey. The couple involved here had to relocate for at least a month while their property was remodeled.

In those earlier days the Black Widow used the assistance of Tommy Bell, one of her criminal defense clients. Besides being the suspect in the burglary of Taylor's apartment, Bell and Mehaffey were named in a $10 million civil lawsuit filed by Tedesco's family as participants in the conspiracy to murder the doctor. This case was ultimately dismissed for want of prosecution after the family failed to press the matter forward. But that's not the real story here. Four months after the initial suit was filed against Mehaffey and Bell, Bell was found dead in his Houston apartment, a slug embedded in his left temple. Investigators ruled accidental death – you won't believe this – while Bell was engaging in Russian roulette. I mentioned this in Chapter 1 but recount a bit of it here to raise a question.

The question: Are you keeping score?

Tedesco was dead. Taylor was wounded. Bell dead under extremely unusual circumstances. All three had one thing in common – Catherine Mehaffey was the lowest common denominator.

If you include the other dead and wounded, add the Hierros, Michael (dead) and Marisa (wounded) to the Black Widow's list.

Oh, and there is another, Christian Harold Hansen, a Mehaffey client in the North Texas segment of the Black Widow chronicles. Howard Swindle's investigation found little details about Hansen's relationship with Mehaffey – who, let me remind you, was by this time known as Catherine Shelton.

Hansen was working off a debt to his lawyer when he was found dead in a bedroom in Shelton's Denton County home. Investigators found that he died of "accidental autoerotic asphyxiation."

Score another in our LCD calculation. That makes it four dead and two wounded.

There is no accurate score for the number of stalkings. If you ask me, we could safely say that Mehaffey stalked every person who worked for her or who were on the other side of a love affair gone bad or, in her later years, people with guts enough to stand up to her bullying. Her motive is always: What's in it for me?

A friend of Sergeant J.W. Lorentz and acquaintance of his surviving sister said she felt stalked by Mehaffey, leaving the impression that she was after all she could get from the estate. There is no evidence that she got anything. Lorentz collected guitars and guns – all of which were given away or sold to other people. Mehaffey stayed resolute in getting her way. She even asked the sister and Lorentz's friend if they would include a quote from her in the obituary. The quote: "He was very good in bed." Again, Mehaffey failed to get her way. Can you imagine reading a review of your sex life in your obituary?

In interviews or investigative reports about Mehaffey's antics over the years the term "stalked" appears frequently. One polygraph operator who worked for Mehaffey when she was known as "Shelton" and worked as a lawyer in the Dallas/Denton corridor, actually got a judge's order forbidding Mehaffey from getting within 500 feet of him. This was a condition placed on Mehaffey at a bail hearing after she was charged with trespassing. The polygraph operator, William M. Parker, a retired Dallas homicide detective and private investigator, declined to discuss the details of the trespassing and stalking from more than twenty years before. I will reference the quote he provided for Swindle's story: "I don't want to do anything to make things worse." This sounds like most of the people involved with Mehaffey over the years.

Still, in 2020, some of the good guys on the side of law and order were pushing for a further investigation of Sam Shelton's death – or should I say *timely* death. In probate court, Mehaffey (Shelton) still ranks as an heir. If you watch TV mysteries, then you know that means she had a motive.

The murder case of Dr. George Tedesco remains unsolved. Mehaffey has always been the main suspect. Houston homicide detectives on cold case assignment were looking into the evidence files, albeit forty years after the initial investigation.

You have to note that in 1979 they didn't have DNA evidence. Is Mehaffey's DNA on the murder weapon – the table leg of a chair (or "lead pipe") used to bash in the head of the doctor? Also, homicide now has sufficient reason to look more closely into the death of Sam Shelton.

I love it! A good investigator never lets anything go in the pursuit of justice. I don't think the radar screen of the law can miss "the Black Widow," "the Townhouse Terrorist," "the Queen of Deception," and "the

Predator of the Weak." I don't care which of these nicknames is used, I prefer "the Black Widow." And I know her address!

SPECIAL ACKNOWLEDGMENTS

To be a secretary, clerk, or intern in Special Crimes, you had to be vetted just like an assistant district attorney or investigator. Many cases on our often complex drawing board always required confidentiality and fierce loyalty to our quest to haul in all the bad guys.

The secretaries knew practically every detail of every case, whether closed or ongoing. They typed these detailed reports for each of us – except for Johnny Holmes who could type faster that any person in Harris County.

Our workweek usually consisted of fifty to sixty hours. When I first started in Special Crimes we didn't have time sheets or comp time accumulations. Priorities changed after a year or two when these calculations became necessary to run a more efficient office operation.

Our first two secretaries were Barbara Crowe and Debbie Burkhalter. Blaylock and I were normally in the office by 6:00 or 6:30 a.m. Barbara would usually arrive early, since she had to type our reports, but not as early as Blaylock or me. We usually made the coffee. We had Dictaphones, but I used to get Barbara and start dictating reports to her. I didn't like talking into a phone. Never have, never will.

Not only did individuals like Barbara do secretarial work, they also served as our radio dispatchers. Both Barbara and Debbie were very hard workers who went far outside their job descriptions together with personable approaches to getting the job done, no matter which individual prosecutor or investigator they worked with. They knew each of us so well that they could almost read our minds or anticipate our next need to accomplish a certain task. I have to say that we couldn't have done these jobs without them.

By reading my accounts of Special Crimes cases, you must have realized that the more complex our operation became, the more backup staff we needed. We finally added a third secretary, Virginia Devine. She didn't miss a beat picking up her share of the vast workload.

When we moved from Texas and Caroline in late 1979 to the main office at 201 Fannin, we had with us a larger, very competent staff of experienced assistants. Besides the first three I've mentioned, there were Melinda Hendrix Funni, Ann Grych, Rosie Martinez, Cheryl McGeough, Katherine McMaster, Becky Fulbright, and Allenda Stevens Elam. And we also had an intern from Sam Houston State University. Her name was Lisa Taylor Pearce.

For many years, I managed each of the "Sam interns" who were students in the school's highly recognized Criminal Justice program. After all, I was a CJ graduate of Sam Houston State and an intern for the Harris County Juvenile Probation Department in 1971.

Actually, I have to say that our first Sam CJ intern was a male who also held the distinction of being a fellow graduate of St. Pius X High School. His name was Cole Lester, who became a Houston police officer and leader in the Houston Police Officers Union.

We had many CJ interns who became DA investigators after they served at least five years as a police officer at a law enforcement agency.

One intern, Steve Januhowski, was later my partner in Special Crimes when I returned to the DA's office in 2009. We arrested more than fifty or more defendants in pending Special Crimes cases in 2009, each of them on the loose for a long period of time. He's still one of my best friends and like my "son from another mother." He's currently a detective with the Fort Bend County Sheriff's Office. Many of those former interns are still on the job with the DA.

My favorite law school intern was Mike Guarino, son of Joe Guarino, a long-time state district judge in the 183rd District Court. Mike later became the district attorney in Galveston County. Mike and his chief investigator, Felix Mares, would call me many times whenever they needed me to assist them in cases where they needed to do surreptitious recordings.

At this writing, another law school intern, Brett Ligon, is serving as the DA in Montgomery County, Texas. We had so many law school interns that became Harris County ADAs, that l have lost count.

Another one of my impressive interns majoring in Criminal Justice and in hopes of a law enforcement career was Mark Newcomb. Before he entered the Houston police academy he served as a dispatcher for us. To this day (2020), Mark is a highly decorated and dedicated HPD sergeant in the Narcotics Division. I like to believe that he got the taste for rounding up the bad guys while a twenty-something intern in Special Crimes.

Clever Bonilla was my CJ intern with my company, Gulf Coast AccuSearch in 2007. He is like another son and is now a computer forensics investigator for General Motors.

These ladies and interns were the backbone of Special Crimes and we couldn't have done it without them.

Allenda Stevens   *Ann Grych*   *Barbara Crow*

Candy Roch   *Cheryl McGeough*   *Debbie Burkhalter*

Virginia Devine and Debbie Burkhalter   *Lisa Taylor Pierce*

Mark Newcomb   *Melinda Hendrix and Pam Durand*

Mike Guarino and Me   *Steve Januhowski*

KNOWN LAW ENFORCEMENT RELATIVES

Thomas Gay (fourth great grandfather) received a league of land in Stephen F. Austin's second colony. He fought at the Battle of San Jacinto and was one of the first Texas Rangers. He along with four other Texas Rangers were killed at the Battle of the Birds in Bell County by some Indians.

Osborn A. Bexley *(third great grandfather) former Sheriff of Lee County, Texas, 1888 - 1890*

Kyle Rodgers (son)
former Harris County
Precinct 5 deputy

Kristin Rodger-Smith (daughter)
former Harris County and Brazoria
County Adult Probation Officer
and former Juvenile Probation
Officer in Harris County and
Montgomery County

Donnie Gay (cousin),
current FBI agent —
he's on the left

Jack Garrett (great-grandfather), Houston Police Department

Frank Hooper (cousin), former FBI agent

Paul Rodgers (cousin), former Houston Police officer

Hillary Roberts (niece), current officer with Houston Police Department

Blake Roberts (nephew), current officer with Houston Police Department

BOOK CREDITS

Chapter 17	**Odds and Ends**
State of Texas vs. Lilla Paulus cause #194130,
The Houston Post various dates

Chapter 18	**Disappeared**
State of Texas vs. Robert Lomas cause #1203841, 469891,
469892, 427173, 803099, 230520, HPD offense report
#032626385

Chapter 19	**The Wiretapping Killer**
Harris County Sheriff's Office case #86-031951

Chapter 20	**Another Halloween Tragedy**
Baytown PD offense report #W-28351,
The Low Zodiac Killer and the Mysteries of Texas

Chapter 21	**Friday Gunsmoke**
State of Texas vs. Sergio, Sergio Borgos, Raul Garcia Jimenez
cause #'s 342157, 449609, 872519, 872519, 370407, 367908,
The Houston Post, Houston Chronicle

Chapter 23	**Later Years (1986-2001)**
State of Texas vs. Revert Weston and Leonard Page
cause #193837, *The Houston Post, Houston Chronicle*

Chapter 25-28	**Yankee and the Dog**
State of Texas vs. Donald B. Yarbrough (Travis County)
The Houston Post, John B. Holmes, Jr. memo to Carol
Vance, 4-12-1978

Chapter 30	**The Black Widow Returns**
State of Texas vs. Catherine Mehaffey Shelton,
208th District Court, cause #1639739

Other information was obtained from notes taken from the author's daily
diaries from 1976 through 1991.

ABOUT THE AUTHOR

Kenneth K. "Kenny" Rodgers spent 33 years as an investigator in the Harris County District Attorney's Office, stair-stepping through the ranks to become chief investigator under District Attorney Johnny Holmes.

He was the first DA investigator to be named Officer of the Year by the 100 Club of Greater Houston.

Rodgers specialized in "finding people," a law enforcement talent that helped in the investigation and prosecution of thousands of suspects and hundreds of convictions over his tenure.

A Houston native, Kenny grew up on numerous football and baseball fields. He played third base on the Houston team that finished third in the 1963 Little League World Series. Rodgers preceded Gary Kubiak as quarterback of Houston's St. Pius X High School, where his grandson, Carson Rodgers, is now the quarterback. He played college baseball at New Mexico Military Institute before transferring to Sam Houston State University, where he earned a Criminal Justice degree.

Rodgers began his law enforcement career as a juvenile detention officer before beginning service as an investigator for Harris County District Attorney Carol Vance. He spent most of his career in the DA's Special Crimes Bureau, which handled major investigations involving political corruption, narcotics, pornography, gambling, and other organized crime activities. He graduated from the FBI National Academy in 1989.

After his retirement Kenny began service as a private investigator. He and his wife Debbie have seven dogs and seven cats – each "rescued" from throughout Houston and the Texas Gulf Coast.

Kenny is the father of three adult children: Kyle Rodgers, owner of a pre-employment screening company, Keith Rodgers, bank internet computer technician, and daughter Kristin, an adult probation officer. He is the grandfather to five grandsons and one granddaughter. He is no relation to Kenny Rogers (no "d"), the late fellow Houston native and famous singer and actor.

ABOUT THE EDITOR

Tom Kennedy is a Houston journalist who walked the beats as a crime and political reporter and columnist for *The Houston Post*.

Kennedy graduated from the renowned Baylor University School of Journalism, pioneered by Dave Cheavens and David McHam. After serving as co-editor of *The Baylor Lariat* with Ed Kelton, he was named Outstanding Journalism Graduate before beginning his professional journalism career at United Press International – the fourth consecutive *Lariat* editor to join UPI. He spent 25 years at *The Post* until it closed in 1995 (RIP).

Kennedy had excellent news sources like Kenny Rodgers, Johnny Holmes, and many other Harris County prosecutors whose work is prominently detailed in *Special Crimes*.

As a *Post* columnist and editorial writer, he crusaded adamantly against violence against women, against faulty sentencing trends for convicted rapists, and against the partisan election of judges and law enforcement officials.

He has written five books and edited five others. He is an inductee in the Gainesville (Texas) Alumni Hall of Fame. Among his works are the co-authorship of *Houston Blue: The Story of the Houston Police Department* (with Mitchel Roth) and as the sole author of *From Waco to Wall Street,* the biography of John Baugh, the founder of Sysco.

A one-time grand jury foreman, he is the current editor of the *Badge & Gun,* the monthly online magazine of the Houston Police Officers Union.

These days, Tom is the owner of a sports memorabilia shop, Tom Kennedy's Collectibles. He and his wife Glenda, a retired public school teacher and guidance counselor, have two adult children – Chris Kennedy, a video producer, and Claire Kennedy Platt, a technical writer and mother of granddaughter Alice Kennedy Platt.

KENNETH K. RODGERS

LIEUTENANT
OF INVESTIGATORS

SPECIAL CRIMES BUREAU

DISTRICT ATTORNEY'S OFFICE

HARRIS COUNTY, TEXAS

Made in the USA
Coppell, TX
25 October 2020